Yuan Shih-k'ai

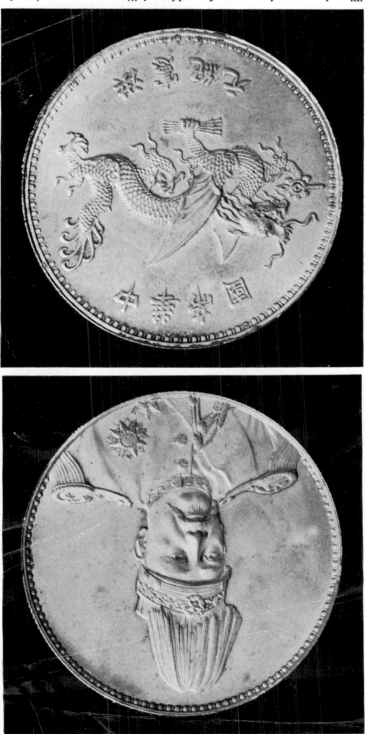

YUAN SHIH–K'AI

1859-1916

Brutus Assumes the Purple

BY

JEROME CH'ÊN

M.A., PH.D.

STANFORD UNIVERSITY PRESS

STANFORD, CALIFORNIA

1961

Stanford University Press, Stanford, California

© George Allen & Unwin Ltd, 1961

Library of Congress Catalogue Card Number 61-14066

PRINTED IN GREAT BRITAIN

To Sir Percival David, Bt.

Acknowledgments

I am grateful to the facilities given to me by the Foreign Office library, the British Museum, the Public Records Office, and the library of the School of Oriental and African Studies, particularly to Mr E. Grinstead of the Museum and Mr J. Lust of the School for their friendly co-operation.

In writing this book, I have depended much on the constant advice and constructive criticism of Dr Purcell of Cambridge, without whose invaluable suggestions, especially with regard to the period before the 1911 Revolution, *Yuan Shih-k'ai* would not have taken its present shape. Mr J. Gray of the School of Oriental and African Studies has read the manuscript and made several useful comments.

Miss J. M. Forshaw has improved the style and Mr H. D. Talbot has drawn the map. I am indebted to both of them.

J. C.
London
October 1960

Abbreviations

Bland, J. O. P., *Recent and Present*: (*Recent Events and Present Policies in China*)

CFKP: (*Cheng-fu Kung-pao*)

CJCC: (*Chung-Jih Chan-cheng*)

HHKM: (*Hsin-hai Ke-ming*)

JATTC: (*Jung-an Ti-tzu Chi*)

Johnston, R. F., *Twilight*: (*Twilight in the Forbidden City*)

Liang Jen-kung, *Nien-p'u*: (*Liang Jen-kung Nien-p'u Ch'ang-p'ien*)

Liang, *Nien-p'u*: (*San-shui Liang Yen-sun Hsien-sheng Nien-p'u*)

LSCFKP: (*Lin-shih Cheng-fu Kung-pao*)

LSKP: (*Lin-shih Kung-pao*)

LWCKCS: (*Li Wen-chung-kung Ch'üan-shu*)

Putnam Weale, *Fight*: (*The Fight for the Republic of China*)

Remer, C. F., *Trade*: (*The Foreign Trade of China*)

T'ao Chü-yin, PYCFTCSCSH: (*Pai-yang Chun-fa T'ung-chih Shih ch'i Shih-hua*)

WHPF: (*Wu-hsü Pien-fa*)

YCTKCP: (*Yü-chai Ts'un-kao Ch'u-pien*)

YSY: (*Yang-shou-yan Ts'ou-i Chi-yal*)

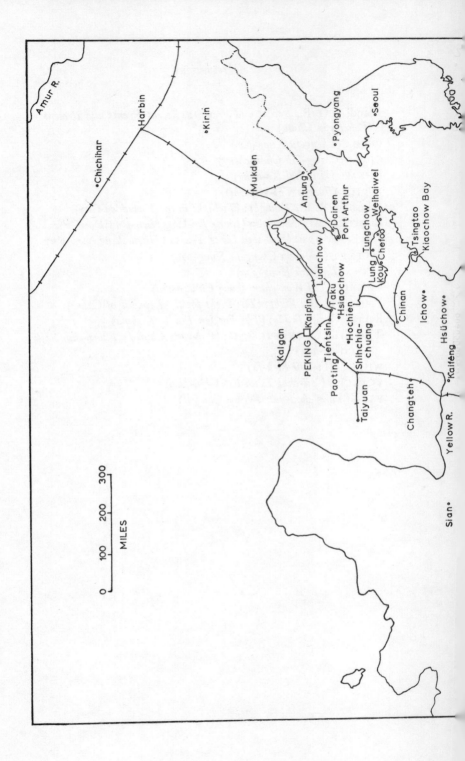

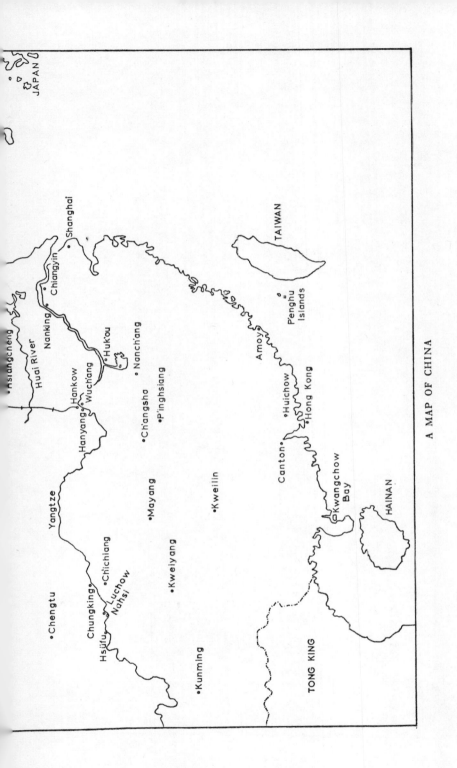

A MAP OF CHINA

CONTENTS

Youth 1859-1882

'When he was a young man, Ts'ao Ts'ao went to see Hsü Shao of Junan and asked what Hsü thought of him. Hsü replied: "Sir, you will be an able Minister during a peaceful reign, but your turpitude will show itself at a time of crisis". He was very pleased.'

(*Tzu-chih T'ung-chien*, ch. 58)

THIS anecdote has come down from the second century, yet the career and the character the author sketched might have been those of the man whose life and times we are about to tell, a man, who lived some 1,700 years later.

Hsiangcheng is a small town of no particular character in the south of Honan. The name of the province means 'south of the Yellow River'; and the town was a long way from the seats of traditional learning or the modern civilization which began to take root in China after the Sino-British War in 1839; at that time, too, the region was already poverty-stricken by the visitations of floods and drought. A little to the north of Hsiangcheng, a farmer named Yuan Shou-ch'en made his home and brought up four sons; one of these, born on September 16, 1859, he named Shih-k'ai.

It was a time of foreign invasion and armed rebellion. The Anglo-French expeditionary troops were occupying Peking—the Imperial Capital—and the Manchu Emperor was in exile, while the rebels—the T'aip'ing (1850-1864) and the Nien (1852-1868)—devastated the lower reaches of the Yangtze and the Yellow Rivers, and the Huai region. In the spring of 1860, the Nien drove into south Honan and threatened the security of Hsiangcheng. Yuan Shou-ch'en took his family to the east of the town where the Yuan Fortress stood. At that time it was quite common for a large clan to build a fortress for protection against bandits. This refuge of the Yuan clan belonged to General Yuan Chia-san—a prominent leader of Li Hung-chang's Huai Army, who was then fighting against the rebels. The General, who was a classical scholar, had not been touched by modern ideas; indeed, none of his clan was what one might call 'enlightened'. His adopted son, Tu-ch'en, was childless, and became very fond of the sturdy infant, Shih-k'ai, when they met in the Fortress. An adoption was arranged which brought the boy into an influential military family and was to have an important effect on his career.

Yuan Tu-ch'en took Shih-k'ai to Shantung in 1866, three years after the death of General Yuan Chia-san, and secured a classical scholar of some fame as his tutor, with a view to preparing him for an orthodox career. But the boy found books less attractive than boxing or riding. By this time, the T'ai-p'ing had been suppressed and the Nien were on their last legs. Peace was restored in the greater part of the Empire and modernization, intended to strengthen the Manchu rule, was already under way. The leaders of the new movement, among whom Li Hung-chang was the most outstanding, were all military commanders. Their armies were their own and their allegiance to the ruling House sprang largely from the Confucian ethic of loyalty. They were, in many ways (though not in this particular one), the forerunners of the Chinese warlords of more recent times.

Yuan Tu'chen died in the lucrative office of the Salt Gabelle Inspector of the territory south of Yangtze. His close friends, Generals Liu Ming-ch'üan and Wu Ch'ang-ch'ing, arranged his funeral and Yuan Shih-k'ai, then fourteen, escorted the coffin back to the family shrine in Hsiangcheng. Yuan's own father, Shou-ch'en, died two years later, but this did not oblige the son to observe the usual three years of mourning, since he had been adopted. He was therefore free to sit for the autumn examination for the first degree in 1876.

Since much of his time has been spent in riding, boxing, and entertaining friends, Yuan's failure in the examination was as expected. Soon afterwards, at the age of seventeen, he found consolation in an early marriage—though early marriages were not at all unusual in the China of those days. He and his bride, whose family name was Yü, took up their abode in Chenchou, Honan, where, two years later, their first son, K'e-ting, was born.

While in Chenchou, Yuan made the acquaintance of a poor scholar by the name of Hsü Shih-ch'ang (h. Chü-jen) who was then working as a private tutor, but was later to become a Cabinet Minister and eventually the President of the Republic of China. Before long they were loyal friends and sworn brothers. Hsü was a year older than Yuan Shih-k'ai and already the holder of the second degree when they met. In 1879, Yuan financed Hsü's journey to Peking to take part in the Metropolitan Examination for the third and highest degree. This Hsü obtained in 1886. Shortly after Hsü's departure, Yuan tried once more at the autumn examination and, again, he failed.

Two failures convinced him that to seek fame by the orthodox path of obtaining three degrees and an official post was too difficult a task for him. He therefore at once switched his ambition from a career in the civil service to one in the army, and made his way to Tengchou (near Chefoo), in Shantung, to seek a post in the Ch'ing Brigade under the command of a friend of his adopted father's, General Wu Ch'and-ch'ing. Yuan was then already a mature young man of twenty-one.

At Tengchou, in 1880, he met yet another scholar, Chang Ch'ien (t. Chi-chih), who was also working in General Wu's headquarters. He received lessons on poetry and prose from him and addressed him as 'Sir', for he was six years younger and the possessor so far only of a mere 'purchased title' as a secretary-to-be of the Grand Secretariat of the Imperial Court. In 1902, when he became the Viceroy of the Metropolitan Province of Chihli (now Hopei) and concurrently the Imperial Commissioner of North China for Commercial Affairs, he addressed Chang Ch'ien, then a great scholar and industrialist, as 'My brother'. Chang wrote in reply: 'Now your rank is more exalted my address is consequently less deferential'[1].

Chang was deeply impressed by the young man's ability and astuteness, and unreservedly recommended Yuan to the General for a more important post, at the same time exhorting him to give up any lingering hope of a civil career. Through Chang's influence Yuan was made an *aide de camp* in charge of training and discipline in the Brigade.

The leisurely, peaceful years from 1880 to 1882 came to an abrupt end when a mutiny broke out in Seoul, the capital of Korea.

[1] PYCFTCSCSH, I, p. 26, n. 3.

The country was then under China's suzerainty, and for this reason the acting Viceroy of Chihli, Chang Shu-sheng, despatched General Wu and his Brigade to quell the riot. Yuan Shih-k'ai made one of this force.

The King of Korea was gentle and kind, but weak in character. He had come to the throne in 1864 at the age of twelve, being the son of Prince Heung Sung of the Yi House. After his accession, his father assumed the title of Tai Won Kun and the authority of a regent, and was described by his contemporaries as having 'bowels of iron and a heart of stone'.[1] He was certainly rapacious and unscrupulous, but none the less able. In spite of the contacts already established with the United States of America, Great Britain, Germany, and France, he stubbornly pursued a policy of isolationism and was determined to have nothing to do with any foreign power. What had happened to China since the war of 1839 and to Japan since Commodore Perry's expedition in 1853 had not made the slightest impression on his mind. In 1866, some 2,000 Korean Catholics were slaughtered at his orders and, in the following years, when Japan endeavoured to establish diplomatic relations with his country, her embassies of 1868, 1869, and 1872 were all fruitless, owing entirely to Tai Won Kun's xenophobic attitude.

Japan was rapidly becoming a considerable force in the Far East and her interest in Korea grew increasingly evident. Only the size and prestige of the old Manchu Empire held her back from embarking on an adventure of conquest. In 1873, Iwakura's Government sent Soyijima Taneomi to China to exchange ratifications of the Sino-Japanese Trade Treaty, and also to sound out China's attitude towards Korea. The Tsungli Yamen, then China's Ministry of Foreign Affairs and Foreign Trade, reaffirmed their determination to preserve China's suzerainty over Korea at any cost, but it made it clear that Korea alone was responsible for her own internal administration and had the right to choose between war and peace.

The reply, ill-considered perhaps from China's point of view, encouraged Japan's aspirations. In the nineteenth century (as before and afterwards), it was by no means uncommon for a strong state to scheme against a weak one. Furthermore, the frustration of her attempts to establish diplomatic relations with Korea irritated

[1] Mrs I. L. Bishop, *Korea and Her Neighbours*, II, p. 44.

Japan considerably. Still, it was necessary to find a pretext before taking forceful action.

On October 18, 1875, a small Japanese man-of-war, the *Ungo*, approached the shores of Kanghwa Island, near Inchon, to obtain fresh water and was fired upon by the Korean shore-batteries. The Japanese commander sent a boat under a flag of truce to investigate the attack, but this too was fired upon. Thereupon a Japanese war vessel, which by a coincidence happened to have anchored near by, retaliated by bombardment. Japanese marines were landed and sacked the town on the island. Not satisfied with this, the Japanese Government sent more warships to Pusan, threatening further destruction unless a treaty was concluded. The subsequent negotiations which took place in Seoul early in 1876 resulted in an agreement of twelve clauses to be ratified by China. A Japanese envoy was sent to Peking soon afterwards to accomplish this.

The Tsungli Yamen's attitude was conciliatory so long as Japan was willing to respect China's suzerainty. In its reply to Japan, the Yamen once again stated that China did not wish to interfere with Korea's own affairs. 'If Japan has a mind to restore friendly relations with Korea, she should deal with her directly.'[1]

Under the Kanghwa Treaty of 1876, Japan recognised Korea as a sovereign state with full power to deal with her own affairs under China's overlordship; she was to exchange diplomatic missions with Korea; and Inchon and Wonsan were to be opened up to Japanese trade.

Among the Korean leaders, Tai Won Kun and his followers were bitterly opposed to this Treaty, while the Queen and her party, realizing their country's lack of adequate defences and that intercourse with foreigners was inevitable, supported it. China's complacency and Li Hung-chang's refusal to take military action during the Kanghwa episode strengthened the Queen's hand. The Treaty was signed on February 27, 1876.

Tai Won Kun, defeated but undaunted, was vengeful. On July 23, 1882, some Korean troops in Seoul found their rice ration rotten and mixed with sand and worse still this was the first ration they had been given for a whole year. It was small wonder that about 10,000 soldiers mutinied as a result of this discovery. Their leaders went to see Tai Won Kun, who promised to deal with the matter himself, but, at the same time, laid all the blame on the

---

[1] CJCC, I, p. 289.

B

corruption of the Queen's party as well as on the export of rice by the
Japanese merchants residing in Korea. The incitement was too strong
for the soldiers' tempers; on the same day, they killed several of the
Japanese instructors of the army and besieged and burned down the
Japanese Legation. The Minister, Hanabusa, fled home in a British
ship while some of his staff were savagely beaten to death. The next
day, the rioters looted a number of famous houses in the capital,
including the Royal Palace and Tai Won Kun's residence. It was
then rumoured that the Queen had been given poison and was dead;
the Chief Minister, Min Thae Ho, was seen, fatally wounded, in a
ditch, and his son, Min Yong Ik, who was also the Queen's nephew,
shaved his head, disguised himself as a Buddhist monk, and escaped
to Japan. The mutiny which began as an expression of grievances
was now transformed into a movement against Japan and the
Queen. Tai Won Kun, having settled his grudge, reinstated himself
as the civil and military dictator of the country.

Japan reacted swiftly. On July 31st and August 1st, 700 marines
and another 700 infantry soldiers were landed on Korean soil, and,
meanwhile, the Japanese Foreign Minister, Count Inouye, was on
his way to the scene of the riot.

The Queen, as it turned out, did not take the poison: her maid did
so in her place, giving her a chance to escape. Before leaving the
Palace, she appealed to China for help. The great Viceroy Li Hung-
chang was in mourning for his mother's death, but Chang Shu-sheng,
acting under his instructions, sent three warships and the Ch'ing
Brigade to Korea. The naval vessels arrived at Inchon on August
10th and the infantry reached Masampo on August 20th.

The despatch of troops did not mean that Li was willing to resort
to force to obtain a Korean settlement. His intention was to move in
before the Japanese could act, and also to make a gesture which
would appease his political opponents at home. He knew that his
Huai Army, the best fighting force China possessed, was not strong
enough to defeat the Japanese. When the units were on their way
to Korea, his German adviser, C. von Hanneken, suggested that
up-to-date ammunition should be bought from Krupp's to supply
the gunboats, but this was rejected on the ground of lack of
funds.

The Ch'ing Brigade, consisting of six corps or 3,000 soldiers, was
landed on foreign soil as a force from the 'Celestial Empire' coming
to the help of unfortunate vassals, but its discipline was appalling,

Yuan Shih-k'ai had to order several executions before the soldiers
would stop plundering the Koreans. The Chinese set up their
headquarters on the outskirts of Seoul on August 25th. General Wu
Ch'ang-ch'ing and the commanding officers of the gunboats, Ting
Ju-ch'ang and Ma Chien-chung, held a conference to decide in
detail how to carry out Li's instructions. The next day, General Wu,
Ting, and Ma, accompanied by a small escort, paid a courtesy call
on Tai Won Kun and were politely received by the Regent, his sons,
and grandsons. The residence was exquisitely furnished and the
commanders were impressed by its owner's refined taste. Ma
Chien-chung reflected upon this in his Journal, remarking: 'This old
man is very deep.'[1] At 4 o'clock in the afternoon of the same day,
Tai Won Kun went to see the General at the latter's headquarters
where the guest and his hosts, including Wu, Ting, Ma, and Yuan
Shih-k'ai, had a long conversation 'on paper', as then all educated
Koreans could read and write Chinese though the Chinese were too
proud to learn Korean. They used up twenty-four long sheets of
paper before the dusk fell. The 500 guards escorting the Regent
were presently sent away by the Chinese. Shortly afterwards
Ting Ju-ch'ang and Ma Chien-chung seized the Regent and pushed
him into a sedan-chair. Ting, taking a company of soldiers, then
escorted the chair to Masampo, a distance about fifty-five miles. It
was a rainy night. They marched the whole way at one stretch and
arrived at noon on August 27th. The Chinese warship, *Teng-yin-chou*,
was waiting to take the Regent to Tientsin. For the next three years
he was kept a prisoner in China.

The chief trouble-maker thus neatly removed from the scene, this
crisis of 1882 was peacefully settled. On August 30th, the Chemulpo
Treaty between Japan and Korea was signed, giving the former the
right to station garrison troops in Seoul to protect the Legation.
These forces were to be withdrawn after a year, if no further incidents
had occurred and the Japanese Minister deemed that their presence
was no longer necessary. Korea, for her part, realized that China's
suzerainty alone was not enough to shield her in the modern world.
It became obvious that she herself must have adequate defensive
power to deal with an emergency. The King therefore proposed to
train a corps of 500 soldiers in modern warfare, and the man appointed
to undertake this task was Yuan Shih-k'ai, then a young man of
twenty-three. A group of Korean youths was selected to study

[1] *Tung-hsing-san-lu*, ch. 6, quoted from CJCC, II, p. 196.

engineering in Tientsin, and China also promised to purchase machinery on Korea's behalf to equip modern arsenals.

For the part which he played in settling the crisis, Yuan Shih-k'ai was recommended for promotion by Li Hung-chang in a memorial on October 10th. The Emperor approved the appointment two days later and Yuan was also given the rank of a sub-prefect and the privilege of wearing the much-coveted decoration of peacock's feathers in his hat, while his friend, Chang Ch'ien was given the rank of a magistrate and the privilege of wearing the peacock's feathers of the fifth grade. Both were to remain in Korea.

CHAPTER II

Korea 1882-1895

THERE was a noticeable change in the political situation after the removal of Tai Won Kun. Although the Government was still corrupt, its power divided, the currency debased by inflation, and the country threatened with semi-starvation, the Queen and her party were now supreme without any serious opposition in sight. They were at that time pro-Chinese, for the Queen's family, the Mins, were of Chinese origin. They were also the largest noble clan and the biggest landowners in Korea. Their attitude to their two contending neighbours was ambivalent. Japan urged the Koreans to adopt progressive measures which they loathed to contemplate, while China respected their rights to govern themselves and was more, easy-going; China, after all, was still in the 'eighties the most power-ful nation in the Far East. The Koreans liked the Chinese but sneered at them, hated the Japanese but admired them. Hon. G. N. Curzon (as he was then) remarked: 'The race hatred between Koreans and Japanese is the most striking phenomenon in con-sneered at them, hated the Japanese but admired them. The Hon. Japanese developed in Korea a faculty for bullying and bluster that is the result partly of national vanity, partly of memories of the past. The lower orders ill-treat the Korean on every possible opportunity, and are cordially detested by them in return.'[1]

Japan was, however, not prepared to sit back and watch this un-favourable situation develop. She did not suppose that her struggle with China for the control of Korea could be peacefully solved. She therefore concentrated on building up a strong navy, at the same time encouraging her people to settle in Korea as merchants. By 1884 there were about twelve times more Japanese at Korean trading centres than Chinese. Furthermore, Japan took every opportunity to foster political opposition against the Queen. She

[1] *Problems of the Far East, Japan, Korea, China*, revised edition, p. 194.

found the many Korean visitors, among them Kim Ok Kiun, Hong Yong Sik, Pak Yong Hio, Song Kwang Pom, So Chi Phil and others, willing to listen to her suggestions respecting this last matter. Kim, a young nobleman of most attractive manners, was by far the ablest of them and was regarded as the leader of an expanding party. He went to live in Japan in 1881, willingly obeying the King's command, for it put him out of reach of Tai Won Kun's ruthless dictatorship. In 1882, when the crisis subsided, he returned home with the Japanese Minister Hanabusa. By then the Korean Royal Court was engaged in selecting an envoy to Japan to negotiate a loan of Fr. 120,000 and Kim's name was suggested for the post. He himself, however, declined this; instead, he recommended the king's brother-in-law, Pak Yong Hio, as the head of a delegation, with himself as adviser. After the mission, he stayed on in Japan and in the meantime widened his contact with Japanese political leaders. He made a deep impression on his European and Japanese friends and, in turn, was thoroughly convinced of the merits of European civilization and particularly impressed by Japan's social and economic progress. He knew of her aspirations respecting his own country through an interview with the powerful Count Inouye, who remarked to him: 'Our armament programmes are not solely for our own defence, but also aim to assist your country to achieve full independence.'[1] His other Japanese friends thereupon intimated to him that if he could gain power in Korea, a great deal would be achieved. Therefore he decided to go home.

Upon return, Kim Ok Kiun was placed in charge of colonization, and later of foreign affairs. He found the pro-Chinese Min party firmly in the saddle. Although the Chinese troops stationed in Seoul had been reduced from 3,000 to 1,500, the modern Korean army under the control of four commanders and Yuan Shih-k'ai was now four battalions strong—with 5,500 men and about 3,000 Peabody-Martini rifles. The commanders were Min Yong Ik of the Right, Yi-Ho Yun of the Left, Han Kiu Chik of the Front, and Yun Thae Jun of the Rear Palace Guard Battalion. These battalions formed one pillar of the Min party's strength; the other, strangely enough, was a German, who had been sent to Korea in 1883 by Sir Robert Hart, the British Inspector-General of the Imperial Maritime Customs of the Chinese Empire. P. G. von Möllendorf was a Chinese agent, undoubtedly able but headstrong and opinionated. He dressed and

---

[1] Kim's *Diary*, see Hirobumi Ito, *Hisho ruisan*, I, p. 430.

behaved like a Korean and controlled the finances of the Korean Government.

Yuan Shih-k'ai and the King and Queen of Korea were on very good terms and early in 1883 the King went so far as to request that Yuan should be made a marshal of the new army. General Wu Ch'ang-ch'ing did not agree, but this did not interrupt Yuan's control of the training of the battalions.

Meanwhile China was engaged in a military conflict with France in Annam and a full-scale war between them appeared imminent. On November 12, 1884, Yuan sent a confidential message to Li Hung-chang, summing up the political situation in Seoul in these words:

'Because of the conflict with France, China cannot deal with an emergency in Korea with armed forces. The King and many of his Ministers are now planning to seize this opportunity to shake off our control in order to achieve full independence. Their policy may be carried out through making alliances with other neighbouring powers. Kim Yun Sik, Yun Thae Jun, Min Yong Ik, and others are opposed to this plan, but the King is rather displeased with them.

I fear that in three years' time the result of this policy will become evident.'[1]

But Yuan did not have three years to wait. Soon after his return, Kim Ok Kiun was received in audience by the King. This was on the eve of the Sino-French War when China's loosening grip on Korea made her overlordship less dependable and the Queen's position more vulnerable. At this critical audience, the King listened to Kim's exposition of a pro-Japanese policy which revolved around the point that Japan might decide to annex Korea, should she, in concert with France, defeat China in a war. An amusing coincidence was that, a few months later, Sir Harry Parkes, the British Minister to China, advised the Tsungli Yamen of the strength of the militaristic elements in Japan and enlarged on the danger of an armed coalition between France and Japan. Kim went on to say that China's protection of Korea had become ineffectual in a changing world and that the preservation of Korea's integrity required an alliance with Japan and a parley with Czarist Russia. The King found his mind well-informed and his reasoning cogent and promised to seek his advice in every important matter.

[1] Wang Yun-sheng, *Liu-shih-nien lai Chung-kuo yü Jih-pen*, I, pp. 216–217.

The rise to power of the pro-Japanese party alarmed the Chinese representatives in Seoul, but the military leaders, General Wu Chao-yu and his deputy, were given to indecision and the Consul-General, Ch'en Shu-t'ang, was described by Kim Ok Kiun as a 'boneless sea-slug'.[1] So it was left to Yuan, a relatively junior official, to inform Li Hung-chang that an 'unexpected event' was afoot.

On November 8, 1884, Kim and his comrades met in secret. One of them reported that Yuan had alerted his troops a few days ago by ordering them to sleep in their tunics and boots. The Japanese Minister, Takezoye's, counter-action was to order his garrison soldiers to practise shooting during the night of November 11th. This might be at his own initiative, but certainly shocked the King and the inhabitants of Seoul. Rumours broke out and ran wild. Yuan imposed a curfew in the neighbourhood of his camp as a precaution, and the Korean Battalions did likewise.

Yuan's firm control over the Korean army and Möllendorf's unrelenting grasp of the Treasury made it extremely difficult for the pro-Japanese party to challenge the Min party. Against this formidable alignment, their only hopes of success lay in winning the soldiers over, which would inevitably take a long time, or in assassination. The Japanese Minister and his American colleague, Lucius H. Foote, believed that Han Kiu Chik, the commander of the Rear Battalion, was sympathetic to the pro-Japanese cause. Even counting on Han's assistance, the pro-Japanese still had no chance in an open conflict against the pro-Chinese. They therefore had to fall back on more covert ways to their goal.

The rumours, whispered from ear to ear, and the busy activities going on secretly in Seoul could not fail to arouse anxiety among all concerned. In the small hours of November 17th Min Yong Ik, the commander of the Right Battalion, paid a visit to Yuan and, after a long talk, they went together to Min's headquarters at 3.40 a.m. Yuan then went on to visit the Chinese Commander-in-Chief, General Wu Chao-yu, and he was seen riding back to his own camp at the crack of dawn. A week later, the British Consul-General, W. G. Aston, jestingly warned Kim Ok Kiun: 'Something is bound to happen very soon. People like Your Excellency ought to be more careful.'[2] Yet Kim was resolute. On the next day, he and Takezoye discussed the detailed plan of a *coup d'état*. The latter rejected the

---

[1] Kim's *Diary*, p. 436.
[2] Kim's *Diary*, p. 445.

idea of kidnapping the King and taking him to Kanghwa, but agreed to supply 3,000,000 yen as a provisional financial backing for the new government when it was formed. He also consented to send his troops to the Palace as soon as the *coup d'état* took place. Before Kim left, the Japanese Minister asked: 'How am I to send troops to the King's aid?' Kim smiled and replied: 'Your Excellency will get a message from His Majesty'. Takezoye remarked: 'A word will do'. But Kim added: 'It will be delivered to you by His Majesty's brother-in-law, Pak Yong Hio'. 'That will be splendid'[1] was the answer. Parting on this note, they agreed to see each other no more until the day of action.

From November 30th, the plot thickened. The conspirators held a conference at which they decided to stage the *coup* on December 4th when a banquet would be given to mark the completion of the General Post Office building by the newly-appointed Postmaster-General, Hong Yonk Sik—a pro-Japanese leader. All important members of the Government, including the four commanders of the Palace Guards, were invited. The party would be made to last as long as possible and, meanwhile, members of the pro-Japanese group were to burn down the Heir-Apparent's Palace. This, they hoped, would draw the guardsmen thither, leaving the Royal Palace unprotected. The pro-Japanese and the Japanese garrison troops would then rush to the Palace, seize the King, force him to proclaim a new government, and issue reform edicts.

The banquet took place as planned. About twenty people were present including the Korean Foreign Minister Kim Hong Chip, three commanders, Min Yong Ik, Han Kiu Chik, and Yi Jo Yun, the Japanese secretary, Shimamura, and his interpreter, Kawamata, the American Minister Foote and his secretary, C. L. Scudder, the Customs Inspector, von Möllendorf, the Chinese Consul-General, Ch'en Shu-t'ang, and the British Consul-General, Aston. The pro-Japanese included the host, Hong Yong Sik, Pak Yong Hio, and Kim himself. The Japanese Minister and many others, who all declined the invitation, gave the same excuse, 'a slight indisposition'.

The seats were arranged in a very interesting way. The most honourable went to Foote and the four lowest were shared among the Chinese and the British Consuls and two commanders. Kim tucked himself between the two Japanese, for he could converse with them in their own language, and the commanders sat nearest to the door,

[1] Kim's *Diary*, p. 447.

so that they could get away quickly if necessary. The servants were given orders to serve dinner as slowly as they could so as to give ample time for the fire-raisers to do their work. 'The Progressives', as the pro-Japanese were then called, were anxious to see their country modernized and strong, but their efficiency was not as great as their aspirations. Twice they came back to the Post Office to report their inability to start a fire anywhere. They tried the Heir-Aparent's Palace first but simply could not make it burn, so they hurriedly sent a man to Kim for further instructions. Kim had to leave the table to tell the man they should burn any place they saw fit. A moment later another person came to report more incendiary failures and to convey the even worse news that the police had become suspicious. The panicking conspirators then wanted to come to the Post Office and kill their feasting enemies in the banqueting hall. This proposal Kim firmly rejected and advised them to find a place near the Post Office to finish off their assignment. Kim's second absence from the table aroused suspicion among the guests. When the tea and dessert were served, a great commotion broke out and the shouts of 'Fire!' were heard in the banqueting hall. Kim and the others rushed to the windows and saw that a fire was at long last burning somewhere near by. It was then about 10 o'clock.

The three commanders made their excuses. Min Yong Ik, the first to leave, was back in no time at all, covered in blood from wounds on his head, neck, and shoulders. His right ear was almost severed and only hung by a strip of flesh. The Chinese Consul-General, Ch'en, at once took his leave to inform Yuan Shih-k'ai of this foul play. Foote, the American Minister, sent for Dr Allen, an American physician in Seoul, to come to help, and von Möllendorf took the wounded man to his house.

When Yuan arrived with some Chinese troops, the Post Office was deserted. He at once went to the Japanese Legation where he learnt that Min was being attended by Dr Allen at Möllendorf's house. On his arrival there he found a young man with a pistol guarding the entrance. It was Möllendorf's assistant, T'ang Shao-i (t. Shao-ch'uan). Yuan was impressed by his courage and a friendship which was to have great consequences began.

Before Yuan reached the Post Office, Kim and his friends had got out by the window and had rushed to the Japanese Legation. They asked to see the Minister, but Shimamura told them to go to the Palace, which they did. Without much difficulty, they and others disarmed the handful of guardsmen who were on duty, and broke into the King's bed-chamber. Kim reported to the King and Queen that the Chinese soldiers were trying to burn down the General Post Office and advised them to seek help from the Japanese Minister, but the Queen, being sceptical of Kim's story, insisted that the help of the Chinese should also be sought. Two messengers were sent at once, one to the Japanese Legation and the other to the Chinese Headquarters. But Kim saw to it that the latter never set out. He further urged the King to send a personal message to the Japanese Minister and without a moment's delay produced a pencil and a piece of Western paper on which the King was forced to write 'To the Japanese Minister: Come and protect us'. This was delivered by the King's brother-in-law, Pak Yong Hio.

At this moment, the commander of the Rear Battalion, Han Kiu Chik, came running to the Palace, but, without his troops, he was like a fish out of water; all he could do was to stay near the King to preserve his own safety. Soon afterwards, the 'indisposed' Japanese Minister and Pak Yong Hio with some garrison troops reached a small Palace near the Royal Palace itself. Here the King and Queen and their heir were lodged, surrounded by the pro-Japanese party. All the entrances to this Palace were heavily guarded by the Japanese and Japanese-trained Korean cadets.

At this moment, the safety of the King and Queen was the paramount concern in the Capital. High officials flocked into the Palace, like moths to a naked flame, to see whether Their Majesties were safe. The two commanders still at large, perhaps dazed by the speed of events, went to the Palace, also without their men. Three military leaders, the Chief Minister and his deputy, and the Minister in charge of Army Recruitment were all put to death in a matter of a few hours, and the Chief Eunuch of the Court was hacked to pieces. Before dawn, a new Government was proclaimed with Pak Yong Hio now in command of the Left and Right and So Kwang Pom of the Front and Rear Battalions and Kim himself was in charge of the Treasury.

Next morning, Foote and Aston and later the German Consul-General, Captain Zembsch, with their staffs, went to see the King in answer to his own request by a messenger. Upon arrival, they saw Korean and Chinese troops massed around the entrances to the Palaces while, inside it, Japanese soldiers were guarding the gateways. It was some time before they could get the door of the Hall in which the Royal family was lodged opened to them, and even then they found an array of Japanese bayonets flourished unpleasantly close to their eyes. The King had a short and inconclusive talk with them; all the while, the four pro-Japanese leaders and the Japanese Minister were looking on. It was evident that the audience was designed to put a stop to the rumours about the King's safety.

The anxiety was certainly shared by those at the Chinese Head-quarters. For a short time, the King's whereabouts were unknown and the general situation in the capital was chaotic. The Chinese Commander and his deputy evasively proposed to telegraph Li Hung-chang for instruction, Ch'en Shu-t'ang gladly seconded this, but Yuan Shih-k'ai vehemently objected on the obvious ground that there was no time to lose. The disappearance of the King and his heir led Yuan to suggest the installation of the King's nephew, a 7-year-old boy, as the temporary head of the State, but this proposal his superiors rejected. By a coincidence, the conspirators inside the small Palace were also planning to dethrone the King. Hong Yong Sik was of the opinion that the King should be interned on Kanghwa Island while the Japanese Minister insisted that he should be exiled to the Japanese capital. Before they reached an agreement the situation took a sharp turn.

Aston saw the Chinese Consul after his audience with the King and passed on the news of the King's safety to him. Later Ch'en had this confirmed by Möllendorf. This comforting news, however, gave rise to a delicate problem. The Chinese had the legitimate right to protect the King, who was in the hands of the conspirators and the Japanese. This situation called for some tactful handling if war was to be avoided. Therefore, on December 6th, the Chinese Com-mander sent the King a message. Kim would not allow the messenger to enter and made it clear that he and his colleagues would like to see the Commander and Yuan at the Palace. The message was left there and Pak Yong Hio's brother at once drafted and despatched a reply reiterating Kim's statement. For this, the unfortunate author was later killed by Yuan. Yuan accepted the challenge and, taking 600 soldiers with him, went to see the King. But he too was refused admission.

The news of the conspirators' plan to take the King to Kanghwa eventually leaked out and the Chinese and Korean Conservatives had to take action to prevent this. Yuan was for an all-out attack and he managed to carry his superiors with him. At 2.30 in the afternoon fighting broke out. The main point of controversy at this time and in the ensuing negotiations was, who fired the first shot? Kim recorded:

'At 2.30, a letter to Takezoye was delivered. Before he had time to open it, we heard confused shots. The news that the Chinese troops were fighting their way in from the south-east side, threw the whole Palace into a panic.'[1]

He evaded the issue, but the Japanese explicitly stated in Takezoye's notes to the Korean Government and Count Ito's statements at the Tientsin negotiations that the Chinese opened fire upon the Japanese garrison. The Chinese and the King of Korea, on the other hand, maintained that it was the Japanese who fired the first shot. Yuan's biography, the *Jung-an-ti-tzŭ-chi*, says:

'Yuan sent his assistant, Ch'en Ch'ang-ch'ing, to march ahead of the troops with a huge visiting-card in his hands. Before the man proceeded very far inside the Palace, he was shot at from within. Yuan therefore ordered his troops to attack'.[2]

Foote had nothing to say on this question while Aston believed that the Korean soldiers within the Palace walls were the first to begin firing. An independent observer, Young Allen, agreed with this.

The real truth may never be known. As the Chinese and Koreans outside the Palace were numerically strong, amounting to nearly 4,500 men, while the Japanese garrison inside the walls was only two companies, this seems to suggest that the Chinese Commander would have been confident enough to launch an attack; but in fact he was a vacillating man and feared the responsibility. Once fighting had begun, there was a danger that it might spread to other parts of the country and eventually grow into an international conflict between China and Japan. He was also a timid man. He had not the courage to lead the main body of his troops in this onslaught. He gave this task to Yuan Shih-k'ai, while he and his deputy commanded the left and right wings. When the besieged Japanese counter-attacked, the Commander was overcome by terror, and had to be carried back from the firing-line by two soldiers. Turning to consider the situation as it appeared to the Japanese, they too had reason

[1] Kim's *Diary*, p. 465.
[2] CJCC, II, p. 252.

to open fire; they were surrounded by a large force, and may have felt desperate enough to fight their way out at any cost, especially as their plan was to take the King with them to Inchon. However, neither side was united. Among the Chinese, Yuan Shih-k'ai was the most bellicose, being anxious to see the end of the episode; in the pro-Japanese party some were still in favour of taking the King to Inchon in spite of what was happening, but the Japanese Minister refused to continue with the attempt, having realized the hopelessness of the situation. He was anxious to back out while there was still a chance of cutting his losses.

Yuan went on with the siege from half-past two until sundown but made little progress. The wing led by the Commander himself collapsed, following his own example, while the other led by the Deputy-Commander hid under the Palace walls without firing a single shot. Inside the Palace there was panic and confusion. The pro-Japanese leaders were fully occupied with the conduct of their defence, so the Queen and the Heir-Apparent seized their chance to flee to the Chinese camp. The King wished to follow them and said so several times, but Kim and his colleagues naturally would not allow him. At last night fell and there was a lull in the fighting.

At dawn on December 7th, Takezoye decided to fight his way out and insisted that the conspirators should escort the King to the Chinese camp, his argument being that he and his garrison came to protect the King, not to put him in danger. 'I am going to retreat and to plan for the future,' said he. Kim inquired: 'How can you plan for the future without us?' At this, the Japanese Minister replied: 'I shall take you and your colleagues with me.'[1]

The scheming Postmaster-General, Hong Yong Sik, accompanied the King to a temple to the north of the small Palace where they were picked up by Chinese soldiers. Hong was at once executed. Meanwhile, the Japanese and Kim and the other pro-Japanese leaders fought their way to Inchon where they boarded a Japanese liner which took them to Japan. The three days' crisis thus came to an end.

The King then summoned his Ministers to reconstitute the Central Government and to restore foreign relations. A delegation was sent to Tokyo for discussions and another to Peking to express gratitude for the Japanese intervention. The latter carried with it some 100,000

[1] Kim's *Diary*, p. 466.

taels of silver to purchase luxuries for the Queen, while Yuan Shi-k'ai had to borrow money from the Chinese paymaster to relieve the families of the Ministers and commanders who had been victimised during the *coup*. Yuan's indignant words about this extravagance were: 'Such heartless people ought to perish'.[1]

Yuan had worked incessantly day and night during the few days of the crisis. Although he was only twenty-five, his biographers say: 'His hair had already half-turned grey.'[2] Chang Ch'ien, who had already returned to China by this time, commented on his handling of the situation in a letter to one of Yuan's relatives:

'Shih-k'ai has both courage and tenacity, but, unfortunately, he also has bureaucratic habits, and so he does not always live up to people's expectations. In spite of this, he is fit to be a Prime Minister.

Please ask him to take care what he does in that chaotic country'.[3]

The people of Seoul, less critical, put up stone-tablets to record his merits.

The *coup* was rounded off by two treaties—the Seoul Treaty between Japan and Korea and the Tientsin Treaty between Japan and China. The negotiations began on January 7, 1885 and ended two days later in an agreement on three main points:

1. The Korean Government was to offer an official apology to Japan;
2. It undertook to pay a compensation to Japan for the damages suffered by Japanese citizens in Korea and the Legation buildings;

and

3. The Legation garrison was to be increased to 1,000 men.

This treaty dealt only with the direct consequences of the crisis. Its wider implications had to be settled between China and Japan. Counts Ito and Saigo Yorimeichi went to Tientsin where Ito and Li Hung-chang began a series of negotiations which lasted from April 3rd to 15th. Much of their time was taken up by squabbles

[1] JATTC, CJCC, II, p. 254.
[2] JATTC, ibid, p. 254.
[3] *Chang Chi-tzu Chiu Lu*, CJCC, II, p. 315.

over problems such as the authenticity of the King's message to Takezoye and the question of who fired the first shot. Eventually, on April 18th, a treaty of three clauses was signed under which China and Japan agreed to withdraw all their troops and the garrison stationed in Korea within four months; to urge the King of Korea to reform his defence forces; and to inform each other when either deemed it necessary to send troops to Korea. The last of course was the most significant, since it put Korea under the 'co-suzerainty' of both China and Japan. It was this resounding victory for Ito which caused Li Hung-chang to report to the Chinese Emperor immediately after the signing that:

'This Japanese envoy [Ito], who has been to both Europe and America and has been concentrating his attention to their emulation, is a competent statesman. At the moment, he has no intention to start a war of conquest. Instead, he pursues unwaveringly a policy of commercial expansion in order to enrich his people and strengthen his country. In ten years' time, Japan is sure to become a powerful empire. She is not yet but will in time be our great worry.'[1]

The Tientsin Treaty between China and Japan was negotiated and concluded at a time when China was suffering a defeat at the hands of the French, and her international prestige sank to a new nadir. It was little surprising that Korea should seek help from other quarters in order to preserve the balance of power and a precarious peace at home. The pro-Chinese Min party was now secretly parleying with Czarist Russia, through von Möllendorf, with a view to obtaining Russia's protection for Korea. Li Hung-chang heard this and felt that he ought to reconsider his Korean policy at once. Yuan Shih k'ai was therefore recalled to Tientsin for consultation. At Yuan's suggestion, von Möllendorf was dismissed, and, in his place, two Americans were appointed—H. F. Merrill to take charge of the tariff and O. N. Denny to be the King's political adviser. Li and Yuan also agreed upon the release of Tai Won Kun, the aged prince interned near Tientsin, for both Li and the Imperial Court of China were now convinced of Tai Won Kun's loyalty and the necessity to foster an opposition to the Min party. Finally, it was obvious to Li that he must send an able man to Korea to carry out the reorientated policy and to compensate for the influence China had lost through the withdrawal of Chinese troops according to the Tientsin Treaty. Yuan Shih-k'ai was the only choice, for he had the required knowledge, contacts, and the qualities. Having obtained Yuan's consent to this appointment, Li reported to the Manchu throne on September 6, 1885:

'The reason for the appointment of a Commissioner for Trade is to station a high-ranking official there whose duties are to report the political development of that country. . . . Yuan Shih-k'ai twice went to the King's aid, his meritorious deeds have earned him admiration among Korean officials and common people, and he has shown great promise and loyalty. Furthermore he and the Korean Ministers Kim Yun Sik, Kim Hong Chip and others are very close friends. . . .

When Ch'en Shu-t'ang was there in charge of commercial affairs, other diplomatic representatives in Seoul considered him lower in rank than a Consul-General. This made it rather difficult for him to behave according to etiquette on social occasions. It seems advisable that Your Majesty should appoint a *Consul-General* as other countries. . . .'[1]

The Imperial approval was granted soon afterwards and Yuan was once more on his way to Korea, but only with the vague title of a Commissioner of Trade of the third rank, equivalent to that of a senior prefect. He arrived at Seoul on October 5, 1885 with two fellow passengers. One was Tai Won Kun and the other was T'ang Shao-i—formerly von Möllendorf's assistant and now Yuan's. T'ang had been educated in the United States of America; his knowledge of English and the courage he had shown during the *coup* may have been the reasons why Yuan recommended him for this post.

No member of the Royal family went to meet the returned father of the reigning King; the air of Seoul was full of apprehension and enmity against him. As soon as he landed at Inchon, one of his most trusted *aides* was poisoned and two others executed at the Queen's order. The return marked the first cleavage between Yuan and his comrade-in-arms, General Min Yong Ik—now the Commander-in-Chief of the Korean Palace Guards and the leader of the Min Party.

No one was more surprised to receive Yuan in Seoul than the new American Minister G. C. Foulk, who had been informed of this

[1] cjcc, II, pp. 48-49.

c

'significant' appointment beforehand and knew that Yuan was, in his own words, 'a young man, vigorous and active'.[1] But when T'ang Shao-i called on him and presented Yuan's visiting-card, he was shocked. For it read: H.I.C.M. Resident, Seoul.

Yuan's contemporaries seemed to have widely accepted the translated title 'Resident'. J. H. Longford tells this in his *Story of Korea*, 1911:

'Yuan, Li Hung-chang's deputy, little if at all less able and astute than the great chief, was at the Capital, no longer as a Commissioner, but as *Resident*, a semi-gubernatorial office, and he was *de facto* the King of Korea. Nothing was done without consulting him, nor without his sanction.'[2]

And the celebrated Putnam Weale records in his *Fight for the Republic in China*, 1918:

'Yuan, who had gone to Tientsin to report in person to Li Hung-chang, returned to Seoul triumphantly in October 1885, as *Imperial Resident*.'[3]

But Foulk did not like the title and sought for clarification through diplomatic channels from Li Hung-chang. Li replied:

'Some policies of the Korean Government may have wide implications which require direct consultations with a Chinese official stationed in Seoul in order to preserve peace and order of that country. Therefore His Imperial Chinese Majesty commanded the creation of a post to meet such requirements. Its functions are different from those of a Minister, hence it has a different name. . . .

Yuan Shih-k'ai does not hold the title of a Minister, nor is his rank clearly marked, but he has the same authority and status as other Ministers in Seoul.'[4]

China's difficulty in selecting an adequate title for this post was clear. Being the suzerain, she could not appoint a Minister; nor

---

[1] Foulk to Secretary of State, 15.10.1885.
[2] p. 327. Author's italics.
[3] p. 19. Author's italics.
[4] CJCC, II, p. 86.

could she send a Resident outright, for she had repeatedly declared a policy of non-interference in Korean internal affairs. The previous experiment of stationing a Consul-General was an obvious failure. Thus Yuan was sent there ostensibly as a Commissioner for trade but actually as a political Resident as Longford's and Putnam Weale's observations indicated. This was also borne out by later events.

Yuan's arrival was preceded by the rumour that Kim Ok Kiun, the leader of the *coup d'état*, was returning to Korea with a contingent of a Japanese expeditionary force. The Min party was believed to have started this story, for the Mins knew that both Tai Won Kun and Kim hated them and feared an alliance between these two opponents. The rumour persisted till the end of the year, causing China, Britain, and the United States to send their gunboats to Inchon, but nothing happened. Yuan's arrival was also coincided with that of the Russian *chargé d'affaires*, K. I. Waeber, and with the report of a secret agreement between Russia and Korea. Therefore Yuan did not wait long before presenting an essay, *On Treachery*, to the King. The fact that this composition was called an 'essay' instead of either a 'note' or a 'memorial' was in itself very interesting. In the 'essay', Yuan expounded China's magnanimous policy towards Korea. Being a close neighbour, China would under no circumstances shirk her responsibility in defending Korea, yet, at the same time, she had no thought of encroaching upon Korea's autonomy. Had Korea been under Russian or Japanese protection, the King would never have enjoyed such a great measure of sovereignty. He therefore went on to propose that any attempt to make an alliance with Russia should cease and that the traitor, Kim Ok Kiun, should be put quietly out of the way by assassination. The King received the 'essay' with all due courtesy.

The corruption and intrigues in the Korean Court and officialdom continued. Li Hung-chang and Yuan planned to avert Korea's tendency to move away from Chinese domination by purging the undesirable elements in the Korean government with the help of Tai Won Kun. But since his return, the prince found his wings clipped and was forced to live in semi-retirement. Yuan also arranged to have his confidant, Kim Yun Sik, installed as the Foreign Minister. This was done, but shortly afterwards, in June 1886, Kim was suddenly dismissed. The policy of fostering an opposition to the Min party, ironically reminiscent of its Japanese predecessor, was fruitless.

On the other hand, the Min party continued to dally with Russia. Waeber's presence in Seoul, the fact that von Möllendorf remained there long after his dismissal, and frequent visits of the members of the Min party to St Petersberg pointed to a continued flirtation with Russia—soon to be exposed. On August 13, 1886, Yuan telegraphed Li Hung-chang the text of a secret document:

'My country . . . nominally autonomous, is still under the control of another power. His Majesty the King of Korea is deeply ashamed of this fact and is resolved to adopt reform policies in order to strengthen his country and to free it from foreign domination. Yet there are many hindrances to this. . . . It is therefore sincerely hoped that the Russian Government would agree to protect Korea whenever such protection is needed. If Korea's interests are threatened by another power, it is hoped that Russia will send her warships to Korea's assistance.'[1]

> The 495th Year since the Founding of the Kingdom, the 7th month
> From the Home Secretary of Korea to the Russian *chargé d'affaires*
> (The Imperial Seal)

The date on this document was 'the 7th month, the 10th day' (August 11, 1886). Yuan claimed that a copy of it was smuggled out of the Palace by Min Yong Ik and passed on to him, and the Japanese Minister also informed him of its existence in two copies. Fearing an open conflict, Yuan suggested to Li Hung-chang that he (Yuan) should stage a *coup d'etat* himself by kidnapping the King and his pro-Russian retinue in the same manner as Tai Won Kun had been taken to China in 1882. Li, however, was more cautious. He inquired about the authenticity of the document through the Chinese Minister at St Petersberg and by direct communication with the King of Korea, with the result that both the Russian Foreign Ministry and the King categorically denied any knowledge of it. But by now the news of the discovery had stirred Seoul to no little degree. The King's adviser, Denny, called on Yuan on or about August 16th and demanded to see the copy. At the time, Min Yong Ik was with Yuan. Following Yuan's refusal, there was a heated argument when Denny 'vigorously charged Mr Yuan with being the sole author of any such

[1] Yuan to Li, 13.8.1886, LWCKCS, Naval Affairs, ch. 2, p. 7b.

information'[1]. Having got no useful result through the exchanges of recrimination, Denny proceeded to Tientsin, where he tried to persuade Li Hung-chang to remove Yuan, but the old man would not listen to him. Yuan stayed on, and his relations with both Min Yong Ik and Denny naturally deteriorated.

This incident shows up Yuan's lack of diplomatic experience; it also induces us to ask whether Min really stole a copy of the document, and, if he did, whence and how? The answer to this is provided by a recently published letter from Merrill to Sir Robert Hart in which Merrill said that the British Consul-General in Seoul, Baber, was the forger. Baber's successor, Parker, unearthed this intrigue and reported in detail to Merrill who wrote:

'Parker had found out that Baber alone was responsible. Having invented the story of Korea requesting Russian protection, Baber forged the document which deceived Yuan Shih-k'ai.'[2]

When the contents of the documents became common knowledge, all the foreign representatives in Seoul denounced it as a forgery, except Baber[3]. Baber might have intended to prolong the British occupation of Port Hamilton at the southern tip of the peninsula; and, Min Yong Ik, perhaps in league with him, made use of the forged document to discredit Yuan. For after the 1884 crisis, Britain, fearing that Russian influence in Korea and the Far East might grow to actual domination, occupied Port Hamilton in May 1885, and Min's scheme could thus be regarded as yet another attempt to maintain the balance of power in his country and to check Yuan's increasing interference in Korean affairs. Min Yong Ik was asked to offer an explanation of his dubious part in this incident to Li Hung-chang in Tientsin. He was naturally reluctant to accept this invitation, but was put under great pressure, and eventually arrived at Chefoo in August 1887, where he explained his position to Sheng Hsüan-huai, a trusted lieutenant of Li Hung-chang, and then sailed for Hongkong to live in exile.

In order to appease Yuan Shih-k'ai, the King sent a courtier to call on him and asked what should be done to counteract China's suspicion of Korea. Yuan proposed that Kim Yun Sik should be

---

[1] Foulk to the Secretary of State, No. 3, 8.9.1886.

[2] 26.12.1886, *Chinese Customs Documents*, semi-official letters, 1884-1886, M. 571, IIa, p. 120, Peking University.

[3] Foulk to the Secretary of State, No. 13, 14.10.1886.

re-installed as Foreign Minister. This was subsequently done. But this pro-Chinese Minister and his deputy forged a Royal Mandate and borrowed 5,000 yen from Japan, presumably for their own benefit. When this irregularity became known, both culprits were banished.

Korea's endeavour to shake off Chinese domination continued after the Russian incident. In 1887, the King was to appoint a plenipotentiary through the mediation of O. N. Denny to the United States and to appoint another to Europe. This was a shrewd gambit, since even China did not then have a plenipotentiary representative anywhere in the world. Once appointed, the Korean envoy would hold a higher rank than his Chinese colleague and be treated with more respect in the country where he was stationed. Once more the author of this policy was the exiled Min Yong Ik. Yuan, fully aware of its implications, was opposed to it on the ground that Korea did not have enough trade with either the United States or Europe to justify the appointment. Li Hung-chang also insisted that the appointment, even if absolutely necessary, must be sanctioned by the Chinese Emperor.

The Korean Court was adamant. At midnight on September 23, 1887, the envoy to the United States left Seoul but stopped on the outskirts of the town, waiting for further instructions. Upon hearing this, Yuan strenuously urged that he must be recalled and, at 4.30 in the morning, the envoy returned. There then ensued a stream of protests from the King to the Chinese Government, which eventually conceded that the appointment should be subject to three conditions:

1. Upon arrival at his destination, the envoy should report to the Chinese representative in the same capital and be introduced to the Foreign Ministry of that country by the Chinese representative;
2. The Chinese representative must accompany him to every social occasion which the envoy chose to attend;
3. The Korean envoy must consult the Chinese representative on all important matters.

The Korean Government evidently could not accept these terms. The negotiations went on for nearly two years without an agreement and meanwhile Denny was furious over Yuan's obstruction. Consequently, another feud began between them. In this matter, the

Department of State did not give Denny its full backing, so, in the end, he had to go. He left his post in 1888 and at once published a book—*China and Korea*—in which he charged Yuan with being 'a smuggler, conspirator, and diplomatic outlaw'.[1] Such was Judge Denny's swan-song.

In 1889, there was another attempt to depose Yuan, but once again it did not succeed. During his ten years' incumbency (1885-1895), Yuan worked with industry and decision to keep Korea within China's sphere of influence. At times he overplayed his hand, making enemies and bringing adverse criticism on himself, but, on the whole, Li Hung-chang had reason to be satisfied with his services and twice had him promoted. He took only two short leaves in this decade: one early in 1886 and the other from September 1891 to May 1892 to attend his mother's funeral. On both occasions his assistant, T'ang Shao-i, deputized for him.

Apart from carrying out China's political policies, Yuan also played his part in enhancing her economic influence in Korea. In this, he achieved considerable success by three innovations. First, he introduced a telegraphic service in competition with the submarine cable between Pusan and Nagasaki. This, Korea's only overland line of communication with the outside world whose political and strategical significance was explicit, was begun in 1885 and completed in 1888. It was an important triumph from Yuan's point of view, but later it bedevilled Sino-Korean relations, for towards the end of the decade, Korea tried to take over control of the line by replacing the Chinese operators with her own. Secondly, Yuan's endeavour to expand Sino-Korea trade also met with some success. He arranged with Chinese merchants in Korea to send a petition to Li Hung-chang, requesting that one or two cargo vessels of the China Merchants' Steam Navigation Company should run a regular service between Chefoo or Shanghai and Inchon. Until then Chinese merchants had employed Japanese ships and found the charges exorbitant, so Yuan and the Chinese merchants proposed a twice-monthly service and were willing to pay 12,000 yen per annum. The Steam Navigation Company was then under the control of Sheng Hsüan-huai, who did not favour this suggestion, for the sum proffered would not cover the expenses. Through Li's mediation, an agreement was eventually reached between Yuan and Sheng by Li's promise to grant another subsidy of 12,000 yen per annum. The

[1] p. 38.

route began operation in 1888 with little success. This, incidentally, was Yuan's first direct contact with Sheng—and it was not a propitious one. Thirdly, through a Cantonese firm in Seoul, T'ung-shun-t'ai, Yuan arranged two loans of 100,000 taels of silver apiece for the Korean Government, enabling it to pay for the German ship which it had bought on credit from a German firm.

In Korean trade and financial affairs, China's chief rival during this decade was Japan, although the setback of 1884 had kept Japan quieter in Korean politics. Japanese banks were established in Pusan and other Korean trading ports and Japanese cotton goods were exported to Korea in exchange for rice, soya beans, and gold, the last of which was particularly important for it helped Japan to adopt the Gold Standard. The rice too was useful in solving Japan's chronic food shortage, and in 1889, when Korea had a poor crop

Imports of Chinese and Japanese Goods[1]
at Inchon, Wonsan, and Pusan (in U.S.)

Year	Chinese	Japanese	Ratio	
			Chinese	Japanese
1885	331,342	1,377,342	19	81
1886	454,015	2,064,353	17	83
1887	742,661	2,080,787	26	73
1888	860,338	2,196,115	28	72
1889	1,101,585	2,299,116	32	68
1890	1,660,075	3,086,897	32	68
1891	2,148,254	3,226,468	40	60
1892	2,055,555	2,555,675	45	55

and prohibited the export of rice, Japanese protested vigorously. As a buyer of Korean goods, Japan's position was unequalled by any other country. She alone took 95 per cent of Korean exports in 1891. She also undertook to mint coins for and to lend money to the Korean Government and the number of her people, who had taken up residence in Korea, reached 10,000 in 1892. This economic supremacy was gradually challenged by China whose exports to Korea rose continuously from 1886 to 1892. Japan could hardly watch this development without apprehension. As the decade drew to its end, Japan awaited with sharpening vigilance her opportunity

[1] Li Ch'ing-yüan, Modern Korean History, Chinese translation, 1955, p. 73.

to sever Korea from China. The opportunity came; the inevitable happened; and Li Hung-chang's prediction, made after the Tientsin Treaty of 1885, came true.

Two events set the Far East ablaze. Early in April 1894 the leader of the 1884 *coup d'état*, Kim Ok Kiun, arrived at Shanghai with the son of Hong Yong Sik. Hong was the Postmaster-General who had accompanied the King of Korea to the Chinese camp after the *coup* and had at once been executed. His son resented the fact that his father had been jettisoned by other pro-Japanese leaders and had been planning to take revenge. First he won Kim's trust and then travelled with him from Japan to Shanghai where, after a short stay, he shot him dead in a hotel. The Shanghai authorities, acting under Li Hung-chang's instructions, arrested the man and sent him and the corpse of his victim back to Seoul. The King at once gave him a high post in the Government and the corpse was shown to the public of eight provinces before it was quartered during the night of April 18th—all against the advice of Li, Yuan, and the British Minister to China, N. R. O'Conor. In Tokyo, about the same time, an abortive attempt was made on the life of Pak Yong Hio—another prominent leader of the 1884 crisis. Later, the Korean assassin confessed to the Japanese authorities that he had acted on the King's orders. In an ensuing debate in the Diet, these two assassinations were regarded as actions hostile to Japan, and the Government was urged to take action. However, both the Premier, Ito, and the Foreign Minister, Mutsu, refused to be rushed. They were still biding their time, while Korean-Japanese relations worsened.

Another, even more important event was the Tong Hak Rebellion. The Tong Hak Society was a religious organization founded in or about 1860. Its tenets were a mixture of Confucianism, Buddhism, and Taoism, hence the name Tong Hak (Eastern Learning) chosen to show strong antagonism to the Western Learning, i.e. Roman Catholicism. After 1864, the Society underwent a drastic change and began to direct its followers' activities against excessive taxation. governmental corruption, and foreign encroachment. Two petitions were made in 1892 and 1893, expressing the Society's views, but the Government took no notice. The Society continued to grow; the famine of 1893 drove many hungry people into its fold and a short-lived revolt broke out. In 1894, the extortionate taxes imposed on the people in the south lent more force to the Tong Hak appeal and another revolt occurred. This time the insurgents went from strength to strength until the situation was completely out of hand. The modern troops of Korea proved useless in their campaigns against the rebels, and the King turned to China for help.

The 1885 Treaty between China and Japan stipulated that if either of the signatories were to send troops to Korea, the other must be informed. Korea's request was made at the end of May and on June 2nd, an interpreter of the Japanese Legation called upon Yuan, expressing Japan's anxiety over her trade and the safety of her people in Korea. He asked why China had not sent troops to pacify the rebellion. 'Japan,' he added, 'has no other designs, if China despatched her troops.' The next day, the Japanese *chargé d'affaires*, Sugimura, repeated the suggestion to Yuan.[1]

In response to these requests, Li Hung-chang sent 1,500 men of his Huai Army to Korea, and, at the same time, informed the Japanese Government of his action. On the day the troops sailed, the Japanese Consul in Tientsin urged him to despatch Chinese troops to Korea as soon as possible. Li was ignorant of the fact that Japanese forces were also on their way to Inchon under the pretext of protecting Japanese subjects and their property. Alarmed by this move, Yuan called on Sugimura to ask for an explanation and was once more assured that 'Japan had no other designs'. The presence of both Chinese and Japanese forces in Korea overshadowed the news of the rebellion. The tension suddenly rose and the Russian and French Legations began to evacuate their staffs on June 10th. Two days later the Japanese Minister, Otori, who had returned to Seoul with 1,000 Japanese soldiers, told Yuan that Japan would withdraw her men as soon as the rebellion was supressed and peace and order restored. He then informed Yuan of his country's intention to take part in the campaign against the rebels.

Li Hung-chang, who had no thought of waging a war against Japan, realized what was now at stake and ordered his troops to halt at Kwangju, south of Pyongyang. Meanwhile Yuan and Otori entered into a verbal agreement that neither country was to send more troops to Korea. The Korean Government, faced with this explosive situation, now requested the Viceroy to withdraw his troops, for in its own words, 'the rebels, having heard of the arrival of the troops from the Celestial Empire, are scared out of their wits and know that their days are numbered'.[2]

[1] Yuan to Li, LWCKCS, telegrams, ch. 15, p. 34a.
[2] Yuan to Li, 13.6.1894, LWCKCS, telegrams, ch. 15, p. 40a.

Japan, by her shrewd manoeuvres, had by now stolen the initiative from Li Hung-chang, and her troops in Korea had increased from 1,000 on June 12th to over 3,000 a week later. On June 21st, they amounted to 15,000. They were, moreover, stationed at such vantage points as Inchon, Pusan, and Seoul, and outnumbered their Chinese counterparts by two to one. China thus found herself in an extremely awkward position. Her soldiers had come to Korea to suppress the rebels in the south, who had now become inaccessible, for the Japanese troops blocked the way, somewhat prophetically, along the 38th Parallel; and their withdrawal at this stage would mean the surrender of China's suzerainty to Japan. Li Hung-chang did not know what to do. One thing, however, was clear in his mind: he must avoid a war against Japan at any cost.

At first Li made direct contacts with Japan, trying to secure a simultaneous withdrawal of troops on both sides. This being fruitless, he sought the good offices of both the British and the Russian Ministers to China, O'Conor and Cassini, to find a *modus vivendi*. On June 28th, the representatives of Britain, Russia, the United States, and France sent joint notes to the Japanese and Chinese Ministers, requesting the simultaneous withdrawal of their countries' troops. China agreed, but Japan did not. Count Mutsu, recalling this failure in his *Memoirs*, said that it 'gave my country a free hand and personally I was pleased'.[1]

On the day the diplomats delivered their notes, Japan demanded that the King of Korea should declare his country independent and reform his Government. Kim Hong Chip was appointed Premier to negotiate with Japan on a reform programme. Mutsu again recorded:

'The political reform was in fact devised to settle the complex problem between Japan and China. . . . We made use of this either to promote a peaceful solution to the worsening Sino-Japanese relations or, if that was impossible, to hasten a final "show-down".'[2]

The negotiations, conducted under flagrant duress, did not make much progress. On July 22nd, Japanese troops entered Seoul and broke into the Palace; the King, Queen, and their children were all seized and carried off as prisoners to the Japanese Legation, and, in place of the kidnapped monarch, the aged Tai Won

[1] Quoted from CJCC, VII, p. 150.
[2] *Memoirs*, p. 300.

Kun was reinstated as Regent. At last the velvet gloves were off.

In the Imperial Court of China, the war party under the leadership of the Grand Council, particularly the Grand Secretary and the Imperial Tutor, Weng T'ung-ho, who was concurrently the President of the Board of Revenue, launched a relentless attack on Li Hung-chang's bungling and appeasement. Weng was advised by Yuan Shih-k'ai's scholar-friend, Chang Ch'ien, and Yuan himself also advocated a strong policy towards Japan. In despair, Li Hung-chang resolved to fight and despatched more troops to Korea. On July 25th the British steamer *Kowshing*, with 1,220 Chinese troops on board, was intercepted off the coast of Korea and sunk by the Japanese cruiser *Naviwa*, and two days later the imprisoned King was forced to declare war against his suzerain. This was followed by the Mikado's declaration of war on July 31st and the Chinese Emperor's on August 1, 1894.

From July 1894 to March 1895, the two sides fought first in Korea, and then in Manchuria and on the Yellow Sea. China's defeat in three major engagements was complete. Sir Robert Hart wrote:

'China has given no offence—has done no wrong—does not wish to fight, and is willing to make sacrifices: She is a big "sick man", convalescing very slowly from the sickening effects of peaceful centuries, and is being jumped on when down by this agile, healthy, well-armed Jap—will no one pull him off?'[1]

Early in July, after the failure of the Four Power mediation, Yuan asked to be recalled, since his continuance in his post served no useful purpose. This request was refused by the Tsungli Yamen. Once a powerful 'Resident', he was now a pathetic figure, as no one called upon him and all his servants deserted him. He soon fell ill, and T'ang Shao-i carried on the routine work of his office. In the end, through Li Hung-chang's efforts, he was ordered to make a report in person about the latest development to the Tsungli Yamen in Peking, *before going to Tientsin*. The melancholy journey began on July 19th and ended a week later. But on August 4th, Li sent him to Pyongyang as the quartermaster of the Chinese army. Before arriving there, Yuan received the news of the fall of Pyongyang. With Chou Fu and Hu Yü-fen, he stayed in Manchuria supplying provisions and

[1] Hart to Campbell, 28.10.1894.

equipment to the fighting forces. Then he had another opportunity to witness the corruption and the utter inefficiency of the Huai Army —and its shattering defeat. It was a thought-provoking experience and may have helped him to decide to resume his career as an army trainer. Indeed, Hu Yü-fen even suggested to him, while they were both retreating with the beaten soldiery, that he should at once organize an army of his own.

Upon the signing of the Shimonoseki Treaty on April 17, 1895, the War came to an end and a new epoch in the modern history of China began. From many points of view, it was to be a far worse period than any that had in modern times preceded it.

CHAPTER III

The Army 1895-1899

THE war and the peace of 1895 put an end to China's suzerainty over Korea and her sovereignty over Taiwan (Formosa) and Penghu (the Pescadores). In addition, she agreed to pay an indemnity of 200 million taels of silver in eight instalments which virtually reduced her maritime customs to a debt-collecting house for Japan; and to allow the Japanese and, by applying the most-favoured-nation clause, many other nations as well, to build factories on her soil, thus inaugurating a period which Lord Salisbury termed the 'Battle of the Concessions'. However, the war's more profound effects were the sense of panic that now seized upon the Chinese mind and the absolute bankruptcy of the policy known to historians as the 'Self-strenghtening Movement' or the 'T'ung-chih Revival'.

In Chinese eyes, Japan owed her civilization to China; she was a much smaller country and her people, though of the same stock as the Chinese, were shorter in stature; her modernization policies began about the same time as those of her continental neighbour, and yet China had suffered this staggering defeat at her hands. Never before had China been humbled by an Asian power. The shame was overwhelming and stupefying, and her statesmen threw up their hands in despair.

During the T'ung-chih Revival (approximately from 1865 to 1895), new armies were trained, a navy was established, and arsenals and factories built. With these as a security, China enjoyed peace and order for nearly thirty years. As long as the Huai Army and the Northern Fleet remained supreme, the dynasty was safe, for the Imperial Domain and its adjacent provinces were all under their protection. That was why Li Hung-chang accepted the Japanese challenge with such reluctance. Others with less precise knowledge of the real strength of these fighting forces blamed him, forced him to change his policy towards Japan, and, after he had been ruined,

sent him abroad on a long tour. The Viceroyalty and Commissionership which he vacated were taken over by Wang Wen-shao, but
the actual power fell into the hands of Jung-lu, the Manchu
Commander-in-Chief of the army, whose immediate task, with
the other policy-makers, was to see the Imperial Capital secured
again and made safe. Inside the Government, discussion was
concentrated on the recruitment and training of a modern army;
outside it scholars loudly criticized the 'Self-strengthening' policies
and proposed a drastic governmental change. Two quotations out
of many available ones will suffice to show this:

'Li Hung-chang in his heyday was entrusted with the defence of the
Empire. But the humiliation and losses . . . of 1895 made him a
laughing stock among all barbarian peoples. Afterwards, those who
talked about self-strengthening were often sneered at.'[1]

and

'Have we not seen Li Hung-chang's navy, foreign-style army, and
military and medical schools? Have we not seen Chang Chih-tung's
colleges, foundries, and Self-strengthening Army? Those were the
results of Li's effort for thirty years and Chang's for fifteen years.
If we allow other Lis and Changs to pursue the same policy for
another fifty years, to proceed at the same snail's pace, . . . in the end,
we shall have another crop of schools and foreign-style troops, who,
in another emergency, will turn back and run for their lives as their
predecessors did in 1895. What good will this do to our country?'[2]

Two schools of thought appeared. One, which prevailed in government circles, continued to accept the traditional social and political
systems as perfect but admitted China's military weakness. According to them, all that China needed was a modern and more efficient
fighting force. In the 'sixties, the self-strengthening had been
financed by the newly reorganized and expanded customs service
which provided more than one-third of the Government's total
revenue each year. These sources of revenue were now one by one
pledged against foreign loans, which were raised to pay the Japanese
indemnity. Without them, the new fighting force was unlikely to be

---

[1] Hu Ssu-ching, *Wu-hsü-lü-shuang-lu*, WHPF, I, p. 399.
[2] Liang Ch'i-ch'ao, *Wu-hsü-cheng-pien-chi*, 1954 ed. pp. 83-84.

bigger than the old and had to be confined to the army alone. This led to the raising of the Newly Created Army, quartered at Hsiaochan near Peking. The other school of thought was far more radical, for it advocated the adoption of a constitution and a thorough governmental reform. Those who believed in it refused to trust any modern measure to the corrupt and archaic administrative machine. This eventually culminated in the 1898 Reform. In both the Army and the Reform, Yuan Shih-k'ai had his part to play.

Let us look at the Army first.

Prior to 1884, China had a sizeable navy divided into two fleets—the Southern which was seriously crippled in the 1884 war against France, and the Northern, annihilated ten years later by Japan. Now financially handicapped, China found herself unable to revive the dream of becoming a maritime power. The existing army, on the other hand, consisted of a large number of the traditional archers and lancers, equipped with a few outmoded Mausers, and the remnant of the Huai Army which was left after the 1895 War. China in fact could not afford to maintain these troops and, at the same time, train a new army. But the internal situation preserved the former while foreign pressure made the latter necessary.

What was left of the Huai Army after the War included General Nieh Shih-ch'eng's Tenacious Army and General Sung Ch'ing's Resolute Army. Together with General Tung Fu-hsiang's Kansu Army, which was actually a swarm of brigands, these formed the inadequate defensive force of the Imperial Capital and North China. These troops amounted to no more than 70,000 men, with a measure of bloodthirsty bravery but neither training nor discipline, equipped with Mausers and rifles of various makes and calibres. The dire need for a new army was obvious. Late in 1894, at a crucial stage of the War, von Hanneken submitted a plan to both the Grand Council and the Tsungli Yamen, in which he suggested the training of 100,000 modern troops with the funds controlled by Sir Robert Hart. Weng T'ung-ho, the Grand Secretary, favoured the idea and considered it to be 'China's only way to survive'.[1] The British Minister O'Conor put forward a similar suggestion; moreover, he thought Sir Robert was the most suitable person to take full charge. Under Weng's instructions, with the blessing of the Council and particularly that of Jung-lu, Hu Yü-fen worked out a detailed programme which emphasized both drilling under foreign instructors

[1] Weng's *Diary*, 28.10.1894, CJCC, IV, p. 505.

and uniformity with regard to arms and organization. He also proposed that North China should be responsible for the training of 50,000 soldiers, South China 30,000, and Hupei and Hunan 20,000, at an estimated total cost of 14,000,000 taels of silver.

Sheng Hsüan-huai, Li Hung-chang's lieutenant in commercial and economic affairs, also presented a plan for training a new army. He put the number of new troops required at 300,000, but insisted that the 800,000 traditional troops should be demobilized. A soldier, according to his plan, should be in active service for fourteen years— three in the standing army with full pay; three in the reserve; three as a retained soldier, and five in militia units. After the first three years, a soldier was to be free to return to civilian life, except for taking part in annual manoeuvres; and throughout the fourteen years he was to be exempted from other forms of *corvée*. Other memorialists on this subject included such illustrious personages as the Viceroy of Hupei and Hunan, Chang Chih-tung, and the new Viceroy of Chihli, Wang Wen-shao.

The Grand Council's own and less ambitious programme fixed the quota for the first four months at only 4,000 or 5,000 men and selected Hsiaochan as the location. The place lay between Peking and Tientsin. It was here that Li Hung-chang had maintained the barracks of his Huai Army for more than twenty years. Hu Yü-fen, not Yuan Shih-k'ai, was appointed the Supervisor and von Hanneken the Chief Instructor. Hu, a competent and enlightened official, could not get on well with the German, because, as he said, Hanneken was greedy and arrogant. Before long, he gave up administration of the army in favour of building railways and Yuan Shih-k'ai was appointed to succeed him.

Apart from the discredited generals of the Huai Army, Yuan was the only one among his contemporaries who had the required experience and knowledge for the task. Furthermore, he had an unstained reputation and showed considerable interest in the work. Before the end of the War, on May 17, 1895, he wrote to Li Hung-tsao, a Grand Councillor:

'The weakness of our troops does not lie so much in quantity but in quality; not so much in their physical strength as in their lack of training. The worst of all is their lack of a uniform organization, unified command and stern discipline. They can neither be controlled nor whip up enough courage to face their enemy. . . .

D

Under these circumstances, we should do our best to rectify the mistakes of the past—by eliminating superfluous units, economizing on excessive expenses, dismissing incompetent officers, and tightening up discipline. In addition, we should select a few generals of high repute, giving them a free hand and generous financial backing, so that they can proceed to reorganize our existing troops into several big units and station them at strategic points. We ought to employ foreign instructors to assist in the work of reorganization. Both our own traditional and European methods will be adopted after careful deliberation in order to evolve a new system. . . . At the same time, military academies must be set up, staffed with foreign experts, to train selected cadets; and, later on, these cadets should be sent abroad for further studies. On their return, they would be given command in the army according to their merits.'[1]

As a result of this letter Yuan was called to the Capital for consultation in June. He and Hu Yü-fen, and indeed a host of others, were fully aware of the meaning of this task, not only to the nation as a whole, but also the man chosen for the job. Competition between Yuan and Hu became unavoidable. Hu wrote to Li Hung-tsao describing Yuan as 'arrogant'.[2] Chang P'ei-lun, another highly-placed lieutenant of Li Hung-chang, in a personal letter addressed to the same Grand Councillor, criticized Yuan in these words:

'I have had several talks with him and found him boastful and utterly unreliable. His past history shows that he is conceited, extravagant, lecherous, treacherous, and ruthless. Sir, you would be right to treat him as the son of a friend, but gravely wrong to esteem him as a man of rare qualities. I am compelled to speak up about him, for having misled Li Hung-chang, he may now attempt to mislead you and, indeed, our country!'[3]

In spite of these attacks, Li Hung-tsao had formed rather a distinctly good impression of Yuan; so had Jung-lu and Weng T'ung-ho. But one fact weighed heavily against him and in favour of Hu Yü-fen, namely that Yuan had joined Liang Ch'i-ch'ao's Strengthening Society, a Reformist organization, prior to the appointment. As Hu

[1] Yuan to Li Hung-tsao, 17.5.1895, CJCC, V, p. 219.
[2] 8.7.1895, CJCC, V, p. 221.
[3] Few weeks after the conclusion of the Shimonoseki Treaty, CJCC, V, p. 231.

had now left his post due to his quarrels with Hanneken, Jung-lu instructed Yuan to make a report on army training. This he did in several thousand words, advocating the use of German techniques. Li Hung-tsao, seconded by Jung-lu, then recommended him as capable of training an efficient army. The notorious but powerful Prince Ch'ing and the Grand Eunuch, Li Lien-ying, both supported Yuan's appointment. The Grand Council therefore memorialized the throne on December 8, 1895 that Yuan be appointed to command and supervise the instruction of the Newly Created Army.

Yuan Shih-k'ai took over the Army in the middle of December 1895, when he was thirty-six years of age. There were ten corps at Hsiaochan—3,000 infantry, 1,000 artillery, 250 cavalry, and 500 engineers. The infantry was divided into two regiments, consisting of rapid-fire gun, heavy artillery, and reserve units; and the engineers into six sections—bridge-building, fortification, ordnance, repair, surveying, mine-laying, and telegraph detachments. The arms and equipment were far from standardized. According to the report which Yuan made to the Grand Council, the foreign-style drilling would be continued and the number of foreign instructors increased from two—a German and a Norwegian—to five. He also proposed to expand the Army from 5,000 to 7,000 men who would be paid according to the scale recommended by Yuan and under his personal supervision. The total monthly pay, amounting to 70,000 taels of silver, and other expenses were to be allocated by the Board of Revenue.

His headquarters had a chief-of-staff in the person of his old friend, Hsü Shih-ch'ang and a secretary, T'ang Shao-i—his erstwhile assistant in Korea. There were also four bureaux—supply, ordnance, transport and foreign affairs (intelligence), and two officers in charge of military law and drilling. The German-trained Manchu General Yin-ch'ang, who was the head of the military academy at Tientsin, recommended to Yuan four of his best students —Feng Kuo-chang, Tuan Ch'i-jui, Wang Shih-chen, and Liang Hua-tien (of whom the last named was later drowned during a night manoeuvre). Feng and Wang were from Chihli and Tuan from Anhwei. They were to become the Big Three of the Northern Army and leaders of two powerful factions. Feng was made Yuan's *aide-de-camp* and concurrently the head of the infantry school; Tuan commanded the artillery corps and was concurrently head of the artillery school; and Wang commanded the engineers' corps and was also head of the engineering school.

A year later, on December 10, 1896, Yuan reported to the throne the formation of a full-scale division including two wings, infantry and artillery, and four companies of cavalry. He took special steps to prevent his officers and men from smoking opium and embezzling funds. Soldiers were paid individually under his personal supervision instead of the money being issued to the commanding officers in the customary way. Discipline was so stern that there were said to be only two ways of noticing subordinates, either by promoting or beheading them. Yet in April 1897 a censor memorialized to the Emperor, charging Yuan with brutal killing and corruption. In response to this, Jung-lu went to Hsiaochan to investigate; on his return he paid unreserved tribute to Yuan's accomplishments. Two years later, when Yuan and the censor met in Shantung, all was forgotten and forgiven and Yuan took him into his secretariat.

A big moment in Yuan's career came when Rear-Admiral Lord Charles Beresford visited Hsiaochan in October 1896. The Admiral was deeply impressed by these 7,400 Shantung men. The infantry was equipped with standardized Mauser rifles, cavalry with both Mauser rifles and lances, and artillery with six-gun batteries from one to six pounders as well as Maxim machine-guns. 'By Western standards,' he commented, 'Yuan Shih-k'ai's troops were the only completely equipped force in the Empire.'[1] For his good work at Hsiaochan, Yuan was promoted to the rank of a provincial judge of Chihli in July 1897 and people began to notice him. Wu Ju-lun, a great scholar, wrote to him on January 17, 1896: 'I have heard that your troops have adopted the Western-style drilling. This is undoubtedly the most urgent task of our time.'[2] Above all both Jung-lu and Weng T'ung-ho retained their good impression of him. The former was a staunch supporter of the Dowager Empress and the latter the Emperor's tutor.

The Newly Created Army continued to grow; and, at the same time, Chang Chih-tung's Self-strengthening Army was taking shape in Hankou and Wuchang and General Nieh Shih-ch'eng's Tenacious Army was being reorganized. Nieh's troops amounted to nearly 10,000, but could not match Yuan's in drilling or equipment. With these separate efforts, however, the defence of the Empire was

[1] *The Break-up of China*, 1899, pp. 4-5.
[2] CJCC, V, p. 303.

gradually consolidated. At the beginning of 1898, there were five armies stationed around the Capital. General Nieh guarded the entrance to Tientsin; General Sung Ch'ing the north-east pass to Peking; Jung-lu's own troops were on the outskirts of the Capital; General Tung Fu-hsiang was near Chichou and Yuan himself at Hsiaochan. Although the Hsiaochan troops were reputed as the strongest, they had not yet been tested in battle. Furthermore, their commander, being a shrewd man, was fully aware of their importance to his own position. The Newly Created Army was to Yuan as the Huai Army to Li Hung-chang, the Hunan Army to Marquis Tseng Kuo-fan, or the Chekiang Army to Tso Tsung-t'ang. It was clear to him that it was no coincidence that the loss of the Huai Army and Li's eclipse were simultaneous. On the other hand, his stay in Korea had enabled him to observe at close quarters the decline of two powers due to their adherence to traditional methods and their refusal to adopt new political and economic measures according to the need of the time. Therefore he was also fully aware of the necessity of a thorough-going reform.

Indeed the demand for such a reform had been growing since 1895. K'ang Yu-wei, a candidate in the Metropolitan examination of that year, together with more than a thousand others, had submitted a memorial to the throne, requesting immediate reform. He and his comrades, including Liang Ch'i-ch'ao and T'an Ssu-t'ung, also organized numerous societies all over the country to promote the cause. Yuan joined one of them, thereby manifesting his support. But it was understandable that for him there was a limit beyond which he would not go. He would not jeopardize his position and future by casting in his army with the Reformists' lot.

Before June 1898, K'ang Yu-wei, the Reformists' leader, had six times submitted memorials to the Emperor and presented to him essays on Peter the Great, the Japanese Mikado Meiji, and the tragedies of Poland and Turkey. These submissions were delivered to the Southern Study of the Palace where they were read with awe and admiration by the highly respected Grand Secretary, Weng T'ung-ho. It was mainly through Weng's advocacy that the Emperor made up his mind to adopt the drastic measures proposed by this commoner. Soon after the Shimonoseki Treaty, reform was discussed by the young ruler with his ageing tutor. News of it, however, leaked out, and the Dowager Empress deprived Weng of the prerogative of access to the Southern Study. This gentle warning put an end to the first attempt.

From 1895 to 1897, the 'Battle of the Concessions' began with British and French encroachments on China's sovereignty in the south-west provinces and, at the end of 1897, German troops occupied Tsingtao on the pretext of two German missionaries having been murdered by the hostile people in Ts'aochou. The fear of dismemberment suddenly gripped China and K'ang Yu-wei hurried to Peking to make another urgent plea for reform. With Weng T'ung-ho working for him inside the Palace and his 'Huxley', Liang Ch'i-ch'ao, outside it, the Reform movement gathered momentum. Weng T'ung-ho recommended him as a hundred times more competent than himself and suggested that the affairs of the whole Empire should be placed under his direction. K'ang sent up his most famous memorial, the sixth, on January 29, 1898.

The ultimate aim of the proposed Reform—national wealth and strength—did not differ from that of the policies pursued by Li Hung-chang, Chang Chih-tung, and others; nor did the Reformists' economic programmes. But in one major respect, the Reformists were opposed to the Conservatives. The latter regarded all invading foreign powers since 1839 as barbarians, implying that they were nations of inferior culture in spite of the superiority of their military forces. Therefore, according to them, all China needed was to have the same guns and warships. As time went on, their view was gradually modified, but never came to the point of admitting her cultural inferiority. The Reformers saw the world in a different light by attributing the prosperity and strength of the West to a more efficient administration and a more robust civilization. If China decided to preserve her integrity and to catch up with the West, she should change herself, but not in Li's and Chang's piece-meal fashion. It was not enough 'to mend the cracks'[1]; the root of the trouble lay in China's 'rigid adherence to her archaic traditions'.[2] The Reformers suggested that the Emperor should resolutely proclaim a reform, change the way of selecting talented people for the civil service, and establish an office to draft a constitution.

The proclamation was duly issued on June 11th and K'ang was appointed the head of the Office of Constitution. Five days later, the Emperor granted him a long audience of nine hours. The Hundred Days Reform was well under way. The Conservatives, under the leadership of the Dowager Empress, alarmed by this rapid development,

---

[1] Liang Ch'i-ch'ao, *Yin-ping-shih-ho-chi*, I, p. 8.
[2] K'ang Yu-wei, *The Sixth Memorial*, WHPF, I, p. 198.

were planning to nip it in the bud. They made three decisions on the day before K'ang's audience: Weng T'ung-ho was relieved of all his duties and 'graciously commanded to go home'; Jung-lu was appointed Viceroy of Chihli and concurrently Commissioner for North China, commanding all troops in the Empire; and both the Empress and the Emperor were to inspect the army in Tientsin at a date to be determined later. The news of the dismissal fell upon Peking like a bombshell; and Jung-lu's new posts were interpreted as a step to tighten up the Conservatives' control over the army. The meaning of these two moves was evident, but, for the moment, the full significance of the trooping ceremony was not generally understood.

The dismissal of his tutor of more than twenty years grieved the Emperor, but did not discourage him. Reform edicts were still more frequent than his filial visits to the Empress at the Summer Palace. Alterations were made in the traditional examination system and the traditional army, many old and superfluous offices were abolished, and new people were appointed to responsible posts. Meanwhile dignitaries were busily making their three-hour journeys between Peking and Tientsin to consult Jung-lu. General Nieh Shih-ch'eng's Tenacious Army was moved from Taku to Tientsin and Tung Fu-hsiang's Kansu Army from Chichou to the outskirts of Peking. It became obvious to the Reformers that their success or failure now depended upon the attitude of the military leaders, in particular, Yuan Shih-k'ai, who had expressed his support for the movement. On September 14th, Yuan was ordered to come to Peking to be received in audience by the Emperor. The meeting took place on the 16th and afterwards it was announced that Yuan was elevated from being a provincial judge to the post of Vice-President of the Board of War in full charge of training modern troops in the Empire. The next morning, Yuan went to the Palace to show his gratitude. It was then that his liege intimated to him the irrevocable decision and future plans of the Reform. On September 18th, he paid a visit to Li Hung-chang and later called upon Prince Ch'ing. At dusk, he received a telegram from Jung-lu, urging him to return to Tientsin at once, for there were, according to Jung-lu, reports of British and Russian gunboats sailing towards Chefoo. Yuan and his secretary were just drafting a reply at his temporary home, the Hua-fa Temple, when a porter came in to announce the arrival of an uninvited guest, T'an Ssu-t'ung.

T'an was a young philosopher of considerable influence both during his life and after his death and a radical leader of the Reform. By this time, he held an important position in the Grand Council. The crucial meeting between him and Yuan was fully recorded in Yuan's journals:

'I know of him as a newly-appointed and trusted adviser to His Majesty. His unheralded visit at this hour must mean that he has serious matters to consult me about, so I put down the writing-brush and go out to greet him. Mr T'an is in informal clothes. Having congratulated me on my promotion, he says that he wants to talk to me alone. This strikes me as odd. However, I lead him into a chamber at the back of the Temple. Our conversation begins with the usual compliments and then turns to physiognomy. Mr T'an sees in me the makings of a great military leader. Suddenly he asks me: "Are you going to say good-bye to His Majesty on the 20th?" I refer to the news of British warships approaching the coast and my intention to request His Majesty's permission to leave for Tientsin tomorrow. T'an's comment on this is "Our worries lie at home, not abroad". I immediately ask him for an explanation and he says: "Mr Yuan, you have just been given exceptional favour for which, I am sure, you are anxious to show your gratitude. His Majesty is in great danger and Mr Yuan, you are the only one, who can help!" My face turns pale and I ask him again: "My family have received Imperial kindness for generations, of course I must place myself entirely at His Majesty's command. But I am afraid I do not understand what you mean by danger." T'an replies: "Jung-lu lately proposed to dethrone and murder the Emperor. Did you know that?" I deny any knowledge of it, for I often see His Excellency Jung-lu at Tientsin and know him through both his words and deeds to be an upright and loyal man. I also suggest to T'an that the rumour about Jung-lu's scheme is completely groundless. But T'an adds: "Mr. Yuan, you are a straightforward man, and therefore may not be aware of his guile. He is outwardly very nice to you, but in fact he is both suspicious and jealous of you. Your hard work for so many years has won admiration from people at home and abroad, yet you have been promoted only once. Why? It is entirely due to Jung-lu's obstruction. The other day, Mr. K'ang [Yu-wei] spoke highly of you to His Majesty, but the Emperor merely said that you were arrogant and disobedient according to both the Empress and Jung-lu. Many people can prove this. It is perfectly true. I myself repeatedly recommended your promotion, but Jung-lu objected. His Majesty often says that you are a fine man, but untrustworthy. Your recent promotion did not come at all easily. If you really mean to help His Majesty out of the present difficulty, I have here a plan for you."

'Mr T'an thereupon produces a piece of paper like a large visiting-card, on which are these words:

"Jung-lu plans to dethrone and murder H.M. Traitor! Must be done away with as soon as possible. Else H.M.'s position is untenable. Yuan leaves for Tientsin on the 20th. Give him a mandate in the Vermilion Pencil, ordering him to call on Jung-lu with his troops, arresting and executing Jung-lu. Yuan takes over the Viceroyalty and Commissionership. Make known Jung-lu's treachery to the public. Stop telegraph and railway services. Yuan and his troops come to Peking to guard the Forbidden City and besiege the Summer Palace. Commit suicide in H.M.'s presence, if plan rejected."

I am petrified and, at length, ask him why I should besiege the Summer Palace. Mr T'an explains: "The old rotten —— [the Dowager Empress] must be got rid of, or our country will perish. Nevertheless, that will be my job. You need not bother." I tell him: "Her Majesty's regency of over thirty years has delivered China safely out of many disasters. She is widely loved. My soldiers are taught to be loyal. I cannot turn them into rebels." T'an goes on: "I have recruited scores of brave men and sent for many more from Hunan. They will be here soon. It is my job to do away with the old rotten ——, you need not trouble yourself. What you, Mr Yuan, must do is: first, kill Jung-lu; second, besiege the Summer Palace. If you refuse, I shall die here and now. Your life is now in my hands just as mine is in yours. We must come to a decision tonight before His Majesty receives me in audience." The conversation continues—
I: "This is a grave matter which cannot be decided in haste. I would sooner die than give you my word tonight. Furthermore I do not believe that His Majesty will grant his permission without due consideration."
T'an: "I have ways to make sure of that. I can promise that you will get a mandate in the Vermilion Pencil on the 20th."
He spoke with authority and inflexibility. That he is in the Sovereign's trust makes me wary of refusing him outright. I fear that

unpredictable harm may come my way. All I can do under these circumstances is to find excuses and to avoid committing myself. I explain to him: "Tientsin is a cosmopolitan city. The assassination of the Viceroy there is bound to arouse a great outcry among its Chinese and foreign inhabitants and may lead to the tragic consequence of China being carved up like a melon by the foreign powers. Moreover, there are three armies, each about 40,000 or 50,000 strong, commanded by Generals Sung, Tung, and Nieh. There are also nearly seventy corps of the Huai Army and other troops, In the Capital, there are several thousands of Manchu troops. I have only 7,000 men of whom 6,000 can be thrown into battle. How can I possibly hope to succeed in what you ask me to do? As soon as I make a move, the Capital will be heavily guarded. The Sovereign's position certainly becomes untenable." "But Mr Yuan," T'an argues, "I am sure you can deal them a lightning blow. As soon as you act, a mandate in the Vermilion Pencil will be issued to all the armies and the embassies will be informed as well. No one dares to oppose you." I then submit: "The ordnance and supplies of my army are mostly kept in the city of Tientsin, only a small part is at Hsiaochan. I must have time to accumulate enough ammunition and provisions before taking action." T'an suggests: "I shall ask His Majesty to give you a mandate in the Vermilion Pencil and, at the same time, you will go on with your preparations. When you are ready, please let me know, so we can act in concert." "I am not thinking of my own safety," I add: "but if there should be a leak which places His Majesty in peril, how are we to answer that? No, nothing should be put in writing. There must not be any mandate in the Vermilion Pencil. Please allow me time to think. I shall let you know in a fortnight or twenty days." But T'an insists: "His Majesty wants this to be done quickly. We must come to a decision tonight, so I shall have something to report back to him. In fact I can show you a mandate in the Vermilion Pencil now." When T'an shows it to me, I see it is written in black ink. The handwriting is exquisite and the style similar to that of the Sovereign's. It reads:

"We have resolved to reform, but old Ministers are reluctant to lend their support. We cannot force the pace, lest Her Gracious Majesty, the Dowager Empress, should be displeased. We hereby command Yang Jui, Liu Kang-ti, Lin Hsü, and T'an Ssu-t'ung to find a better approach. . . ."

'The overall tone of the mandate seems to suggest that the four people mentioned in it want to quicken the pace of the Reform while His Majesty refuses to do so. I therefore say: "This is not in the Vermilion Pencil and it mentions neither the execution of His Excellency Jung-lu nor the siege of the Summer Palace." T'an offers this explanation: "The copy in the Vermilion Pencil is with Lin Hsü and this one was made out for me by Yang Jui. There is no doubt of its authenticity. It was issued three days ago. I was upset that Lin Hsü did not let me have it at once. His negligence may lead to harmful consequences. What is referred to here as a better approach implies both the points you have raised." His explanation confirms my suspicion of a forgery. There seems no point in carrying on with the discussion, so I make it clear to him: "Heaven above me, I, Yuan Shih-k'ai, have never been ungrateful to His Majesty. I will not put my liege in jeopardy. The whole subject must be thought over with care, and a fool-proof plan is required. I must confess that I have no courage to become a public enemy." However, T'an is most insistent. He argues vehemently that I must agree with him before he leaves for the Palace tonight. I have also noticed that something like a weapon bulges out from under his jacket. I have a feeling that he is determined not to leave empty-handed. Therefore I tell him: "There will be a trooping ceremony in Tientsin next month. All the armies will congregate there. If His Majesty cares to give us even only a scrap of paper, who dares to disobey and what cannot be accomplished?"

'T'an goes on: "That is too far away. His Majesty might be murdered before that." I say: "I do not believe anything of that kind will happen before the ceremony. Besides, our plan must take time to mature." T'an asks: "If the ceremony is called off, what then?" My reply is: "The ceremony is being prepared and thousands of taels have been spent on it already. I do not think that Their Majesties will change their minds. Furthermore I shall request His Excellency Jung-lu to make sure that Her Majesty the Empress will not revoke her decision. I shall see to that." T'an warns me: "It is now entirely up to you either to repay the Sovereign's kindness, to help him out of the present difficulty and to render an exceptionally meritorious service, or to betray him, to endanger his life in order to obtain power and wealth." I retort: "What sort of man do you think I am? My family has received Imperial benevolence for three generations now. Do you think I am crazy enough to turn traitor?

I will risk my life for what is good for my Emperor and his country."

'T'an is visibly moved. He stands up, salutes me, and calls me a good man. . . .

'On the 20th, I bid farewell to His Majesty. . . . When I arrive at Tientsin, *it is already dusk*. I pay a visit to His Excellency Jung-lu at once and report to him the latest development in the Palace. I have also said that His Majesty is filial to the Empress, but there are rogues forming cliques in the Capital, who are putting the throne in a dangerous position. The blame lies with those serving under His Majesty. In order to maintain peace it is necessary to protect the Sovereign.

'*It is midnight already*, so I ask permission to leave and promise to pay another visit tomorrow. *The next morning*, His Excellency comes to see me instead. It is then I report everything to him in detail. Jung-lu turns pale and cries: "If I had any intention to assassinate the Emperor, Heaven will condemn me to death! . . ." I plead with him: "His Majesty had nothing to do with this at all. If anything happens to him, I will take poison!" '[1]

The same incident was also recorded in T'an Ssu-t'ung's biography by Liang Ch'i-ch'ao:

'In the evening of September 18th, he went to the Hua-fa Temple to see Yuan. He asked him openly "What do you think of His Majesty?" Yuan replied: "A great and sagacious ruler." Tan asked again "Did you know the plot behind the forthcoming Tientsin trooping ceremony?" Yuan said that he did. Then Mr T'an showed a confidential edict to Yuan and said: "You, sir, are the only man, who can help our wise Emperor. The decision is entirely yours." Mr T'an also touched his neck with his hands and added: "If you decide against it, please go to the Summer Palace to report to Her Majesty. You will get wealth and power there." Yuan retorted sternly: "What kind of man do you think I am? We both serve our Sovereign and receive his favour. The duty of protecting him is not yours alone. Tell me what to do." T'an went on: "Jung-lu's scheme will be carried out at the trooping ceremony. Your army and the other two commanded by Tung and Nieh are both under his control. He is going to use you all as the instruments of his plan.

---

[1] *Wu-hsü Jih-chi*, written at Hsiaochan, on October 10, 1898, and published in four instalments in the *Shen Pao* on February 2, 4, 6, and 8, 1926. Author's italics.

But Tung and Nieh are nothing, only you, Mr Yuan, are a strong man. You can crush the other two armies and protect His Majesty. The decision to restore authority to His Majesty and to clear up the chaos in the Palace is completely yours." Yuan declared: "At the ceremony, if His Majesty rides into my headquarters and gives me the order to execute the villains, I shall certainly do my best in concert with you and your friends. . . ." Mr T'an asked him: "Would it be easy to deal with a cunning man like Jung-lu?" Yuan replied with anger in his eyes: "When His Majesty is in my head-quarters, I shall kill Jung-lu as if slaughtering a dog. . . ." [1]

Yuan's own account is considerably different from Liang Ch'i-ch'ao's, and from other records too. Several points will emerge from collating them.

1. T'an Ssu-t'ung, although a radical, was an accomplished scholar, who would not resort to threats as Yuan described. They were simply not in keeping with his character. Furthermore he should know the futility of threatening a man renowned for his audacity in Korea.

2. Prior to Yuan's audiences with the Emperor, T'an had suggested enlisting Yuan's help for his liege. Therefore the confidential mandate in question was very likely a genuine one in the Vermilion Pencil, not in black ink.

3. In both accounts, Yuan had, on his own initiative, pledged his support of the Emperor and promised not to betray the Reformers' trust. According to himself, Yuan did not tell Jung-lu about the plot at the trooping ceremony until the morning of September 21st, after the *coup d'état* had already been staged in Peking. Two questions are pertinent here: Why did Jung-lu fabricate the news of the movement of British ships in order to bring Yuan back? What did he and Jung-lu talk about from sunset to midnight on the 20th?

4. In fact, Yuan arrived at Tientsin, not after sunset as he said, but at 3.00 in the afternoon. The newspaper, *Kuo Wen Pao* (21.9.1898) reported that he took the 11.40 train from Peking, reaching Tientsin at 3.00. At Tientsin station, there was a large party waiting to welcome back the new Vice-President of the Board of War.

All accounts agree on one point—Yuan went to see Jung-lu directly he arrived and made a full report on his doings in the

[1] WHPF, IV, p. 52.

Capital. According to the Shanghai newspaper, *Shen Pao*, Jung-lu immediately telegraphed the contents of Yuan's alarming report to the Empress (8.10.1898), whereas many other accounts say that Jung-lu left for Peking by train to make a personal appeal for action to the Empress at the Summer Palace. There was time for either or both.

At dawn, September 21st, the Empress progressed from the Summer Palace, about six miles west of Peking, to the Forbidden City, proclaimed her second regency and interned the Emperor in a lake palace. K'ang Yu-wei and Liang Ch'i-ch'ao with the help of their British and Japanese friends managed to escape abroad in the nick of time, while six other leaders of the Reformers, the 'Six Gentlemen' as they have been called ever since, were arrested and executed. The offices which had been abolished were restored and the changes in the examination system reversed; and all Reformers in the civil service were purged by dismissal and various degrees of punishment. The Reform was over. On September 25th, Jung-lu was recalled to Peking and Yuan Shih-k'ai took over the Viceroyalty and Commissionership until Yü-lu's appointment was announced three days later. On September 29th, Yuan was richly rewarded by the Empress for his kiss of death on the cheek of the Hundred Days Reform. He remained her henchman until her death in 1908.

The short-lived Reform left a long-lasting impression on the history of China as it marked the beginning of her search for a political system which could offer peace and prosperity to the people and power and authority to the Government. Was the system to be a constitutional monarchy or a republic, a dictatorship or a democracy? Was it to be achieved by gradual reform or by a revolution? In any case, few would agree that the tottering dynasty should have been kept alive for so long as it was. During the search, people of differing experience and training were bound to disagree, and disagreement often resulted in confusion. Their experience or training was obtained either from residence abroad or from reading foreign books. Different countries thus provided China with different models and often with contradictory advice. Everyone was eager to tell her what to do, so that she suffered from an excess of information and counsel which is never conducive to critical-mindedness or originality. It was therefore during this period that China appeared in the eyes of the world as muddled, diffident, dishonest, and disunited, and there were further humiliations in store for her as the Battle of the Concessions went along its shameless course.

CHAPTER IV

The Governor 1899-1901

THE search for a political system continued after the Reform; the next stage of the experiment was the Boxer Movement.

Like the Reform, the Boxer Movement was a direct result of foreign aggression. It began in the peninsular province of Shantung which, since 1840, had been comparatively free from the foreign interference which affected all the other coastal provinces. When, in the spring of 1898, the Germans forced their way into Tsingtao and secured rights to build railways and prospect for mining resources there, the inhabitants cast angry looks upon them. These Shantung people were renowned for their physical and mental toughness. Yuan Shih-k'ai s new recruits at Hsiaochan mostly came from this province. The Shantung peasant was backward and superstitious, the main sources of his knowledge being the hardship of his life, rudimentary religious tenets and, above all, myths. Incidentally, the post-1895 period in China was a golden age of myths, the result of popular indulgence in reading or listening to weird stories as an escape from reality—the nation-wide frustration—made possible by the introduction of the modern printing-press. The belief in physical invulnerability, lethal lights emitted from the eyes, nostrils, or finger-tips, and the ability to command invisible generals and armies was analogous to that of a modern child's in the 'split-second draw' of a Jesse James novel. Relying upon such beliefs, the Boxers endeavoured to realize their political ends. They, like their hard-pressed country, had almost no other known resource against the never-ending infringements on Chinese sovereign rights.

The Boxer Movement and the Reform not only sprang from the same cause but also had identical aims. They were both working to strengthen the Central Government of China and to repel foreign influence. The Boxers' slogan, 'Strengthen the Manchu Rule and Wipe Out Foreigners', could easily, phrased more elegantly, have been adopted by the Reformers. An eye-witness of the movement, Sir Robert Hart, described it as 'patriotic in origin and justifiable in its fundamental ideas'[1]; and another, Putnam Weale, said: 'a blight is setting on us, for we are accused by the *whole population* of North China'.[2] C. F. Remer put it more penetratingly: '. . . the movement may be regarded as evidence of a growing feeling of *national patriotism* in China. From this point of view the Boxer Movement may be looked upon as foreshadowing the overthrow of the dynasty.'[3] Both the Reform and the movement, apart from their similar origin and object, could also claim to have a long tradition in China. The former derived its philosophical basis from Confucianism and the latter found popular support by exploiting the superstitions of the people in the same way as the Red Eyebrows and the Yellow Turbans had done in the first and the second centuries AD.

But the superficial similarity ceases here. The Reformers were all scholar-gentry, well versed in the traditional political philosophy of China and with some knowledge of the statecraft of the West, who argued their case at that level. They had no trust in those of their own class already in power, and therefore proposed their replacement. The Boxers, on the other hand, knowing nothing that was sophisticated, put forward their case crudely and violently. They had no trust at all in the gentry. Instead, they proposed a marriage between the Manchu Government and the peasantry whose invulnerability and omnipotent incantations would soon put China back on her feet again.

The movement began to attract official attention early in 1898, shortly after Germany had threatened China with force and secured the lease of Kiaochow, as Russia had done in the Liaotung Peninsula, Britain in Weihaiwei, and France in the Bay of Kuangchou, but the provincial authorities took no effective steps to stamp it out. It was regarded as no more heretical than were the Christian churches being built side-by-side with the Boxers' altars. From May 1898 to March 1899 the Boxers went from strength to strength, plundering and slaughtering their way to popularity. Many Christians as well as railway and mining engineers fell victims to them. The situation took a sharp turn in March when German troops were sent to Ichou, in the south of Shantung, to protect the missionaries there. The

---

[1] *These from the Land of Sinim*, p. 4.
[2] *Indiscreet Letters from Peking*, p. 85. Author's italics.
[3] *The Foreign Trade in China*, p. 105. Author's italics.

Peking Government, fearing unpleasant consequences, cashiered Chang Ju-mei, the Governor, and appointed Yü-hsien, a Manchu, in his place. The new Governor soon fell under the spell of the Boxers. Instead of suppressing them, he became their patron, and the situation went from bad to worse, as each new concession made by the Government to a foreign power could not fail to enhance the Boxers' appeal among the peasants. They went on killing and burning, while the Government had to pay compensation for their deeds. The damages claimed by the Germans as a result of the looting and killing of Christians in Ichou amounted to 100,000 taels, and another 60,000 taels was demanded for the damage to the Ts'aochou churches in the summer of 1899. Towards the end of the year, clashes between the Boxers and Christians became more and more frequent. On December 6, 1899, Yü-hsien was recalled and Yuan Shih-k'ai appointed as the acting Governor of Shantung, from which post he was shortly promoted to be the Governor.

This important appointment did not come as a surprise. In the first place, Yuan himself was already a very high official—he had been junior Vice-President of the Board of Works since June. In the second place, the Government was looking for a man who had sufficient experience in dealing with foreigners and also sufficient strength to quell the Boxers. In the third place, Yuan had been consulted about the Boxer troubles for some time before his appointment, and besides he knew the province and its people well.

Since the collapse of the Reform, Yuan's horizon had widened considerably, perhaps a sign of the Empress's increasing reliance upon him. His memorials covered an extensive range of subjects such as tax reform, coal-mining, foreign relations and, of course, military training, the last of which was still his main responsibility. He made two important proposals in 1899 on national defence, urging the Government to make China self-sufficient in the supply of ordnance and to bring the number of modern troops to 100,000. On July 4th, he submitted a memorial on the religious incidents in Shantung. According to him, these conflicts could be stopped by sending thither a well disciplined force to act as police, and by informing local officials in Shantung and other provinces of the contents of China's treaties and agreements with other powers, so that they could tackle problems with foreign representatives with the required knowledge. The only man, who had such a force at his disposal and such knowledge, was Yuan himself.

E

Two corps of Yuan's troops were despatched thither in May for the announced reason of a joint manoeuvres with the twenty corps of the provincial garrisons. Upon his appointment, Yuan took the rest of his division with him. At the same time, he received Imperial instructions to give strict orders to his subordinates that, in cases of conflict between common people and the Christians, they should handle them fairly and 'in no way should rely solely upon military force, lest the people be frightened into revolt'.[1] Yuan also discussed the question of the movement with a former Shantung local official, Lao Nai-hsüan, who had made a special study of the Boxers and was then considered an authority on this subject. Lao was of the opinion that the Boxers were heretical rebels, who should be supressed, but not by force alone. Looming at the back of his mind was perhaps the wise saying: 'Conquer not only men's cities, but their hearts.' The first thing that Yuan did was to test the Boxers invulnerability. His firing squad shot at and killed a number of them. Similar tests had been held before, but the reported results were different. This may have been due to the greater reliability of Yuan's men. His other observations were that the Boxers obtained their supplies by looting and that once 400 to 500 of them had attacked a church but failed to take it. 'How can they wipe out foreigners? Even if they could recruit millions of people into their ranks, roaming around everywhere like spreading bush fires, what would happen to our country?'[2] Yuan proposed to take both long-term and short-term measures in dealing with them. In the long run, he was to promote understanding between ordinary people and Christians; and, in the short, he was determined to maintain order, liquidate bandit elements, and pardon the wayward people, allowing them to redeem themselves. Yuan's suppression of the movement was both severe and thorough, causing the anxious Empress to demand that he be more lenient, but soon incidents became few and far between and the rebels fled from the tight corner they were in in Shantung to the roomier province of Chihil. In this way, Yuan laid the foundation of stability in that province throughout the turbulent year of 1900. 'Shantung is all right, never fear. . . .' Putnam Weale recorded in his *Indiscreet Letters*, for 'the provincial Governor is a strong Chinaman, one Yuan Shih-k'ai'.[3]

[1] *Ch'ing Te-tsung Shih-lu*, 26.12.1899, ch. 455, p. 11b.
[2] *Yuan's memorial to the throne*, 13.1.1900, YSY, ch. 2, pp. 2b–3a.
[3] pp. 8–9.

For the suppression of the Boxers, Yuan requested the expansion of his division and was instructed to reorganize and incorporate the twenty corps of the provincial garrison into his army as its vanguard. Feng Kuo-chang, who with Tuan Ch'i-jui and Wang Shih-chen was at this time holding a rank equivalent to prefect, was given full charge of this work. The morale of the officers and men was high, for the operations against the rebels were successful and the prospects for the troops and their leader were extremely bright. Compared with the four other divisions of the Imperial Guards, Jung-lu's Central, Sung Ch'ing's Left, Nieh Shih-ch'eng's Front, and Tung Fu-hsiang's Rear Divisions, Yuan's Right Division was by far the strongest and had the good fortune to be stationed at some distance from Chihli.

Yuan's meat was other people's poison. Once the Shantung Boxers entered Chihli they found among their new supporters many Manchu dignitaries through whom they won the favour of the august Empress Dowager. Under her patronage rebels and officials worked together in attacking Christians as well as those who were suspected of foreign contacts, killing and plundering being the order of the day. Hu Yü-fen, the Commissioner for railway affairs, nearly lost his life and had to flee to Yuan Shih-k'ai for protection. Tung Fu-hsiang's Kansu army was particularly active in giving the Boxers its support. Nieh Shih-ch'eng at first was not convinced of the efficiency of the Boxers' magic powers or the good that they might do to the country. He tried to suppress them, but was severely warned against such rash action by the Empress. The Commander-in-Chief of all the infantry, Jung-lu, was in two minds, fearing the consequences of the Boxers' provocations as well as the Empress's wrath. As those who spoke against the movement within the Imperial Court were being cashiered, the situation outside deteriorated.

With June came the siege of the Legation Quarter in Peking. The embassies were waiting for reinforcements to arrive on the 11th, but none arrived. Hope soon dwindled into despair and Sugiyama, a chancellor of the Japanese Legation, volunteered to break through the ring of Boxers and troops to find out what had happened. His driver returned shortly to report that he had been decapitated and mutilated by Tung Fu-hsiang's army near the Altar of Heaven.

The news of the murder and the siege reached the capital of Shantung on the next day, and Yuan thereupon addressed a telegram to Jung-lu, exhorting him either to do all he could to protect the

Legations or to give a safe conduct to all the diplomats in Peking. At the same time, he telegraphed Sheng Hsüan-huai:

'About 8,000 foreign troops near Tientsin and Peking; 10,000 more on their way. Dare not surmise what will happen. Please advise me. Have Viceroys Liu K'un-i and Chang Chih-tung any good suggestions?'[1]

Being still the junior among the Viceroys and Governors, Yuan was not in a position to advocate an independent policy and assume the leadership. But this telegram dropped an unambiguous hint to the provincial leaders that something had to be done to secure South and East China. It also showed Yuan's willingness to co-operate with them in a concerted action. Sheng, Li Hung-chang's lieutenant and a key man in economic matters, had perhaps the best contacts with foreigners in Shanghai but was in the enviable position of not being a local official, so Yuan's telegram was sent to him instead of directly to Liu or Chang. Of these two messages, the first fell upon deaf ears and the second upon sympathetic ones. The incident marked the dissension between Peking and the provinces, as Peking saw in the Boxers an effective force against aggressive foreigners which should be harnessed and made full use of, while the provincial leaders regarded them as dangerous and absurd and as rivals in strengthening China. The local opinion, however, was temporarily invalidated by the defeat of Admiral Seymour's troops.

Sir E. H. Seymour, the British naval commander at Tientsin, was anxious to raise the siege of the Legations in Peking and, with some 2,000 soldiers, was attempting to fight his way thither from Tientsin. He and his men clashed with the Boxers, Nieh Shih-ch'eng's Front Division, and Tung Fu-hsiang's Rear Division on June 18th. They were compelled to retreat after suffering heavy casualties. This in the eyes of many Manchu dignitaries was sufficient proof of the Boxers' ability to extinguish foreigners. The Empress at once called her officials for a discussion in the Palace, and they resolved to award 100,000 taels of silver to the Boxers, set up altars everywhere for people to worship, and attack the Legations. Jung-lu was appointed the Commander-in-Chief of the operation. Still indecisive, he wrote to Liu K'un-i, forecasting the lamentable

[1] YCTKCP, 14.6.1900, ch. 35, p. 226a.

result of a weak country fighting against several strong ones.

By then eight powers—Britain, France, Russia, Germany, the United States of America, Italy, Austria, and Japan—had already formed a loose alliance and their reinforcements had arrived at Taku. On June 17th, the strong fortress at Taku fell and Tientsin was consequently laid bare to attack. Yet in the capital, provocations continued. The German Minister, F. von Ketteler, was murdered at the order of a Manchu prince on June 20th, and, on the next day, the Empress declared war. The battle of Tientsin ensued. General Nieh Shih-ch'eng died in action on the outskirts of the town on July 9th and five days later his troops were completely wiped out. Another division, the Left of the Imperial Guards, now under the command of General Ma Yü-k'un, who firmly believed the Boxers' ability to block the foreigners' gun-barrels and ordered an attack, received a crippling blow in the same battle, and, on August 5th, when the city fell, was put out of action. With the city went the biggest arsenal in North China. On the same day the Viceroy of Chihli, Yü-lu, committed suicide.

The victorious expeditionary forces then drove towards Peking where, outside the city wall, they engaged in a fierce battle against General Tung Fu-hsiang's troops on August 13th. The Empress realized her own folly and miscalculation, and, in a desperate attempt to rally her supporters together to find a way out, called a Palace meeting on August 14th—but no one attended. The city was broken into on the next day just after the Empress, the Emperor, and their entourage had fled in disguise. The siege of the Legations was thus lifted and the infamous sack of Peking began.

While disaster fell upon Tientsin and Peking, peace reigned in the south-east. Local authorities declined to follow Peking's lead; in preference, they adopted a policy of protecting their own territories. Yuan clearly expounded this policy in a memorial to the throne on June 29th with a view to saving parts of the Empire from catastrophe and protecting the economic resources in the south-east which were vital to the dynasty. Through Sheng Hsüan-huai, he came to a *rapprochement* with the British based at Chefoo. He and his colleagues, such as Li Hung-chang of Kuangtung, Chang Chih-tung of Hupei, and Liu K'un-i of Kiangsu, maintained a friendly attitude towards the foreign powers throughout the whole episode. His initial diffidence gradually gave way to the urgent need of the time, and eventually he took up the leadership in pursuing this policy.

Sheng Hsüan-huai, in his telegram to him on July 14th, put it candidly:

'Ho-fei (Li Hung-chang) is too old. Sir, you are now the man of destiny!'[1]

As the war went on, Yuan's position became increasingly important. His office in Chinan, close to the Capital, was the centre of telecommunications between the Imperial Court, the provinces, and the Chinese Legations overseas. He was not only the best-informed but also the strongest man in the Empire, as by the time Peking fell four of the five divisions of the Imperial Guards had met their doom, and the only one remaining, the Right Division, was the one modern army in North China. Supreme power was within his grasp, the stage was cleared, and he knew full well who had paved the way for him!

Power, however, did not fall into his hands like a ripe apple; his own astute judgment played its part. The master never made a false move. It was clear in many minds that, after the Boxer crisis, North China would once again become a power vacuum as it had been after the fall of Li Hung-chang five years before. The much coveted Viceroyalty of Chihli would have to be given to a strong man. Among those who were eligible for the post, Li Hung-chang had prestige at home and abroad, seniority and experience, and a large number of henchmen holding important posts all over the country; Chang Chih-tung and Liu K un-i were both possible choices, for they were also senior officials and had their own troops. However, if defence and security was the supreme consideration, Yuan's army might just tip the balance, and its destruction consequently would pave the way for the senile statesmen. For Yuan himself, the maintenance of his military supremacy was naturally of paramount importance. When the Empress commanded him to despatch troops to Tientsin on June 17th, he merely sent a token force of 3,000 men under the command of Sun Chin-piao. They went as far as Techou in north Shantung and were ordered to turn back, for Yuan had noticed their lack of discipline and therefore sent the six battalions under Hsia Hsin-yu's command instead. These delaying tactics gained a day or two and on June 20th, two days after Seymour's defeat, the Empress confidently ordered Yuan to recall them. This was swiftly done, but

[1] YCTKCP, ch. 37, p. 17a.

another two days later the situation, as well as the Imperial mind, changed. Two urgent calls for help suddenly came from Peking, both of which Yuan refused on the ground that the troops having just returned could not be sent again. Sheng Hsüan-huai also urged him to clear up the Augean stables in Chihli and to protect the diplomats in Peking, but Yuan remarked 'the critical illness is undergoing a change; better not hurry with medicine'.[1] At the beginning of July, Li Hung-chang too was of the opinion that Yuan should lead his troops to Chihli to suppress the Boxers, and Yuan replied: 'If I lead my troops to save the foreign Ministers at Peking without Imperial orders, I am afraid that, on the way, I shall be defeated. This I really cannot do.'[2] When Sheng Hsüan-huai entreated him again, he tersely said: 'The less we talk about it, the better.'[3] However, as a gesture of Yuan's loyalty to the throne, Hsia Hsin-yu's small contingent eventually arrived at Peking, only to vanish in the tide of events.

A hunting dog is needed as long as there are foxes and he has his master's trust. Yuan was useful to the Empress for similar reasons. True, he did not do much in 1900, not because he could not, but because there were other dogs about and the Boxers were not 'on his beat'. His loyalty was never suspect. He was the first to send money, silk, and even food to the Imperial travelling lodge; and though he was the Governor of a relatively poor province, his contribution to the 1901 indemnity was the second largest. When there was talk that foreign powers should demand the termination of the Empress's regency, he was the first to oppose the idea. He left no room for anyone to stand between the mistress and her servant.

It would be unfair to blame Yuan alone for his lack of action in the Manchu interest in 1900, for other viceroys and governors in fact did less. Li Hung-chang, for instance, flatly refused to lend any support to the Boxers; and Chang Chih-tung and Liu K'un-i declined Yuan's suggestion that troops should be sent to Chihli and Shansi to mop up the Boxers after the fall of Peking. Li Hung-chang, the wily old fox, was perhaps the most impassive of them all. At the end of 1899 when both the movement and the plot to dethrone the Emperor were gaining support, Jung-lu, under the Empress's instructions, went to see him, when he was living in semi-retirement

[1] YCTKCP, 28.6.1900, ch. 36, p. 20a.
[2] LWCKCS, 7.7.1900, ch. 23, p. 20b.
[3] YCTKCP, 2.8.1900, ch. 38, p. 23a.

in the Capital and was anxious to get out of the place. Jung-lu's mission was to ask Li to find out whether the diplomats would favour the accession of Ta-o-ko. Li seized the opportunity to propose: 'If Her Majesty would appoint me to a viceroyalty somewhere, the Ministers will come to congratulate me. I shall then find out what you want to know.'[1] A few days later, the appointment of Li to the Viceroyalty of Kwangtung and Kwangsi was announced. Having got out of the Capital, all that Li had to do was to sit back and wait. The more the situation in the north deteriorated, the more his services would be needed, for he was the only elder statesman who could command enough respect abroad to deal with the deluge after the Boxer uprising. In June, the Empress ordered him to come to Peking, but he refused; and, at the beginning of July, he was again urged to come; this time he took a boat as far as Shanghai, whence he reported his illness and the necessity of a short stay there for treatment. He was well again after the fall of Peking and arrived at Tientsin in September under Russian escort as the Chinese Plenipotentiary to sue the eight allied powers for peace. With Prince Ch'ing as his co-negotiator, he signed the twelve-article Peace Protocol of 1901 on September 7th under which several princes, presidents of boards, and governors were punished as war criminals. Tung Fu-hsiang, the commander of the Kansu Army, was cashiered and died in disgrace in 1908. A prince and a vice-president were to be sent to Germany and Japan respectively to offer an apology for the murder of von Ketteler and Sugiyama. In addition to these stipulations, China agreed to stop purchasing weapons from abroad for two years and to pay an indemnity of 450,000,000 taels (£67,500,000) within thirty-nine years, the revenues from the customs and the Salt Gabelle being the guarantee.

Li Hung-chang's other appointment was to the office of Viceroy of Chihli, where his immediate duties were to maintain order and to unravel a tangled situation. For these purposes, he took over command of the remnant of the Central Division of the Imperial Guards from Jung-lu and summoned Hu Yü-fen to Peking to gather together what was left of Nieh Shih-ch'eng's and Sung Ch'ing's troops. At the same time, he had to negotiate with Russia for the evacuation of her troops from Manchuria, for the Czar, fishing in troubled waters, had occupied the whole Imperial Domain. These heavy duties broke the feeble health of the ageing statesman

[1] Lo Tun-jung, *Ch'üan-pien-yü-wen, Jung-yen*, I, No. 4, p. 2.

and on his death-bed, on November 7, 1901, he dictated a valedictory memorial to the Empress—'Looking around the whole Empire, I see Yuan Shih-k'ai standing head and shoulders above the rest'[1]; and recommended Yuan to succeed him.

Thus ended Yuan's two years' tenure of office in Shantung, the beginning and end of which coincided with the rise and fall of the Boxer movement. During this period, the star of the misled Governments sank to its nadir while that of Yuan rose to its zenith. The Boxers had made his fortune. As far as more constructive measures were concerned, his governorship was a success. He improved the efficiency of tax collection to produce a surplus in 1901 of more than a million taels. This enabled him to finance the expansion of his army and to supply the needs of the Empress Dowager in retreat, first at T'aiyuan and then in Sian. On military development Yuan spent more than 900,000 taels, and, by the time he took over the Viceroyalty at Tientsin, his army had grown to 20,000 men. In this he offended Viceroy Chang Chih-tung, for in July 1901 he was ordered to assume command and responsibility for the training of a large section of Chang's Self-strengthening Army, stationed in Kiangsu. Chang at once telegraphed Viceroy Liu K'un-i for an explanation of the change in command, and both Liu and Yuan memorialized to the throne against this decision. But their protests came to nothing, except that Yuan gained a regiment and an enemy in Chang Chih-tung.

Shortly before his departure, Yuan laid the foundation of a provincial college in Chinan. This ambitious project was designed for children from seven to fourteen years of age. The college was to be divided into three sections—the preparatory, eight years, for lessons in the classics, history, astronomy, geography, and mathematics; the secondary, four years, for the same lessons but at an advanced level; and the tertiary, another four years, for specialized subjects such as languages, commerce, engineering and so on. An American missionary was appointed the chief instructor and the fund was to come from the estate dues of the province. Yuan did not remain long enough in Chinan to see this project being brought to fruition.

In Chinese politics of that time, it was essential to have the right connexions and the right sort of followers. A high official should know, and be known to, other dignitaries and, particularly, have a

[1] Li Chien-nung, *Chung-kuo Chin-pai-nien Cheng-chih-shih*, p. 216.

sizeable secretariat consisting of his trusted lieutenants. By the time he was ready for the State in Tientsin, Yuan had on his side in the Imperial Court the Empress, Prince Ch'ing, Na-t'ung the President of the Board of Revenue, and Li Lien-ying the Grand Eunuch. In his secretariat, there were his sworn brother Hsü Shih-ch'ang, the loyal assistant T'ang Shao-i, and a host of officers of the Hsiaochan days among whom the most notable were Tuan Ch'i-jui, Feng Kuo-chang, Wang Shih-chen, Chang Hsün, Chiang Kui-t'i, Ni Ssu-ch'ung, Ts'ao K'un, and Tuan Chih-kuei. The last-named addressed him as 'Father', and most of the others regarded him as their teacher. In many cases, the relationship between the head and his subordinates was strengthened by personal considerations of one kind or another. They were loyal to the throne because he was. With this devoted group of men working under him, Yuan was well prepared for a more important post than the governorship of Shantung.

Although his appointment as Acting Viceroy of Chihli and concurrently Commissioner for North China Trade was announced on the day of Li Hung-chang's death, Yuan could not accept this most powerful office without the proper ritual. The word 'pride' in Chinese also means 'conceit'. To accept a responsibility of such magnitude with pride but without making some gesture of self-doubt might show Yuan lacked modesty. After all Chang Chih-tung, Liu K'un-i and the newly-appointed Viceroy of Shensi and Kansu, Jung-lu, were all senior to him, and he should take their feelings into consideration; moreover, the influence he had built up in his two years in Shantung should not lightly be left unexploited. He therefore immediately telegraphed the Empress declining this Imperial favour. On the same day, Sheng Hsüan-huai urged him to take up this key post in the north and Yuan replied in an apparently firm tone:

'My waning health and confused mind do not permit me to do as I am commanded. If I go, Shantung will certainly fall into chaos like Mukden. How can Chihli look after itself, if both Shantung and Mukden are in turmoil? My departure from Chinan can only mean harm to the delicate situation. Please think it over and please drop this matter altogether.'[1]

Sheng, reading between the lines and anxious to be on good terms

---

[1] YCTKCP, 7.11.1901, ch. 56, p. 28a.

with this new dignitary, took the initiative in proposing that Shan-tung should be added to the long list of duties of the Viceroyalty; Jung-lu seconded this, and the Empress's approval was granted about the middle of November. On the 17th, Yuan accepted his new seal of authority. Three days later, he relinquished the governorship to a subordinate and began his journey to Chihli. He must have remembered that seven years ago, on the eve of the Sino-Japanese War, he was on a much less pleasant journey back to China from Seoul. Then he held the rank of a prefect and was virtually unknown in the internal politics of China. His rise to power in seven years had indeed been spectacular, and he was still only forty-two years of age.

CHAPTER V

The Viceroy 1901-1907

THE authority of the Viceroy of Chihli had never been clearly defined, but had always been greater than that of other governors-general. It grew considerably during Tseng Kuo-fan's incumbency, starting in 1865; and, with Li Hung-chang's appointment five years later, it reached a new peak. In addition to taking full charge of the civil administration and defence of the province, dealing with foreign affairs of local importance and making suggestions on national policies, Li obtained Imperial permission to incorporate the duties of the Commissioner for trade of North China into the Viceroyalty. The defence of the north, the maritime customs at Tientsin, the railways, mining and other modern economic development were all his concern. This practice became a rule. The war against Japan of 1894, though marking the decline of Li, set up a precedent for the Viceroy's participation in the defence of Manchuria—hitherto the sole responsibility of the throne. Li's successors, who had neither his prestige nor his military power, found his shoes too big for them, and consequently their authority waned. Yuan Shih-k'ai's wish upon his appointment was to restore, if not to surpass, the glory of the Li Hung-chang period.

The seat of the Viceroy had always been in Tientsin despite the fact that the capital of the province was Paoting, further to the west. Yuan, however, could not go to Tientsin in 1901, for the city was under foreign military occupation, which was not withdrawn until August 8, 1902. Yuan set up his temporary headquarters at Paoting, whence he directed a mopping-up campaign against small bands of Boxers who were still roaming the countryside, with the assistance of Tuan Ch'i-jui and Ni Ssu-ch'ung. Once again the Manchu Bannermen proved utterly useless in these operations and it was Yuan's Right Division that scored the victory. Peace and order were restored early in 1902, and Yuan was free to proceed with his long-term policies.

The young Viceroy's supreme task was to secure the defence of North China from the Amur to the Shantung Peninsula. His 20,000 soldiers were scarcely enough for this and it was imperative that he should expand his army. Army expansion needed funds which he could not expect from the depleted Treasury, nor from the regular revenues of the devastated province. Therefore he had to tap such sources of revenue as the customs office of Tientsin, the coal mines of K'aip'ing, and the railways under the control of Sheng Hsüan-huai. In these economic enterprises as well as in the area now under his care, there were foreign interests to be considered, especially the Russian and Japanese aspirations in Manchuria. Thus Yuan's share in conducting China's diplomacy also increased. Let us look at his defence policies first.

In his department of military administration in Paoting, there were three offices—planning, training, and supplies—headed by Tuan Ch'i-jui, Feng Kuo-chang, and Liu Yung-ch'ing respectively. The chief of the department was Yuan himself, while his other lieutenant, Wang Shih-chen, was given the command of the First Brigade and was concurrently in charge of training other troops in Chihli.

Yuan's plan, of course approved by both the throne and the Grand Council, was to standardize the organization, the drilling, and, if possible, the equipment of Chinese armies. As the importing of arms was forbidden for two years by the 1901 Peace Protocol, Yuan had to be content with the first two tasks. His initial step was to reorganize the remnants of the traditional Green Corps of archers and of the Huai Army, getting rid of the old and sick and recruiting new soldiers to take their place. On February 20, 1902 he memorialized suggesting the recruitment of 6,000 men from 20 to 25 years of age, able to lift up 100 lbs. and to walk 6 miles an hour, more than 5 feet tall and free from the opium habit. The non-commissioned officer's monthly pay was to be 5 taels of silver and that of the private 4·2 taels. Each man was to serve 3 years in the standing army after which he would go back to civilian life, but still be registered as a member of the army reserve, drawing the monthly pay of 1 tael. Another 5 years later, his salary was to be reduced by half when he was registered as a retained soldier. In other words, a recruit was to serve altogether 11 years in the army, but nevertheless during the last 8, he was to return to civil life except in the last month of each year when he must report for training. This plan was reminiscent of that drawn up by Sheng Hsüan-huai after the 1895 War, but was less ambitious. Yuan aimed to have 1 division only completed at the end of 1902, when there would be 2 divisions in Chihli, the other being Yuan's own Right Division, to make a total of 42 corps or 19,120 men at an annual cost of 1,990,000 taels of silver. By October 1902, the new division, the Left, was completed and Ma Yü-k'un assumed command over it.

In the meantime, a group of Manchus in the Court were also contemplating setting up a division of their own, consisting of Bannermen only. In June 1902, there were 7,000 such troops and nearly half of them were given to Yuan to train. Yuan accepted this demonstration of good-will from the Manchus, in spite of the innuendo of distrust implied in the formation of the division, and gracefully recommended T'ieh-liang to take command. This was the nucleus of another division.

The Fourth Division was formed almost by accident. Under the Peace Protocol of 1901, Chinese troops were not allowed to be stationed within six miles of Tientsin after the city had been handed over to Yuan on August 8, 1902. As a countermove to this restriction, Yuan had set up a police training college in Paoting, so when the time of transfer was at hand he had some 2,000 policemen under the command of Tuan Chih-kuei for maintaining order in the city. The occupation troops also left him another 1,000 officers and constables. As soon as Yuan moved his office, the police college found new accommodation in the same city. Later a fire brigade and a coastal patrol unit were added to this, the first police force in China; and, still later, during the Russo-Japanese War of 1904-05, it was reorganized into a division.

The gathering clouds of the Russo-Japanese War enhanced China's need for armaments. This soon resulted in the abrogation of the prohibition against importing arms into China. At the end of 1903, the development of the Northern Army entered a new period. On December 4th, the Commission for Army Reorganization was established in Peking with Prince Ch'ing as Commissioner and Yuan and T'ieh-liang as Assistant Commissioners. The Chief-of-staff was Yuan's sworn brother, Hsü Shih-ch'ang, and three departments —administration, command, and training—went to Yuan's faithful lieutenants, Wang Shih-chen, Tuan Ch'i-jui, and Feng Kuo-chang.

The venerable Prince, the seller of official titles and posts, was Yuan's Manchu mouth-piece and his Commissionership was devised to quell Manchu opposition to the ambitious young Viceroy. T'ieh-liang, however, had ideas of his own. As the junior Vice-President of the Board of War, he did not favour the creation of a body to supersede his own Board; nor did he like the widening of Yuan's power. Still, he realized that he was not strong enough to challenge Yuan at once. Meanwhile, he introduced a great number of Japanese instructors as well as returned Chinese cadets from Japan, most of whom were Manchus, including a young man by the name of Liang-pi, for he knew that although Yuan did not dare to offend the Japanese, but disliked and was disliked by them.

Having planted his men in the new Commission, Yuan presented the first plan for military reorganization. For the defence of Chihli including Peking, according to him, 30,000 additional soldiers were needed, considering that a Russo-Japanese conflict might be imminent. The estimated cost of this expansion was 3 million taels, of which he offered to contribute one-third from the treasury of Chihli, leaving the Board of Revenue to make up the rest. At the end of 1903 and the beginning of 1904 the troops under his direct control amounted to 60,000 men—the Right Division numbering 7,000; the Left Division 10,000; a new division completed early in 1903, 9,000; Chiang Kuei-t'i's units 5,000; the Self-strengthening regiment 2,000 and the Bannermen being trained by him 3,000, besides the 20 corps of the vanguard of the Right Division stationed in Shantung under the command of Chang Huai-chih. With the new recruits, Yuan's military strength would grow to nearly 100,000 men, all capable of serving in a modern war.

The expansion was carried out without major mishaps. In 1904, there were three divisions in Chihli commanded by Wang Ying-k'ai, Wu Ch'ang-ch'un, and Tuan Ch'i-jui; in the year following, they increased to six. The First was evolved from T'ieh-liang's Bannermen; the Second was the Left Division; the Third a mixture of the Self-strengthening regiment and new recruits; the Fourth, Yuan's own Right Division; the Fifth, stationed in Shantung, came from the vanguard; and the Sixth from the Tientsin police force. Yuan frequently changed their commanders to avoid the danger of their men forming personal loyalties; he also attached great importance to the Fourth and the Sixth Divisions, which were always controlled by his most trusted officers such as Tuan Ch'i-jui and Feng

Kuo-chang, and later Ts'ao K'un. In the formation of the Sixth
Division, a man by the name of Chao Ping-chun came to Yuan's
notice. He was a mysterious figure. Apart from the fact that he was
born in Honan and was therefore a fellow provincial of the Viceroy,
no one knew much about him. He claimed to have been born on the
first day of the first month of the cyclical year chia-tzu (the combina-
tion of the first of the Heavenly Stems and the first of the Earthly
Branches), i.e. February 8, 1864; and his family name was the first
of the Hundred Names. This concentration of 'firsts' was not
impossible, but hardly credible. To add the unlikely to the im-
probable, he was named Ping-chun—meaning the first man under
the son of Heaven. He began his career under Yuan as a gaol
warden and was subsequently selected to train the police force.
Therefore, when the Ministry of Police was created in 1905, he
emerged on the horizon as the solitary expert, and was made its
Vice-President. He owed his astonishingly quick promotion to his
master and was to place himself exclusively at his disposal.

At the end of the Russo-Japanese War, Yuan's influence spread
out from Chihli and Shantung to other provinces. Liu Yung-ch'ing
was sent to north Kiangsu to command the newly organized brigade
of 4,000 men; Chang Hsün and his men were transferred to the Huai
River area; and Wang Ju-hsien with his brigade was garrisoned in
Honan. The War, though a quarrel between Russia and Japan
alone, was fought in Manchuria. As soon as it was over, the Empress
despatched Chao Erh-hsün, Hsi-liang, and Hsü Shih-ch'ang
thither 'to organize relief and rehabilitation'. In fact their main tasks
were to organize the Banner troops and to call upon the bandits
commonly known as the Red Beards to surrender. In these, they
had the invaluable assistance of an old soldier, General Chang Hsi-
luan, who was one of Yuan's several sworn brothers. General Chang
captured a notorious bandit leader, Chang Tso-lin and was about to
deal with him as the law bade him. But suddenly, for reasons unknown, Tuan Chih-kuei's father, who was a friend of both the
General and Yuan, intervened. He guaranteed the bandit leader's
good conduct in future and also persuaded the prisoner to take an
oath to become General Chang's sworn son. This was the humble
beginning of the leader of the Mukden Group of the Northern
Warlords.

The administration of Manchuria also underwent a drastic change
at this time. The Imperial Domain was divided into three provinces,

to be ruled by a viceroy and three governors. The viceroy was Hsü Shih-ch'ang and the governors were T'ang Shao-i of Fengt'ien, Chu Chia-pao of Chilin, and Tuan Chih-kuei of Helungkiang. *The Times* commented on these appointments on April 22, 1907:

'It is a notable fact that every one of these new posts is entrusted to a Chinese instead of a Manchu, and every one to a Chinese who owes his advancement to Yuan Shih-k'ai.'

To ensure Hsü's effective control, Yuan reinforced Chang Hsün's troops which he had sent thither with a mixed brigade drawn from the Second and the Fourth Divisions and appointed Wang Ju-hsien to lead them. Meanwhile T'ieh-liang also ordered a division and a brigade of his men to Manchuria. All these troops were placed under Hsü Shih-ch'ang's authority.

In Chihli and elsewhere the work of military expansion continued. The First Division under T'ieh-liang was now stationed at Paoting and Peking; the Second under Ma Lung-piao in the norther-east of Chihli; the Third under Ts'ao K'un in Manchuria; the Fourth under Wu Feng-ling at Hsiaochan and Mach'ang; the Fifth under Chang Huai-chih in Shantung; and the Sixth under Tuan Ch'i-jui near Nanyuan. These were all completed units. One other was being formed by Wei Kuang-t'ao, to be numbered the Seventh and the Ninth was being shaped by Chou Fu and Tuan-fang in Nanking. In other provinces, some ten brigades were being trained, largely due to Yuan's proposal to reorganize the Green Corps of archers, except Chang Chih-tung's Eighth Division—the Self-strengthening Army under Chang Piao's command.

This military expansion kept pace with the surging tide of revolution, and it was deemed necessary to hold annual manoeuvres as a demonstration of strength in the hope of subduing insurgent elements at home and abroad. In October 1905, the first of such display of strength in the history of China took place in Hochien in Chihli. It was ill-prepared; the operation itself was chaotic and the parade at the end had to be called off because of a sand-storm. The next manoeuvres took place at Changteh in Honan. This time, the preparations showed an appreciable improvement. The participants included units of the First, Fourth, Fifth, and Sixth Divisions of the Northern, and the Eighth of the Southern Army, amounting to 33,000 men under the direction of Tuan Ch'i-jui and Chang Piao.

F

T'ieh-liang and Yuan Shih-k'ai were appointed inspectors and Wang Shih-chen, Feng Kuo-chang, and Liang-pi umpires. It was a prim affair. On October 18, 1906, Yuan was given an *ad hoc* audience; he left Peking for Changteh on the 20th. The manoeuvres lasted from the 22nd to 25th, and left a splendid impression on the 487 foreign spectators.

Prior to these events, adverse criticisms of Yuan had been heard frequently. In the Inner Court, a plot to clip his wings was well under way. As early as 1903, when the Commission on Military Reorganization was established, a censor spoke pungently against him:

'The Viceroy, just over forty years of age, has no outstanding service, but has received favours far greater than those conferred upon Tseng Kuo-fan and Li Hung-chang. . . . It is a long standing tradition that the Imperial Guards in the Forbidden City must be Bannermen. Yet now the Viceroy's troops are everywhere in the Palaces. . . . Yang Shih-ch'i is made a counsellor and Hsü Shih-ch'ang a member of the Grand Secretariat, so the Viceroy's henchmen are in the Inner Court as well. The appointment of Na-t'ung to the Grand Council has aroused a great deal of unfavourable criticism, for through Prince Ch'ing's recommendation the Viceroy has extended his power into vitally important offices. Why does the Prince trust and rely on him ten times more than Jung-lu ever did?'

The censor specifically remarked of the Commission itself:

'The venerable Prince Ch'ing knows nothing about military affairs while T'ieh-liang has still to prove his worth. The Commission is in fact entirely in the Viceroy's hands. Its three departments are all headed by his men.'

He justifiably pointed out: 'Military force, if not coupled with an enlightened civil administration, is not enough to keep the state from harm.' He went as far as to compare Yuan to the third century usurper, Ssu-ma Chao, with a quotation from the ancient chronicles of the Three Kingdoms—'His designs are clear even to the men in the street'.

Yuan at once tendered his resignation from the Commission in order to display his loyalty, but it was not accepted. Meanwhile the

Manchu Cabal led by T'ieh-liang was being formed with the aim of strengthening Manchu control in both the Government and the Army. Yuan, lacking the temerity to disobey the throne, had to appease his foes. After the second manoeuvres, he voluntarily surrendered the First, Third, Fifth, and Sixth Divisions to the Manchus, retaining only the Second and the Fourth under his direct control. The four divisions were given to a Manchu commander, General Feng-shan, who did not wait long before beginning to sell officers' posts at prices ranging from 3,000 taels for a brigadier to 500 for a captain. He abolished saluting, to bring back the outdated deep bow and kneeling on one knee. The administration of national defence also underwent a change. The Commission for Army Reorganization was assimilated into the new Ministry for the Army on November 6, 1909 with T'ieh-liang as Minister and Shou-hsün and Yin-ch'ang as Vice-Ministers.

These changes do not suggest that Yuan had lost all his influence over the army; on the contrary, the German-trained Yin-ch'ang was his agent. In May 1907, Prince Ch'ing was named the controller of the Ministry of the Army and General Feng-shan's overall powers were shared by Wang Ying-k'ai, who upon Yuan's recommendation was appointed the deputy commander of the four divisions. As we have mentioned above, in 1907 the Third division and a brigade were in Manchuria at the disposal of Hsü Shih-ch'ang, and the Fifth Division was in Shantung under Chang Huai-chih. The lately created Seventh Division in north Kiangsu was taken over by Wang Shih-chen. Of the leading commanders, only Tuan Ch'i-jui resigned. Thus what T'ieh-liang and his fellow Manchus had achieved was nothing more than formal control. The troops remained loyal to their absent master.

Two other aspects of the infantry under Yuan—instruction and finance—ought to be discussed before passing on to the Viceroy's other many-sided activities. When he took over Chihli in 1902, the military academy established by Li Hung-chang in Tientsin was lying in ruins, having been destroyed by the joint expeditionary troops. Yuan had to make do with an officers' training class in Paoting under the directorship of Lei Chen-ch'un. It was an eight-month course mainly on trigonometry and ballistics. Rudimentary as it was, Paoting was one of the two officers' training centres in the Empire. On December 12, 1902, it was decreed that a selected number of officers from Honan, Shantung, and Shansi should go to Paoting while those from Kiangsu, Anhwei, Kiangsi, and Hunan should be sent to Wuch'ang for training. Yuan thus succeeded in killing two birds with one stone—China was to have her urgently needed officers and Yuan personal contacts with troops other than his own.

In 1903 several military schools were built in Tientsin. The military academy was restored to give a two-year course, and the class in Paoting was transferred to Tientsin. In addition, there were a staff college with a one-year course, a non-commissioned officers' training school with a three-year course, a topographical school and a school for old-style officers. Large numbers of officers were selected from Yuan's Right Division to study in Japan. The military academy, however, remained the most important of all these schools. Under Tuan Ch'i-jui, it provided a twelve-year course in three stages. By 1906 nearly a thousand officers and non-commissioned officers from other provinces and from the Capital had passed through the training at one of these schools. To put this figure into proper perspective, there were in 1906 35 military schools and training classes in China with an estimated total enrolment of 787 officers, 3,448 officer candidates and 2,072 non-commissioned officers. Tientsin was not only the best, but also the largest training centre in the whole country. In June 1906 yet another officers' college was inaugurated in Paoting giving a short course of one year and another of three years. The former could accommodate 40-60 students, and the latter, 50-80. A year later, a school for military police was set up in Taku.

An interesting feature of Yuan's training programme was the use of a new alphabet of more than forty letters, based on the Peking pronunciation, as a means of overcoming the officers' and the men's illiteracy.

The financial aspect of Yuan's armament programme is a more complex matter. The stipulation in the 1901 Peace Protocol that China was not to import arms and ammunition for two years, imposed at a time of extreme fiscal stringency, gave the Treasury a breathing space. Neither Yuan nor Chang Chih-tung made any demand for funds for purchasing arms in that period. The army expansion was almost entirely carried out with local financial resources. Yuan for instance transferred one million taels earmarked for relief and rehabilitation to finance the recruitment of 6,000 soldiers in 1903. By 1905, when the six divisions were completed, the financial responsibility was shared thus:

Division	Annual Expenses		Source
1	1,640		Chihli
2	1,500		Board of Revenue
3	1,500	1,000	The Board
4	1,498	taels	Shantung and Hupei
5	1,500		Shantung and the Board
6	1,498		The Board

The total was then just over 9 million taels. But this swelled to 60 million in 1908 and to nearly 68 million taels in 1910.

It is impossible to ascertain what proportion of the annual expenditure on defence went to the purchase of weapons from abroad; all we have to go on is that imports were resumed in 1903, and the arms came mainly from Japan. The pace, after an interruption in 1904 and 1905 due to the Russo-Japanese War and China's declared neutrality, was quickened in 1906 and 1907. This may have been the cause of the inflation of the military budget in those two years. But, for our limited purpose at this juncture, we are more interested in the ways and means by which Yuan managed to strengthen the defence of the North between 1902 and 1907.

Chihli after the collapse of the Boxer Movement was not exactly a Gladstonian goose that laid the golden eggs. The young Viceroy had to look elsewhere for the income needed for his goal. He posted the ubiquitous T'ang Shao-i to the customs office in Tientsin, but its yield since the 1895 War had to be deposited in foreign banks for the payment of the Japanese indemnity. This being out of his reach, Yuan, through the assistance of Jung-lu and Lu Ch'uan-lin, the President of the Board of Revenue, established a bank in Tientsin in 1902 on behalf of the Board in the hope of being able to issue paper notes as well as to attract private deposits to finance public expenses. Indeed, banking was considered a profitable business in China. But this again did not produce the expected results. In 1905, Yuan tried his hand at floating public loans, the first provincial loans in Chinese history. The total amount was fixed at 4,800,000 taels at the annual rate of 7 per cent and a sinking fund of 1,200,000 taels. Yuan's biographers recorded a great success in this experiment as the big bonds, according to them, were sold out 'in a short period of time'[1]; but Liang Ch'i-ch'ao, the 1898 Reformer, had a different story to relate: 'Only some 100,000 taels worth was sold and consequently compulsory allocation was resorted to. A big county [of the province] was ordered to buy 29,000 taels and a small one, 12,000 taels. . . . Even so, the total sale was less than 1 million.'[2] Under such circumstances, it was not surprising that Yuan turned his attention to two lucrative semi-governmental enterprises to seek money as well as power—the K'aip'ing Coal Mine Company and the railways.

The K'aip'ing Company, situated in the north-east corner of Chihli, was founded by Li Hung-chang in 1875. It was under official control, but the capital came from private investors of whom one of the largest was Chang I, better known abroad as Chang Yen-mou. Chang was its director-general in 1900 when the allied troops were fighting their way from Taku to Peking. He was arrested by the troops in Tientsin. Fearing that the mines might fall into the hands of the Russians or the Japanese, Chang turned to G. Detring, a German who served under Sir Robert Hart as the customs inspector of Tientsin. Detring advised Chang to change the Company into a British limited company in order to safeguard it. In June 1900 Chang and Herbert Hoover, who was then the agent of Bewick Moreing and Co. in China and later became the President of the United States, reached an agreement to sell the K'ai-p'ing mines and other attached property to C. A. Moreing. Three documents were signed: The Agreement of Sale on July 30, 1900, the Agreement of Transfer on February 19, 1901, and a Memorandum also on February 19, 1901. Chang himself did not sign the first, Detring deputized for him and the Company. According to the Agreement of Sale, all the property of the Company was transferred to Bewick Moreing and Co., and the old Chinese shares of 1,500,000 taels were to be replaced by 375,000 new ones of £1 each. The total capital of the new company was to be registered in London at £1 million. Chang was not satisfied with the conditions, and refused to put his name to the document; but Detring, without his or the Company's authority either to sell or to sign, signed on their behalf!

The face value of the old shares amounted to only one and a half million taels, which according to the rate of exchange of the time was equivalent to only £165,000, but the actual value as reckoned by Moreing himself in his letter to Detring on November 9, 1900 was no

---

[1] JATTC, ch. 3, p. 20b.
[2] *Yin-ping-shih-ho-chi*, ch. 21, pp. 94-96.

less than £850,000. This was one of the reasons for Chang's refusal
to sign. Negotiations went on until the other two documents were
signed on February 19, 1901. The Agreement of Transfer confirmed
the first agreement; while the Memorandum made some titular
concessions to Chang, for instance the new K'aip'ing Company was
to be a Sino-British limited company and Chang himself a permanent
Chinese director, having the same power as other directors residing
in China. On the basis of these nominal changes, Chang reported to
the throne in June 1901 that the new company had *added* foreign
capital to make a total of £1 million of which 50 per cent belonged to
the old Company and the rest to foreign shareholders. The ageing
Empress, completely ignorant of the niceties of modern economics,
approved Chang's report in the traditional manner: 'All right!'[1]
quite unaware of the fact that one of the major coal-mining enterprises of her Empire was no longer Chinese.

The matter came to a head in November 1902 when the Chinese
staff of the new company quite innocently hoisted a dragon flag, the
Chinese Imperial Standard, beside a Union Jack on the company's
premises. The British representative in Peking, Sir Ernest Satow,
at once took up this matter with the newly created Ministry of
Foreign Affairs (Wai-wu Pu) and lodged a protest. It was only then
revealed to the Manchu Government that the new company was not
a Chinese concern.

Yuan at the same time asked Chang about the ownership, but all
that he could get out of him was lies and evasions. Chang said that
the K'aip'ing property had not been sold to the British company and
that he had already briefed counsel in Britain to fight this out in a
court of law. Yuan was promised a definite answer in January 1903,
but in February the answer was still not forthcoming. Thereupon he
submitted a memorial to the throne, arguing that the transaction was
invalid, on the ground that Chang did not sign the Agreement of
Sale. The Empress, no wiser then than before, instructed Yuan to
order Chang I to recover the mines without delay.

This terse command in the Vermilion Pencil set the ball rolling.
The two unauthorized venders—Chang and Detring—reacted
differently. Chang, in spite of the fact that his wife was related to the
Dowager Empress, was, after all, a Chinese and had to be obedient
to his superior, the Viceroy of Chihli; but Detring, on the other hand,

[1] Dated 11.7.1901 in the Vermilion Pencil, see the *K'ai-luan Files*, the *Hopei Mining Journal*, September 1930.

did not care a fig for Yuan's or any Chinese authority. According to Hart, Detring drew up an attack on Yuan and sought Hart's advice on it. Hart replied:

'What I suggest . . . is this, 1. Remove any allusion to Yuan by taking out passages marked blue; 2. Let it be a simple résumé of the facts of the case and the arguments they support; 3. Address it—not to Wai-wu Pu but to—Yuan himself; he will see that it cannot be taken or treated as an attack on himself, but as a simple statement of the case for his consideration, and it may thus, without irritating him, supply him with a ladder to climb down by; . . .'[1]

Instead of taking Hart's advice, Detring addressed his statement directly to the Wai-wu Pu and sent a copy to Yuan. The action reaped its just reward; the Viceroy promptly returned the document.

Meanwhile, nearly a year had slipped away, during which Chang I could not produce a single definite word in answer to Yuan's repeated inquiries. As a result, two weeks before Detring's statement, Chang lost his exalted rank of the Vice-President of the Board of Works and was cashiered. This did not mean that Chang had done all there was to be done about the mines. The dispute was to be finally settled in the Chancery Division and, if necessary, in the Court of Appeal in London, early in 1905. As a matter of 'face', Chang I was graciously given a rank of the third grade and sent to Britain as the plaintiff in the case against Bewick Moreing and Co.

The case, heard in the presence of Mr Justice Joyce, began on January 19th and ended on February 13th. It was revealed during the hearings that, 1. H. Hoover, according to his own admission, had gone so far as to threaten Chang I in an attempt to complete the transaction; 2. the documents, as pointed out by Mr. Justice Joyce, did not even provide for the £375,000 shares being given or paid to the shareholders of the Chinese Company for the purchase of that Company's property; and 3. two other documents signed by Chang I —one during his imprisonment in Tientsin in June and July, 1900 dated June 23rd entrusting Detring with the care of the Company's property, and the other, dated Kuang-hsü 26th year, the fourth month, the nineteenth day (May 17, 1900), instructing Detring to borrow foreign capital or to float shares in foreign markets in order to

[1] 22.1.1904, to Detring.

transform the Company into a Sino-foreign joint ownership, had not authorized Detring to sell! Chang himself knew not a word of English and his adviser, Yen Fu, the translator of Adam Smith, Darwin, and J. S. Mill, left something to be desired as a legal interpreter. As a result, the understanding between counsel and his client was far from being perfect. For instance, the counsel understood that the second document mentioned above was dated July 16th instead of May 17th. Mr Justice Joyce's verdict, in short, was that the Memorandum was binding, and unless complied with within a reasonable time, the defendant company was not to be allowed to retain the property at K'aip'ing. If necessary, the Court itself would issue an injunction to this effect. The defendants were ordered to pay the costs of the case.

Following this, there was an appeal in the Court of Appeal II, but Joyce's verdict was substantially upheld and the case was dismissed.

Unsurprisingly, Chang I's report to the throne was quite different from the above description based on the reports in *The Times*. Chang gave prominence to the fact that he, the plaintiff, was awarded his costs. He was honest enough to admit that the Memorandum was binding, but concluded that, the Company, in Chang's own words, remained a commercial enterprise under the Chinese Government's supervision. 'Our country has recovered its sovereignty over the mines and the Chinese director, his equal power [with the foreign directors] with respect to the administration of the Company. However, it is impossible to change the status of the Chinese-foreign joint concern.'[1] This specious argument did not escape Yuan's discerning mind. In a memorial to the throne, Yuan remarked on Chang's evasiveness and showed deep suspicion of the claim that control of the Company had been recovered. Yuan again urged the throne to instruct Chang I to withdraw the Memorandum and to return the property to its *status quo ante*. 'Yuan did not care for . . . the London decision,' as Hart put it.[2] But there was nothing either he or the Empress could do to alter the *fait accompli*.

Yuan was undoubtedly right in principle to inquire into the K'aip'ing ownership, whatever his motive might be. His view was, according to the Revolutionary paper published in Tokyo, the *Min*

[1] Quoted from YSY, 33, 1b, 1.4.1905.
[2] Hart to Campbell, 16.4.1905.

Pao, that foreigners had the right to *work*, but not to *own*, Chinese mines.[1] The inquiry resulted in Chang's falling into oblivion with £75,000 new K'aip'ing shares and 340,000 taels of silver in his pocket.[2]

Having failed to recover the K'aip'ing for the finance of his armament projects, Yuan at once planned to set up a rival coal mining company in Luanchou, about 25 kilometres to the west of K'aip'ing. The idea was mooted in 1906 when the hope of regaining control of K'aip'ing faded. Preliminary surveys were carried out in that year under the supervision of one Chou Hsüeh-hsi, a member of Yuan's secretariat in charge of railway affairs. In 1907, the Luanchou Coal Mining Company was registered as a private limited company under government supervision. The initial investment was estimated at 8 million taels, a quarter of which was to come from the treasury of Chihli. Its head office was to be under Yuan's wing in Tientsin. But his incumbency there did not last long enough to see the fruits of the plan.

The Luanchou Company was a long-term project, obviously not intended to produce immediate profit to relieve Yuan of his financial difficulties. It was organized out of spite more than anything else. As sources of funds, the railways and other means of communications attracted Yuan's attention.

Upon his appointment to the Viceroyalty, he was simultaneously made the Commissioner in charge of the nation's railway affairs. At that time, the railways south of the Great Wall were under British military control while those in Manchuria were under the Russians, both being temporary arrangements after the Boxer Movement. Yuan took up the matter with the British and Russian representatives and on October 16, 1903, the lines were handed back to Hu Yü-fen and Yang Shih-ch'i. The former being Yuan's erstwhile colleague and the latter a new henchman of his.

We must at this stage digress and say a few words about Chinese railway administration prior to the Boxer Uprising. To begin with, the power was divided between the Commissioners for Trade of the North and South. In other words, Li Hung-chang had a great deal to do with it, and, consequently, his lieutenant in economic affairs, Sheng Hsüan-huai, played a major part in both the building and running of the lines. After Li's downfall in 1895, Sheng was severely

[1] No. 2, p. 10, 1905.
[2] Hoover to Detring, 24.10.1907.

criticized by some censors and was cashiered pending an inquiry into the charges of embezzlement and corruption laid against him. The Viceroys Wang Wen-shao and Chang Chih-tung were appointed to conduct the investigation.

Earlier, in 1899, when China decided to build railways, Chang was the leading advocate of a trunk line between Peking and Hankow, while Li Hung-chang preferred a less ambitious plan for a shorter line in Chihli. Chang's proposal won the day and ever since these two viceroys had been at loggerheads. Chang was also responsible for the Hanyang Foundry, which was designed to make rails for the Peking-Hankow line. Both the railway and the iron mill ran into great financial difficulty when Chang was investigating Sheng's irregularities. A tantalizing situation thus arose—the investigator and the investigated depended upon each other for their political careers. The temptation to bargain, even to the otherwise impeccable character of Chang Chih-tung, was irresistible. The result of the inquiry was a joint recommendation from both Chang and Wang that Sheng should be made responsible for building and administering railways and running the Hanyang Foundry. The argument put forward by these viceroys was that the 1895 war had proved the need for a unified control as well as new lines, in order to facilitate the transport of troops and their provisions during an emergency. Therefore the National Railway Company had been created with Sheng as its director.

To Yuan, the transfer of control of the railways from Sheng to himself had greater significance than merely to facilitate the transport of troops and their provisions. It meant, in the first place, that he could despatch his troops without thinking about the onerous duty of paying fares; in the second place, he would be able to reap the yield of the lines to finance his army; and, in the third place, he could use them as security for foreign loans. To him, the railways were far more important than the feeble friendship between himself and Sheng. It was inevitable that, upon his appointment as the Commissioner in charge of railways, he would clash with Sheng Hsüan-huai.

Rich and powerful as he was, Sheng had his weaknesses. He was greedy and inefficient. A great deal of money had been borrowed during the term of his directorship of the National Railway Company, but very little had been accomplished. His accumulation of vast personal wealth through his monopoly of the railways, the telegraph system, and shipping turned many people green with envy, and, as he lived permanently in Shanghai, he had no opportunity to sweeten his opponents in Peking. But Sheng's greatest blunder, from the point of view of his own interests, was the admission of the Russo-Chinese Bank to financial participation in the construction of the Peking-Hankow Railway in August 1899. This, in the words of Lord Salisbury, was 'an act of deliberate hostility' against Britain. In his instructions to C. MacDonald, the British Minister in Peking, Salisbury said: 'A concession of this nature is no longer a commercial enterprise and becomes a political movement against the British interests in the Region of Yangtze. You should inform the Tsungli Yamen that Her Majesty's Government cannot possibly continue to co-operate in the friendly manner in matters of interest to China, while preferential advantages are conceded to Russia in Manchuria and to Germany in Shantung these or other foreign powers should also be offered special openings or privileges in the Region of Yangtze . . . after consultation with the Admiral, you may give them the number of days or hours you think proper within which to send their reply.'[1] The Tsungli Yamen, faced with this barefaced gunboat diplomacy, 'conceded everything'.[2] In dealing with economic affairs, Sheng, for that matter any other Chinese, had to dance to the tune played by the foreign powers, particularly Britain. Lord Salisbury's wrath and the charge of breach of faith did not do Sheng Hsüan-huai any good at all. Worse still, shortly after Yuan took over the railways, Sheng's father died. According to tradition, he had to observe three years' mourning in semi-retirement. Therefore, on the next day after the sad event, Sheng telegraphed Yuan:

'The only one who really knows me, after Wen-chung [Li Hung-chang], is Your Excellency. You should select able assistants to take over the railways and foreign trade from me in order to round off the outstanding problems concerning them.'[3]

The untimely death of his father rendered the situation hopeless for Sheng. Seeing this, he climbed down gracefully, expecting Yuan would cover up whatever outstanding problems there were, but also

---

[1] China, No. 1, 1899, CIX, No. 286.
[2] No. 324, MacDonald to Salisbury.
[3] YCTKCP, 25.10.1902, 58, p. 30a.

he did it suddenly, expecting thereby to throw trade and communications completely out of gear. But Yuan was not going to fall into the trap. With equal grace he at once sent a telegram to Sheng, exhorting him to stay on and promising to lend him every assistance and support. To make his words more persuasive, Yuan took a trip south at the end of that year to discuss things with Chang Chih-tung in Hankow and to consult Sheng in Shanghai. Once more, he asked Sheng to give up what he called 'jobs for an accountant' for more important work, for he candidly expressed the opinion that Sheng was capable enough to run a Ministry.[1] His unstinted praise comforted and reassured Sheng, who stayed on as the nominal head of the National Railway Company until 1906.

The change in control also meant a change in policy. Sheng advocated nationalizing the railways while Yuan was opposed to it, for it would defeat Yuan's own purpose of procuring money to finance his army expansion. At the end of the Ch'ing dynasty, all the railways in China were managed by Han Chinese. Sheng's policy thus had all the support of the Manchu Cabal while the Han Chinese were all against it. In other words, Yuan's more *laissez-faire* attitude had wider approval. However, Yuan's policy was inconsistent. On the one hand, he patriotically proposed to construct a line connecting Peking and Kalgan with Chinese capital and Chinese personnel; Yang Shih-ch'i was made responsible for the administrative and Chan T'ien-yu, an American-trained engineer, for the technical aspects of the construction. The planning began in 1902 and the 100-mile-long but very hazardous line both to construct and to operate was completed in 1908. It was a proud achievement. But, on the other hand, Yuan was in favour of the Manchurian railway scheme put forward by the American railway magnate, E. H. Harriman. In September 1905, an agreement was reached for joint American-Japanese ownership and working of the Southern Manchurian Railway, but it was never put into practice, due largely to Japan's dislike of it. Patriotism to Yuan was merely a matter of political expediency.

Having acquired control over the railways, Yuan's next move was to encroach upon Sheng's monopoly of the telegraphic service. In January 1903, immediately after his visit to Sheng in Shanghai, he himself was appointed the Commissioner in charge of telegraphic communications. He also managed to gather a large troupe of

[1] Yuan to Sheng, YCTKCP, 17.2.1902, 59, p. 11a.

assistants to run the railways and the telegraph lines for him. These included his old colleagues T'ang Shao-i and Hu Yü-fen and new recruits such as Yang Shih-ch'i and Liang Shih-i. The last named was especially important, for in 1906 when Sheng resigned his directorship on the ground of ill health and T'ang succeeded him, Liang was made superintendent of five railways— the Peking-Hankow, Shanghai-Nanking, Taokouchen-Ch'inghua, Chengting-T'aiyuan, and K'aifeng-Loyang lines. These people also had their henchmen. Together they formed an extremely influential clique, later to be known as the 'Communication Clique', which was no less valuable to Yuan than his Northern Army. Except for short intervals, they were the people who continued to take charge of the Ministry of Communications and also the Bank of Communications established in 1907.

Now we must turn to the political aspects of Yuan's time as Viceroy of Chihli. To do so, we cannot but write our story around the most important single event of this period, the Russo-Japanese War. This is, however, not the place to trace its causes or to describe how it was conducted. It suffices to point out that one of the unique characteristics of the War was that its battlefield was the territory of a third, neutral, and sovereign power. Even the nineteenth century had not seen such a monstrous situation.

When the belligerent powers had settled their disputes, China was called upon to endorse the Portsmouth Treaty of September 1905, which she duly did. Prince Ch'ing, Grand Secretary Ch'ü Hung-chi, and Viceroy Yuan Shih-k'ai were appointed the Imperial Plenipotentiaries to meet the Japanese representative, Baron Komura, in Peking on November 17, 1905. The discussions concentrated on Manchuria in the absence of the Prince, who was indisposed, but nevertheless managed to recover in time to sign the agreement on December 12, 1905. So it was Yuan who in fact led the Chinese delegation, and carried his colleagues along with him to give China's full approval to the Treaty of Portsmouth. From his personal point of view, this was an expression of friendship to the country he had offended during his terms of office in Seoul from 1883 to 1895.

Another unique characteristic of the War was the defeat of a European country, a white man's country, at the hands of an Asiatic, a coloured man's kingdom. Japan's unexpected victory had the greatest possible impact all over the world, particularly on the Chinese mind. This question was posed: how could a small country whose people were of the same stock as the Chinese humble a gigantic European country of the Great West? The ready answer found by most Chinese was that Japan was a constitutional monarchy while Czarist Russia was an autocracy· The Chinese newspapers commented:

Chung-wai Jih-pao (May 21, 1905): 'Russia's weakness would not have been exposed, and the question of the relative merits of a constitutional and an autocratic monarchy would not have been answered, had there not been this war.'

Nan-fang Pao (August 23, 1905), under the headline 'Constitution the Panacea': 'Ruling a country is like piloting a boat. The destination must be determined before the voyage begins, or the vessel will drift into nowhere. A constitution is to a state as a compass to a captain.'

Wai-chiao Pao (November 20, 1905): 'Russia's defeat is not a cause but a result; the result of her autocracy!'

and

Chung-wai Jih-pao again (September 20, 1905): 'This is not only a war between Russia and Japan. It is in fact a war between autocracy and constitutional government.'

The premise that a constitutional monarchy was better than a despotic autocracy was now generally accepted without reserve. The only uncertainty was whether the Chinese people were ready for a constitutional government. Because of this, the memorialists such as Chang Chih-tung, Chou Fu, Chao Ping-lin, and Yuan Shih-k'ai, who jointly proposed the adoption of a constitution, were of the opinion that a preparatory stage was necessary. Yuan advocated this even more strongly than the rest.

Seven years before, at the time of the Hundred Days Reform, the Dowager Empress had been against a constitution which would *ex definitioni* curtail the power of the throne. But now she was convinced of its merits and was ready to yield to the popular demand. It was therefore decided to send five high-ranking officials abroad to study constitutional government. They were Duke Tsai-tse, Tai Hung-tz'u, Shao-ying, Tuan-fang, and Hsü Shih-ch'ang. With them, there was a young man from Hunan, Hsiung Hsi-ling, who had been a school teacher and now worked in Yuan's secretariat. On the day when the party set out at the Ch'ienmen Station in Peking on September 20, 1905, a bomb was thrown at them, slightly injuring the Duke and Shao-ying. The would-be assassin, Wu Yüeh, was instantly killed. He was a revolutionary with unmistakable anarchist tendencies, for he had previously expressed the view, undoubtedly under the influence of Russian nihilism, that the period of assassination had begun in China. The incident delayed the party until December 19th, when they finally sailed from Shanghai without Shao-ying and Hsü Shih-ch'ang but with Shang Ch'i-heng and Li Sheng-to. On the eve of their second departure, Yuan, according to the Revolutionary paper, *Min Pao*,[1] gave them a farewell dinner and asked jocularly: 'Are you really going to study politics? Why do you have to take such trouble? It does no great harm to a country like ours to pay your fares for a world tour.'

At the same time the Institute of Political Studies, an advisory body on constitutional matters, was set up, and the five high officials' report later became the main document for study. This report was submitted to the throne on their return on August 25, 1906. The author was a young man by the name of Yang Tu, who was Hsiung Hsi-ling's friend and was also a fellow provincial of his. This political opportunist was then residing in Tokyo where refugees from China —Reformers as well as Revolutionaries—congregated, and Yang was familiar with them both; in fact he had once been a member of a revolutionary society. His report was said to have incorporated the quintessence of the constitutions of the East and West and laid out a detailed procedure for the adoption of a constitution in China. Because of this composition, Yang Tu became the chief expert in the newly created Institute of Political Studies.

On October 25, 1906, an edict was issued to reorganize the Central Government. The Inner Cabinet, which had consisted of a number of Grand Secretaries and Secretaries, the Grand Council, which had been the highest policy-making body but whose powers had been gradually diminishing, the Grand Censorate, which kept a watchful eye on the discipline of the Civil service, the Han-lin Academy, which was the highest seat of learning, and the Imperial Clan Office remained unchanged. The Ministry of Foreign Affairs, which succeeded the Tsung-li Yamen in 1901, and the Ministry of Education, which was created in 1903, also remained intact. The

[1] No. 7, p. 1, 1905.

traditional Board of Civil Office and the Ministry of Police, which came into being in 1905, were amalgamated into the Ministry of Civil Office; and the traditional Board of War split into the Ministries for the Army and the Navy and the Military Consultative Council. The Board of Rites became the Ministry of Rites; the Board of Revenue, the Ministry of Finance; and the Board of Punishment, the Ministry of Justice. The Board of Works and the Ministry of Commerce, established in 1903, merged into the Ministry of Agriculture, Industry, and Commerce and the Suzerainty Bureau became the Ministry of Suzerainty. The Temple of Justice was renamed the Supreme Court. New offices included the Ministry of Communications, the Audit Council, and the Political Consultative Council which was supposedly the forerunner of a parliament. Each of the Ministries had a President and two Vice-Presidents whose offices might be held by either Manchus or Han Chinese. These changes were followed in August 1907 by the Imperial Proclamation of Racial Equality between these two races and intermarriage between them was officially approved. Even the post of a Tartar General could now be held by a Han Chinese.

In these reform measures, Yuan and Tuan-fang played an active role. But the measures themselves were double-edged. They were designed to appease the surging demand for a change as well as to enhance the powers of the Central Government. The 1906 Government for instance was composed of seven Manchus, one Mongol, and one Han Bannerman, but only four Han Chinese. This could hardly lessen the growing animosity between the two races. The reactionary Manchus and Han Chinese were, moreover, in league against the more progressive forces. In September 1907 Yuan Shih-k'ai and Chang Chih-tung were promoted to the highest offices that the Han Chinese were allowed to hold. They were simultaneously made Grand Councillors, Yuan concurrently in charge of the Foreign Ministry under Prince Ch'ing, and Chang, in charge of the Ministry of Education. It was expected that if they were both in the Council one would cancel out the other's influence, for, apart from their opposition to the traditional examination system, these two old rivals had almost nothing in common. Chang came from Chihli, but his long association with Hunan made him a welcome addition to the group of Hunanese Conservatives in the capital under the leadership of Ch'ü Hung-chi. Together with the Manchu Cabal, they were working against Yuan.

G

Even after this crafty 'promotion' Yuan was by no means a spent force. The Viceroyalty left vacant by his transfer was given to a friend of his, Yang Shih-hsiang—Yang Shih-ch'i's brother. The army of the Empire remained loyal to him, and his colleagues and protégés still occupied many important posts. His faithful support of the Empress Dowager had never waned. On her seventy-third birthday, he presented to her two fox-fur gowns, a large piece of calambac inlaid with precious stones, a pair of filigree and pearl phoenixes and a branch of coral as tall as a man. Earlier, during the anxious period of the Russo-Japanese War, he had presented to her an Indian circus and an automobile. All these helped to cement the relationship between the mistress and her vassal.

Yuan, however, had a deadly enemy in the person of the powerless Emperor, for he feared that once the Empress had passed away and the Emperor was restored to full authority, his betrayal in 1898 would be revenged. If the Emperor, in view of his ill health, should die before the senile Empress, as he well might, then Yuan's future would depend upon the choice of the successor to the throne. Therefore, when the nomination of an heir was being discussed just before the Empress's death, Yuan was in favour of Prince P'u-lun instead of P'u-i, because, as R. F. Johnston put it, 'he knew that this [the nomination of P'u-i] would mean the elevation to power of Prince Ch'un [P'u-i's father and Kuang-hsü's younger brother], with disastrous results to his own career'.[1] This view was shared by Dr Morrison's despatch to *The Times* published on September 8, 1910. The Emperor, Kuang-hsü, did not after all outlive the Empress, having died on November 14, 1908, a day before the Empress's death. The close proximity of the deaths gave rise to much suspicion and speculation. Two valedictory edicts were reported. The one by the Empress named P'u-i, a three-year-old infant, the successor to the throne, and appointed his father, Prince Ch'un, Regent. The other, by the deceased Emperor, the authenticity of which is still open to doubt, urged the Regent to punish Yuan Shih-k'ai for his evil doings during the Hundred Days Reform.

Immediately after the deaths, a censor, Chao Ping-lin, submitted a memorial to the Regent, charging Yuan with having unduly furthered his own interests and with having incurred the disapproval of the deceased Emperor. It was said that the Regent was in favour of having Yuan executed at once, but that Chang Chih-tung

[1] *Twilight*, p. 60.

had stopped him. On January 2, 1909, the following edict was issued:

'The Grand Councillor and President of the Ministry of Foreign Affairs, Yuan Shih-k'ai, in times past has received repeated promotion at the hands of their departed Majesties. Again on our accession, we honoured him by further rewards as an incentive to him to display his energy, for his ability was worth using. Unexpectedly Yuan Shih-k'ai is now suffering from an affection of the foot, he has difficulty in walking, and it is hardly possible for him to discharge his duties adequately. We command Yuan Shih-k'ai to resign his offices at once and to return to his native place to treat and to convalesce from the ailment. It is our resolution to show consideration and compassion.'[1]

This edict was issued in the name of the infant Emperor, Hsüant'ung, and countersigned by the Regent, the Grand Councillors except Prince Ch'ing, who happened to be indisposed, and, of course, Yuan himself.

On December 28th, when the Japanese Minister in Peking, Ijuin, opened negotiations with the Ministry of Foreign Affairs, Yuan, as vigorous as ever, conducted the whole discussion on the Chinese side. On January 2nd, a Saturday, he was present at the Grand Council meeting and was affably received by the Regent. There was no sign that anything was wrong with his foot. Putnam Weale recorded: 'Everyone remembers that day in Peking when popular rumour declared that the man's last hour had come';[2] and *The Times* in a long leader praised Yuan's unusual ability, progressive outlook, and great service to the throne, and said: 'This is the man whom the Manchus have driven with indignity from office.'[3]

Yuan had no option but to relinquish all his offices. His residence in Peking was given to his trusted general, Tuan Ch'i-jui, and, instead of going back to his native place, Hsiangcheng, in the south of Honan, he built a retreat on the outskirts of Changteh, an important railway junction in the north of that province. Good humouredly, he named it the Garden for Cultivating Longevity (Yang Shou Yuan), where, for the next three years he was to 'treat

[1] Based on *The Times*, January 4, 1909.
[2] *Fight*, p. 25.
[3] 4.1.1909.

and convalesce from the ailment' of his foot and to watch the rising tide of the Revolution.

As an eminent man of letters, Chang T'ai-yen, had predicted in 1906: 'The Manchu Government relied on the Han Chinese governors as its claws and teeth to dominate the Han Chinese themselves. Now it decides to adopt centralism, and consequently begins to clip its own claws and teeth. This is advantageous to the Han Chinese, for it makes a revolution easier.'[1]

[1] *Min Pao*, 1906, No. 10, p. 19.

CHAPTER VI

Eclipse 1908-1911

————————

AT this point we must give a brief account of the political development of the country at large. As we have said above, the 1895 War against Japan ended an epoch in modern Chinese history. Before it, the adequacy of the country's political system had scarcely been questioned; after it, many Chinese began to search for an alternative in the hope that, once adopted, it would solve her manifold problems. The *literati* attempted a reform in 1898 and the peasantry started an uprising in 1900, both movements being abortive. Yet the search went on under the leadership of a young medical student by the name of Sun Wen, better known as Dr Sun Yat-sen. He advocated revolution.

In 1894, Dr Sun went to Tientsin to present a letter to Viceroy Li Hung-chang, expounding his theories about strengthening China through reform. Li was impressed, but, on the eve of a great war, it is understandable that he shelved the question. Seeing that it was futile to appeal to an obsolete administration, Dr Sun went to Hawaii, where he formed the first revolutionary group on November 24, 1894. The constitution of the China Revival Society did not specify revolution as the means to political change, but as the war progressed Sun's views changed. When the Hongkong branch of the Society was established on February 18, 1895, each of its members had to take the oath: 'Drive out the Tartars; revive China; establish a federal government.'[1] This was a revolutionary programme, for the Tartars could not, in all probability, be driven out except by force.

Thereafter the name 'Brigand Sun Wen' repeatedly appeared in the official communications of the Manchu Government. As his home-land was unsafe for him, Dr Sun toured Europe in 1896 and recruited many followers among the Chinese students in France, Belgium and England. The tour was profitable for him, for he

[1] Sun, *Nien-p'u*, 1959, I, p. 56.

gained political experience as well as knowledge which was to be of immense value in his later career. On the other hand his long wanderings abroad made him too intellectual, high-minded, and idealistic for his comrades. His assessment of the Chinese political situation was not always right and his aims seemed too abstruse for even the educated revolutionaries to grasp. In Europe, he observed not only the working of a democratic government, but also the rising tide of socialism. These together with his patriotism and hatred of despotism became the bases of his *Three Principles for the People*—nationalism, democracy, and economic welfare, of which only the first was to some extent comprehensible to his comrades.

Revolutionary nationalism between 1900 and 1911 was in fact very little more than racial antagonism to the Manchus. At the height of the Boxer Crisis, an independent army rebelled against the Government in Anhwei. Its declared aim was to seek independence from Manchu domination. Two years later, Hung Ch'uan-fu, a nephew of the T'aip'ing leader Hung Hsiu-ch'uan, rose against the Manchus in Canton and proclaimed a Great Ming Empire. Both these revolts were quickly put down by the Manchu army. On April 26, 1902, Chang T'ai-yen, the eminent scholar and revolutionary, called a meeting in Tokyo to commemorate the 242nd anniversary of the destruction of the Chinese Empire, the Ming dynasty. A year later, a revolutionary by the name of Tsou Yung published in Shanghai a long article—'*The Revolutionary Army*' in which he described the Manchus as barbarians draped in animals' skin and wearing horns on their heads. The Recovery Society of 1903 and the Dragonflower Society (*Lung-hua Hui*) and Society of Justice (Chih-kung Hui) of 1904 were all anti-Manchu.

The last-named was a secret society of the overseas-Chinese in the United States, whose constitution was drafted by Dr Sun himself. It marked the beginning of Sun's alliance with Chinese secret societies. The Society stayed in being and was transformed into a party which took part in the coalition government after the 1949 Revolution. In 1904, its aims were to drive out the Tartars, revive China, establish a republic, and distribute land equally.

These aims were adopted by the Alliance Society which Dr Sun helped to form in Tokyo in 1905. He arrived there on August 13th and more than 1,300 Chinese students turned up to welcome him. When the Society came into existence, Dr Sun was its chairman, and among its members were Wang Ching-wei and Chiang Kai-shek.

At the end of 1905 the first issue of the organ of the Society was published; Dr Sun contributed an inauguratory article in which he enunciated his *Three Principles* for the first time. Still abstruse, the last of the four aims—distribution of land—aroused a great deal of scepticism among the rank and file of the Society. Likewise Dr Sun's exposition of five civil rights in 1906 made little impression upon his followers. The movement remained racialistic and anti-monarchistic.

The name of the Society, *Alliance*, suggested that Dr Sun's immediate aim was to form a united front with other revolutionary organizations on the mainland. This was done by setting up five underground branches in China itself as well as five abroad, with the headquarters in Tokyo. In 1909, the Alliance Society became the Chinese Revolutionary Party and its membership oath was changed to: 'Drive out the Tartar Ch'ing; establish the Chinese Republic; carry out the programme of people's economic welfare.'

The revolutionists, first of various small groups, then of the Alliance Society and finally of the Party, staged altogether ten revolts in the provinces south of the Yangtze and also attempted seven assassinations before they eventually succeeded in overthrowing the Manchu régime in 1912. These kept the revolutionary spirit high and also helped to spread the influence of the radicals; the most notable were Wu Yüeh's attempt on the lives of the five high officials in Peking in 1905, Wang Ching-wei's on the Regent in 1910, and P'eng Chia-chen's successful assassination of a leader of the Manchu Cabal, Liang-pi, in January 1912. These widely-spaced but sensational events punctuated the movement's ever-swifter growth until it became one of the main political forces during the 1908-1911 period.

Another major force at work in the same period was the Constitutionist Party, whose aim was to preserve the dynasty by adopting a constitution. This group included the 1898 Reformers and some of the dignitaries in the Court of Peking. The word 'constitution', like many other political terms, is ambiguous. What can one expect from it is not always the same as what is written in it. However, though their motives were different, the Reformers and the Court dignitaries had two things in common after 1906—monarchism and constitution. But there was also a vital difference between them—the former were mostly Han Chinese and the latter Manchus. This explained their totally divergent positions—the Reformers had to take refuge abroad while the dignitaries were in power.

When K'ang Yu-wei escaped to Hongkong after the 1898 *coup*, Dr Sun wanted to meet him, but he refused his invitation. Later in Japan, the revolutionists made another overture to K'ang and his monarchists; this again was fruitless. The Reformers held fast to their allegiance to the powerless Emperor and their main hope lay in his restoration after the death of the ageing Empress. The Imperial proclamation of 1906 which promised to introduce a constitution in the near future whipped up their enthusiasm. They saw a gleam of hope that their programme might be put into practice in spite of the fact that they themselves were still outlaws in China, so they transformed their monarchist organization into the National Constitutional Society. In the next year, Liang Ch'i-ch'ao organized the Political Information Society in the Japanese capital; its aims were: 1. a parliamentary system and a responsible government; 2. legislative and judicial independence; 3. regional autonomy and a clear definition of the powers of the central and local governments and 4. a cautious diplomatic policy respecting both China's and treaty powers' legitimate rights. The Reformers' enthusiasm rose even higher when Emperor Kuang-hsü's brother became Regent in 1908. Their hopes that the Regent would pick up where the Emperor left off before the 1898 *coup* were soon dashed by an edict which prohibited the activities of the Political Information Society. The Society's support of the throne did not help to improve its relations with the Alliance Society either. The members of the latter went to the inaugural ceremony of the former and turned it into a free fight.

In the Imperial Capital, the Regent, according to Dr Morrison of *The Times*, was 'an amiable, intelligent prince, who . . . will be for the next twelve years virtually Emperor [but] who cannot weaken the position of Yuan Shih-k'ai and whose influence makes for progress'.[1] This earlier assessment was proved wrong by the removal of Yuan on the flimsy pretence of 'an affection of the foot'. In a despatch published before the above quotation on September 7, 1909, Morrison lamented 'the deplorable weakness of the Central Government in Peking, where since the fall of Yuan Shih-k'ai there seemed to be no man competent or willing to assume responsibility'. A Court official's observation, on the other hand, was at variance with Dr Morrison's.

'The Prince is a hard-working man. He reads all the state papers,

[1] *The Times*, 17.10.1908.

but without much understanding; and he also loves to write his decisions on them, but often quite incomprehensibly. . . . Indeed, he is very disappointing. He normally sits through an audience in complete silence. When he is asked to pronounce his decisions, he just mumbles.'[1]

R. F. Johnston, Emperor Hsüan-t'ung's English tutor, agreed with this when he wrote:

'He is well-intentioned, tries in his languid and ineffectual way to please everyone, succeeds in pleasing no one, shrinks from responsibility, is thoroughly unbusinesslike, is disastrously deficient in energy, will-power and grit, and there is reason to believe that he lacks both physical and moral courage. He is helpless in an emergency, has no original ideas, and is liable to be swayed by any smooth talker. After he became Regent, however, the flattery of sycophants tended to make him obstinately tenacious of his opinions. which almost invariably turned out to be wrong. During several years of fairly intimate contact with Prince Ch'un I came to be so deeply impressed by his fatal tendency to do the wrong thing or choose the wrong course in matters affecting the Imperial House or the interests of the young emperor his son, . . .'[2]

The other princes around the Regent 'have been trained either in the guards or in the Court with daily routines. They dress lavishly in furs and feathers and scamper hither and thither between the palace halls. When they are free, they spend their time with their falcons and horses'.[3] Such were the people who tried to play the game of a constitutional government in order to appease the Han Chinese and, at the same time, excluded them from all important posts in the Government.

The principles of the proposed constitution were announced by the Regent in September 1908, giving the throne all the absolute power than an autocrat could possibly dream of. The Manchu dynasty, according to the principles, was to rule forever and the throne was to have the supreme power in legislation, in rejecting any decision taken by the parliament, in calling or dissolving the

[1] *Kuang Hsüan Hsiao Chi*, pp. 111-112.
[2] *Twilight*, pp. 60-61.
[3] *Ch'ung-ling Ch'uan-hsin Lu, Jung-yen*, II, No. 5.

parliament, in appointing or dismissing government officials, and in controlling all the fighting forces in the Empire. The people, on the other hand, were to gain nothing except a respectful parliament. The announcement was followed by an awful silence which eloquently showed the public's agreement with a shrewd remark made by Wang Ching-wei two years before: 'One who hopes that the Manchus would sincerely adopt a constitution is like an Egyptian who fervently prays that the Turkish Government will become constitutional.'[1]

Seeing that the principles were not received with enthusiasm and that the revolutionary movement was gaining strength, the Regent promised in 1909 to adopt a constitution in nine years' time. He also decreed the formation of provincial political councils. The suppressed Constitutionists took the opportunity of extending their influence into these councils, through which four petitions for the election of a parliament and the establishment of a responsible government were made in the following year. Yuan Shih-k'ai's old friend Chang Ch'ien, who was now an outstanding industrialist, played an important role in this. Chang and his fellow-petitioners secured the support of provincial governors and extracted a promise from the Regent to shorten the preparatory period from nine to five years. As a comforting gesture, the Regent also convened the Political Consultative Council in Peking in October. This consisted of people of no consequence, and therefore accomplished nothing.

In April 1911, another decorative measure was taken, namely the formation of the first Cabinet in Chinese history. There were thirteen members—nine Manchus and four Han Chinese. Of the nine, five belonged to the Imperial Clan, hence the cabinet was nicknamed 'the Clan Cabinet'. The four Han Chinese were the deputy Prime Minister, Hsü Shih-ch'ang, Yuan's sworn-brother; the Foreign Minister, Liang Tun-yen; the Minister of Education, T'ang Ching-ch'ung; and the Minister of Communications, Sheng Hsüan-huai. The feeble and corrupt Prince Ch'ing was appointed Prime Minister and all the important posts were occupied by Manchus. The composition of the Cabinet disappointed even the most loyal Chinese supporters of the monarchy. Chang Ch'ien ruefully commented: 'It is contrary to the tradition of the dynasty to entrust the Army, Navy and all other important Ministries to members of the Imperial Clan. This move has altered nothing except by making the situation even more untenable. The country is

[1] *Min Pao*, 1906, No. 3, p. 17.

rapidly disintegrating. . . . It is frightening.'[1] Liang Ch'i-ch'ao, a staunch monarchist, obviously in an agony of despair, said: 'Having been disappointed in this, now the people can only turn to the other [alternative].'[2]

Indeed, the politics pursued by the Regent did not in any way reflect his need of allies. He had created a derisory constitution, thereby losing the support of monarchists like K'ang Yu-wei and Liang Ch'i-ch'ao, and his other measures antagonized many loyal Han Chinese. As soon as he assumed power, he appointed Tsai-t'ao, Yü-lang and T'ieh-liang, all Manchu noblemen, to take charge of the training of an Imperial Guard Army with himself as the Commander-in-Chief. He also established a Nobility College to train Manchu cadets as a hurried step to remedy the ominous shortage of Manchu officers in the army. In the first year of his Regency, the command of all the fighting forces in the Empire was unified under him and a Military Consultative Council consisting of five members of the Imperial Clan was set up. Meanwhile the Ministry for the Army went to Yin-ch'ang and that for the Navy went to Tsai-hsün. T'ieh-liang was given the command of the troops around Nanking and Feng-shan of those in the vicinity of Hankow. All of these men were likewise Manchus. The Regent also created no less than 36 divisions of infantry. Behind this reckless armament programme was the compelling need to strengthen the Government in the face of a growing revolutionary movement, which also accounted for the alarming inflation of the defence budget from 9 million taels in 1905 to 60 million in 1908 and 68 million in 1910.

Where was the money to come from? An answer had been found by Yuan Shih-k'ai and was now rediscovered by the Regent—namely the railways. The usefulness of the 5,800 miles of railways in this connection was not that they made enough profit to finance the increasing military expenses, but that they could be pledged against foreign loans. During the short three years of the Regency, railway loans amounted to 185,352,542 yuan ($£1$ = about 11 yuan). This was 40 per cent of all the railway loans contracted from 1887 to 1911. A feature of the railway loans of the Regency was that, out of nine of them, four came from Japan, while the United States took a very small part in them. This was clearly a change from Yuan Shih-k'ai's pro-American to the Manchu Cabal's pro-Japanese policy.

[1] *Chang Chi-chih Hsien-sheng Chuan-chi*, p. 145.
[2] Li Chien-nung, *Chung-kuo Chin-san-shih-nien Cheng-chih Shih*, p. 154.

Another, even more significant change in the railway policy had to do with state control. Unless the lines were placed at the Regent's free disposal, the Government could not use them as security for raising loans according to its wishes. It was therefore inevitable that the Regent and Yuan's Communication Clique should clash. In this conflict of interests, the Regent had a natural ally in the person of Sheng Hsüan-huai, who was panting for an opportunity of revenging himself.

No sooner had the Regency begun than a memorial was submitted to the throne by a censor accusing the Minister of Communications, Ch'en Pi, and his chief lieutenant, Liang Shih-i, of negligence and irregularities. The Regent at once appointed Grand Secretaries Sun Chia-nai and Na-t'ung to investigate. Sun was a highly respected but powerless man and Na-t'ung was a close friend of Yuan Shih-k'ai. The investigation resulted in Hsü Shih-ch'ang's replacing Ch'en Pi as the head of the Ministry while Liang's control over the railways remained intact. At that time, Hsü had lost his viceroyalty in Manchuria and was temporarily unemployed. His taking over the portfolio actually strengthened Yuan's influence in the Government. But, two years later, when the first Cabinet was formed, he was to be 'kicked upstairs' as deputy Prime Minister and Sheng stepped in to take charge of communications. The battle of the railways had begun.

As a prelude to Sheng's appointment, seven censors and Court officials presented a joint memorial charging Liang Shih-i with abusing his authority and with nepotism and embezzlement. Sheng's first action was to have Liang sent back to Kuangtung to direct the Canton-Kowloon Railway. The Railway Bureau which Liang had once headed was abolished, and the new director-general of the Communications Bank was Li Hung-chang's son, Li Ching-ch'u, who had Sheng's personal instructions to audit Liang's revenue and expenditure at the Bank. Three months later, Duke Tsai-tse and several other high officials urged the Government to nationalize all the railways in China. This Sheng accepted as his avowed policy, but Hsü Shih-ch'ang did not endorse it. The first step was to take control of four trunk lines: Peking-Hankow-Canton, Peking-Kalgan-Kiakhta, Peking-Mukden-Huich'un, and Chengting-T'aiyuan-Tat'ung-P'uchou-Ili; and then Tuan-fang, a Manchu progressive, was sent to Hankow to supervise the construction of railways in Szechwan and Kwangtung.

In theory, a state system offered everything that was desired.

What China needed then was to provide railways. She was not yet in a position to dream of improving efficiency through competition, and private enterprise could not meet her demand for railways for strategic and migration, and famine relief purposes. But, in practice, the *sine qua non* of such a system was a clean and incorruptible administration which the people could trust. This obviously did not exist. To arouse even deeper suspicion, the Government would and could not pay cash but offered to give promissory notes as compensation for nationalization. These notes, in the eyes of the shareholders, were not worth the paper on which they were printed. As an attempt to enhance the Government's credit, Sheng Hsüan-huai borrowed heavily from abroad. This, however, produced diametrically opposite results from those that Sheng expected. People seemed to know that the so-called state system was no more than a camouflage for pawning all the railways to finance reckless armament in order to preserve and prolong the precarious Manchu rule. In September a revolt against the nationalization broke out in Szechwan and the Viceroy, Chao Erh-feng, who had killed many in Tibet, was beheaded by the people. The news spread like a bush-fire. On October 10th, the eleventh attempt of the revolutionaries to overthrow the Ch'ing regime took place in Wuch'ang.

Seeing the disastrous result of his railway policy, Sheng at once sent a telegram to Yuan Shih-k'ai, asking him to come out of his hermitage. Yuan replied:

'My weakening body is constantly troubled by illness. The coming of the autumn does it no good. . . . I beseech you to recommend someone else.'[1]

Sheng needed help badly. Five days later, he tried again:

'Please think of your important duties. How can you possibly be happy in the wilderness? It is better for you to come a day earlier than a day later.'[2]

But Yuan did not budge:

'All the troops in Hupei have mutinied and there is no money left in

[1] YCTKCP, 11.10.1911, ch. 87, pp. 9b–10a.
[2] ibid, 16.10.1911, p. 10a.

the provincial treasury. What can I do with my bare hands? General Yin-ch'ang saw me a few days ago and he was full of hope. I think he will soon suppress the rebels.'[1]

These repeated refusals sealed Sheng's fate. On October 23rd, Tuan-fang was assassinated in Szechwan and three days later an edict announced the dismissal of Sheng Hsüan-huai, promising that he would never again be appointed to an official post. Sheng's successor was the then unemployed T'ang Shao-i.

Since the battle of the railways was over, the focus of our attention, like that of Yuan's contemporaries, must be transferred from the Hall of Great Harmony in the Forbidden City to the much humbler Garden for Cultivating Longevity. In that country retreat, our hero found time to drink with his friends, to travel, and even to compose these lines:

> 'The small pavilion gives room for my knees
> Its eaves level with the old and lofty trees
> I open the door where the Dipper hangs
> And look down at the mountain ranges.'

His pretence of being a recluse deceived no one, but it was a tradition for the Chinese statesman in temporary retirement to behave in such a manner. His aspiration effused through the word Dipper, for Confucius said: 'In governing, cleave to good; as the Dipper holds his place and the multitude of stars revolve about him.' The Dipper was, and still is, a symbol of a sovereign.

Indeed, Yuan was not living in complete seclusion. He was only fifty-two years of age and his residence near a railway junction was easily accessible for officials from Peking. General Feng Kuo-chang frequented the house to keep him informed of the wellbeing of his old subordinates; and, living with the master, there were Yang Shih-ch'i and Yang Tu. The Viceroy of Chihli was Yang Shih-ch'i's brother; the Prime Minister, Prince Ch'ing, was still being paid by Yuan; the deputy Prime Minister, Hsü Shih-ch'ang, remained loyal; and Chao Ping-chun continued to control China's police forces. Yuan's own son, K'e-ting, held a senior secretaryship in the Ministry of Communications. These people supplied him with information about the activities within and without the Imperial Court. As the

[1] ibid, 17.10.1911, p. 13b.

situation deteriorated, their visits to the Garden in Changteh became more frequent.

In the spring of that eventful year, 1911, Yuan had an unexpected but extremely welcome visitor—his old friend and teacher, Chang Ch'ien. It was a pleasantly nostalgic occasion. Chang entered this in his diary:

'We talked about the past and present. I found that, after an interval of twenty-eight years, his judgment and observations had become both mature and incisive. He is head and shoulders above the lot.'[1]

Two days after the Wuch'ang uprising, he had another visitor. This time it was his faithful officer, General Feng Kuo-chang, now in command of the First Army and on the way to Hupei to quell the rebellion. Yuan gave him the laconic advice: 'Go slowly and wait and see.' Another two days later, the Regent appointed Yuan Viceroy of Hupei and Hunan, concurrently in charge of pacification. The recall was declined on the same ground as had been advanced for his dismissal—'the affection of my foot has not yet been cured'.

The revolutionaries in Hupei also sent an emissary to Changteh, soliciting Yuan's assistance with the *quid pro quo* that, if the revolution was successful, Yuan would become the President of the Republic of China. Yuan's son showed considerable interest in it, for he would become the 'heir-apparent', but the old master himself remained inscrutable. When there are foxes and hares about, hunting dogs are needed. If he bided his time and let the wild beasts multiply, this hunting dog would be needed even more acutely. Having spent three years in oblivion, Yuan suddenly found that time was on his side.

The panic-stricken Regent and his uncle, Prince Ch'ing, completely perplexed by Yuan's lack of interest, hurriedly sent Hsü Shih-ch'ang to see him and to find out what could be done to satisfy him. Yuan therefore announced his conditions on October 20th: 1. Call a National Assembly in 1912; form a responsible government; 3. repeal the edict prohibiting party activities; 4. pardon the participants of the Wuch'ang revolt; 5. appoint himself as the Supreme Commander of all the armed forces; and 6. guarantee a sufficient supply of money, equipment and provisions to these forces. On the same day, the Regent proclaimed a general pardon of all those who were

[1] *Chang Chi-chih Hsien-sheng Chuan-chi, p.* 145.

taking part in the revolt. But with regard to the other five conditions, he hesitated.

The two armies now fighting the revolutionaries in Hupei were under the command of Feng Kuo-chang and Tuan Ch'i-jui. Yuan's conditions undoubtedly influenced them, and in the following week there were several minor setbacks on the Hankow front. The pusillanimous Regent bowed to Yuan's demands again by appointing him the Imperial Commissioner in charge of all the troops in Hupei, and by superseding Yin-ch'ang. A victory was scored by Yuan's troops on that very day. But Yuan himself remained in his Garden for Cultivating Longevity. *The Times* reported on October 23rd that Yuan refused to go to the front because of his bad foot. On the other hand, he protested that the army had lost its *esprit de corps* owing to the incompetent officials entrusted with its control since his retirement.

Meanwhile, three provinces—Shensi, Hunan, and Kiangsu—declared independence; and, by the end of the month, this number grew to five. At the end of November, fourteen out of the eighteen provinces in China proper were independent. The Regent, with less than half of the Empire still under his control, was in a state of consternation, but Yuan thought that 'it was easier to deal with the military situation in the south than the political labyrinth in Peking'.[1] The difference in their attitudes showed a difference in their policies. The Regent was anxious to restore his control by military suppression while Yuan was merely interested in preserving the Manchu Government from disintegrating too rapidly before he could reach a favourable agreement with the revolutionaries. He did not feel obliged to be loyal to the man who had disgraced him; nor was he idealistic enough to join forces with a total stranger, Dr Sun Yat-sen. He was fully aware that he alone held the balance and was resolved to exploit the situation to the utmost for himself. For the time being, his main concern was how to consolidate the north in order to provide a bargaining counter with the south.

In the north, there were people who wished to overthrow the Manchu régime as soon as they could; there were also diehards who would fight tooth and nail rather than yield an inch. The leaders of the former were Generals Chang Shao-tseng and Wu Lu-chen and the latter were headed by the Regent and Liang-pi. Yuan had to wipe them out before his ambitions could be realized.

[1] Yuan to Liang Shih-i, 14.10.1911, Liang, *Nien-p'u*, p. 100.

These two generals had both been trained in Japan where they had made friends with many revolutionists. In October 1911 Chang was stationed in Luanchou, commanding the 20th Division; and, with three other commanders, he submitted twelve proposals to the throne on the 29th, requesting the Government to call a National Assembly at once and to form a responsible government. Contacts with General Wu Lu-chen were also made at this time, with the object of planning a mutiny against Peking.

General Wu, the commanding officer of the 6th Division, was then stationed at the important railway junction, Shihchiachuang. His help was sought by General Chang, by the Manchu Cabal to get rid of Yuan, and by the Regent to pacify General Chang and General Yen Hsi-shan who had recently declared independence in Shansi. On November 2nd he went to Luanchou where he held secret discussions with Chang; two days later he reached an understanding with Yen. An alliance was thus formed to stage a *coup d'etat* in Peking and to hamper Yuan's military operations in Hupei. Train-loads of arms and ammunition from Peking to Hankow went no further than Shihchiachung. Yuan therefore bribed an officer under Wu's command to assassinate Wu. The deed was done at midnight on November 6th. Early in the next morning, General Ts'ao K'un and his 3rd Division arrived at Shihchiachuang to take over the garrison duties. Ts'ao was a trusted lieutenant of Yuan's. By murdering General Wu, Yuan dealt a lethal blow to the alliance. Yen Hsi-shan thereupon recalled all his troops to Shansi and Chang Shao-tseng, having relinquished his command on November 19th, and went to live in Tientsin as a private citizen.

The generals' activities in the vicinity of Peking scared the Regent into issuing an edict apologizing for maladministration on the day following the issue of General Chang's twelve proposals. At the same time, he gave praise and promotion to General Chang, pardons to all the political offenders convicted since 1898, and instructions to the Political Consultative Council to draft a constitution. With astonishing efficiency, three days later, they had a constitution of nineteen articles ready for the Regent to take to the Ancestral Temple, where he swore to put it into practice. He also, on November 7th, appointed Yuan Shih-k'ai the Prime Minister of the first and only responsible government of the Ch'ing dynasty. The Regent's surrender to Yuan was complete.

Now the famous 'affection of the foot' was over and the patient

H

went to the front to inspect his troops on October 31st; meanwhile his truce delegation were on the other side of the front parleying with the military leader of the Revolutionary Army, Li Yuan-hung.

On November 14th, the inhabitants of Peking had the privilege of witnessing the triumphal return with full military pomp of the man of destiny. At once he was given an audience during which his avowed loyalty was mingled with Imperial hopefulness. On the next day, he announced his Cabinet of ten Han Chinese and a solitary Manchu, who was given the Ministry of Suzerainty, for two reasons that, in the first place, the Mongols and the Tibetans were loyal only to the Manchu Emperor and, in the second place, the Cabinet could not be called a purely Han Chinese one.

CHAPTER VII

The Revolution 1911

THE causes of many revolutions in history are so obvious as to make explanations superfluous. Twice in this century China found herself in the grip of a revolution; on both occasions the causes were painfully clear. However, the fact that the 1911 Revolution took place at Wuch'ang needs some elucidation.

The Self-strengthening Army, or the Eighth Division, which had grown under Chang Chih-tung's auspices and Chang Piao's command, had been for years a centre of revolutionary political activities. A large number of cadets who had received military training and embraced radical doctrines in Japan were employed as officers by Chang Chih-tung and his successor, Jui-cheng. The central China branch of the Revolutionary Party and the Eighth Division were almost synonymous, and Hupei soldiers were indeed the backbone of all the local revolutionary bodies. The control of the army was the key to the success of the October uprising.

On the eve of the Double Tenth, the 8th Division under Chang Piao numbered about 10,000 and the 21st Mixed Brigade, an independent unit under the command of Li Yuan-hung was some 3,000 strong. Of the former, a battalion and a corps were taken to Szechwan by Tuan-fang to quell the railway riot, leaving 5,500 stationed in Wuch'ang, while of the latter there were about 1,500 men in the same city. As soon as the revolt broke out, the Viceroy, Jui-cheng, and General Chang Piao hastily crossed the river to Hankow, taking with them only 500 troops which were in any case non-combatant. In other words, nearly all the 8th Division units in the city went over to Li Yuan-hung.

From October 10th to December 2nd, there were some skirmishes, but rarely a hard fought battle. The number of casualties during those two months was even less than the toll of a fair-sized famine might be. Li Yuan-hung and his troops started action on the night of

October 9th and two days later they were already the masters of Wuch'ang, Hankow and Hanyang. The Manchu Government reacted quickly, rushing two armies thither under Generals Feng Kuo-chang and Tuan Ch'i-jui; the Commander-in-Chief was the German-trained Yin-ch'ang. Serious counter-attack, however, did not begin until Yin-ch'ang was replaced by Yuan Shih-k'ai who, ironically enough, took two days to recapture Hankow. Hanyang was recovered on November 27th and for this General Feng was made a baron. But he was at once called back to Peking by Yuan Shih-k'ai, who also ordered his troops to stop their onslaught on Wuch'ang on the grounds of lack of money and munitions and fear of causing further suffering to the people. The loss of Hankow and Hanyang could have been a lethal blow to the revolution, had T'ieh-liang and Chang Hsün kept the Dragon Flag flying over Nanking. With the occupation of Nanking on December 2nd by the revolutionary troops, honours were even and a truce of three days was agreed upon.

These operations in fact had more political than military significance. For instance, the recovery of Hankow was simultaneous with Yuan's appointment to the Premiership and that of Hanyang with his peace offers. The revolutionaries, on the other hand, delayed an agreement on a truce until after the occupation of Nanking, in order to elevate their morale and to provide a bargaining counter.

Yuan's assessment of the political situation before the truce was far more realistic than both the Manchus' in the Court of Peking and the revolutionaries' in Wuch'ang and Nanking, for from his point of view (to quote a hackneyed military phrase—with a slight twist in its meaning) 'the situation was under perfect control'. The decadent Manchu régime was unpopular. Instead of being the symbol of loyalty, it had become the target of racial hatred. With its decline went the influence of the constitutional monarchists such as K'ang Yu-wei and Liang Ch'i-ch'ao. Now only two of the political forces which we have mentioned in the previous chapter still remained—the revolutionaries and their supporters and Yuan Shih-k'ai and his Northern Army. The latter stood between the former and the overthrow of the Manchu Government. Indeed, the revolutionary leaders realized this, and Li Yuan-hung and the Commander-in-Chief of the Revolutionary Army, Huang Hsing, had solicited Yuan's support for the republican cause, offering him the Presidency as a reward. The Emperor and his Regent, on the other hand, also realized this, and therefore made Yuan Prime Minister in order to prevent him from deserting to the other camp. Yuan himself knew that without him the ramshackle Imperial House would collapse; and, in the recapture of Hankow and Hanyang, he had discovered that the revolutionaries too were not really worthy opponents. The medley of provincial leaders who declared for 'independence' were in fact sitting on the fence and watching in which direction the wind would blow. The governor of Shantung, for instance, having declared for 'independence', telegraphed a 'memorial' to the throne to explain his action and promised to withdraw the declaration as soon as the situation became more stable. The viceroy of Manchuria, Chao Erh-hsün, although refusing to declare for independence, set up a Peace Maintenance Society which operated side by side with the local government. The governor of Anhwei, Chu Chia-pao, disbanded the revolutionary troops in his province, announced independence and then, three days later, ran away. In Kiangsi, there were three different military governors in a hundred days; in Szechwan, two independent governments; in Kiangsu, thirteen military governors; and in Hunan and Kweichow, confused struggles among local warlords. The revolution was a sham; the independence of the provinces a farce. But Yuan would not destroy them lest he should deprive himself of an opportunity to play them off against the Imperial Court. He openly pledged his word never to betray 'the infant' on the throne and 'the widow'—the Empress Dowager Lung-yü for in his, indeed, in everyone else's mind was the story of the notorious usurper Wang Mang who bullied an infant and a widow into giving up the Empire in the year A.D. 6. Yuan wanted the revolutionaries to overthrow the Manchus and himself to reap the reward. Equally vivid before his own memory, no doubt, was the ancient allegorical tale of a mussel and an egret. The mussel was lazying about on the beach when the egret came and tried to eat it. The two halves of the shell closed and the bird found its bill caught between them. The mussel dared not loosen its grip, while the egret was prepared to wait until its opponent died of thirst. Neither of them was in a position to break the deadlock. But presently a fisherman came and picked up both of them. A deadlock of this kind was every fisherman's hope. Therefore immediately after the recapture of Hanyang, Yuan's delegate approached Huang Hsing and Li Yuan-hung in Wuch'ang and proposed a cease-fire, but without result. Earlier he had asked Sir John Jordan, the British

Minister, to use his good offices to secure a three-days' truce. Through Jordan and the British consul in Hankow an armistice agreement was reached on the day the revolutionaries occupied Nanking.

The truce and the ensuing peace were in fact a foregone conclusion. *The Times* had reported 'early news of peace negotiation' as early as October 28th. Indeed when the first period of three days had elapsed another period of fifteen days was agreed upon, and this was followed by yet another week of armistice. The fighting was over and the peace-making began.

On December 1st, the Prime Minister's statement of policy was published:

'For centuries, China has been known as an autocratic country. But even the autocracy is far from being absolute. The people have neither respect for the authority, nor understanding of the responsibility, of the Government. At the moment, only by advocating anarchy or the complete abolition of taxes can one arouse their willing support. This [pathetic state of affairs] must be ascribed to the lack of a responsible government for a prolonged period.

'There are two schools among the Chinese Progressives—the democratic republicans and the constitutional monarchists. I am not all sure whether the Chinese people are well prepared to accept the citizenship of a republic; nor whether republicanism as put forward by its Chinese exponents has popular support. The present political crisis is entirely due to the utterances of a handful of part leaders. This is a fact overlooked by foreign observers. For the creation of a strong government we must go to the majority of the people for consultation, not to a few for advice.

'Apart from what has been said before, there are also divergent views and interests presented and represented by the intellectuals, servicemen, landlords and merchants. If these differences are left unreconciled and small factions are allowed to thrive, the country will certainly disintegrate.

'Although the Ch'ing Government have no policy to rally the people behind them, the proclaimed nineteen articles of the Principles of the Constitution promise to entrust the supreme power of the State to the people.

'If one compares the system of a constitutional monarchy which restricts the power of a king with one or another of the various systems which our people want to try out in China, one must come to the conclusion that the former is the only lasting solution [of our problems].

'I am positive that my love of my people is no less strong than that of the republican radicals. But I am wary about the means by which the proposed reforms are to be carried out. I fully realize the weight of my duty, and my only objects are to restore law and order and to see that plans beneficial to our country are put into practice without mishap. Personal fame and power are not my concern.

'I remain hopeful with regard to the outcome of the proposed peace negotiations. All those who love China wish to find a settlement that will satisfy all parties concerned, to restore peace and to establish a strong government. I know my fellow citizens, sensible as they are, are willing to entertain the thought that China may be destroyed. Thus it is important that we and the republicans should find a way to end the bloodshed, to break down the wall of misunderstanding, and to remove all that has caused inconvenience to the people.

'According to my view, the declarations of independence by some provincial authorities have had very little effect on the peace negotiations. The Government have had almost no control over the provinces and a state of semi-independence, declared or not, has been in existence for some time. In fact, not all the provinces have severed their relations with the Government. Some are still in the hands of Conservatives of independent tendencies whose main objects for the time being are the maintenance of law and order and the protection of the people and their property. The stronger the Republicans are, the more independent these Conservatives will become. Hence I propose to call on all the people to deliberate on the question of a suitable political system.

'This is a question of immense importance. It should be discussed with both a cool head and a warm heart. Emotional outbursts can lead nowhere.

'I submit that the present dynasty and its reigning monarch should be retained in a constitutional monarchy. The discrimination between the Manchus and the Hans should be eliminated.

'However, my most important concern is the preservation of China. I rely on the patriots of all parties to jettison some of their policies in order to co-operate with me in achieving this goal. Only by so doing, can China escape partition or disintegration and its lamentable consequences. For the sake of our country, we must establish a strong Government at once, because the danger is mounting day by day. I hope the Progressives will not permit our country to sink lower, and it is also my sincere wish that they should co-operate with me unreservedly in seeking an adequate solution to every major issue.

'These high sounding wishes of mine may lead to misinterpretation of my true intentions. I am aware of the attacks against me from all quarters. But I shall not permit myself to be influenced by them and shall never shirk my supreme duties. All I am trying to do is to prevent China from breaking into pieces.'[1]

Five days after this statement, the Regent, Prince Ch'un, abdicated and was instructed by the Empress Dowager Lung-yü to take no further part in politics. Simultaneously Yuan Shih-k'ai was given full authority as Prime Minister and on the next day he was authorized to negotiate a peace with the revolutionaries. The peace delegation was headed by T'ang Shao-i.

The composition of the Government's peace delegation was exceedingly interesting. T'ang Shao-i had been appointed the Minister of Communications in Yuan's Cabinet, but declined to take up office on the advice of a dubious figure called Hung Tsu-shu about whom we shall learn a great deal more presently. Hung, according to Chao Ping-chun, exhorted T'ang to discuss with Yuan a detailed plan for deposing the Manchu Emperor and promoting establishment of a republic by playing off the south against the north. The terms of a peaceful settlement should be that Yuan would become the first President and T'ang the first Premier. T'ang obviously heeded this advice, for when setting out for Hankow, he told a foreign friend of his: 'The only solution will be a republic.'[2] *The Times* endorsed this in a despatch published on December 22nd.

T'ang was assisted by the reticent Yang Shih-ch'i who was believed to be a supporter of the monarchy, but judging by his later career, was no more than Yuan's mouthpiece. The third delegate, Yen Hsiu, did not make the journey. Thus the core of the delegation consisted of T'ang and Yang as the representatives and Yang Tu, Wei Ch'en-tsu, and Wang Ching-wei as advisers. Each province had an appointed representative in the delegation.

Another figure, perhaps even more colourful than T'ang in the

[1] *Shih-pao*, December 1 and 2, 1911.
[2] J. O. P. Bland, *Recent and Present*, op. 162.

Imperial delegation was Wang Ching-wei, who had been in prison since his unsuccessful attempt on the life of the Regent in April 1910 until Yuan Shih-k'ai's recall. Yuan secured his release and later suggested to him and Yang Tu that they should organize a Society of Co-operation in National Affairs. Yuan also asked him to become the sworn brother of his son K'e-ting. It was therefore as Yuan's adopted son, as an official of the Imperial delegation and as an important member of the Revolutionary Party that Wang Ching-wei went to Shanghai to play a major part in the peace settlement of 1912.

As the prospects of peace became better, the Revolutionary Party called a meeting in Shanghai and then another in the British Concession in Hankow to work out a common policy. Early in December they agreed to set up a provisional government in Nanking and also elected a peace delegation including Dr Wu T'ing-fang as the leader, the omnipresent Wang Ching-wei, and five others. The election coincided with the arrival of the Imperial peace representatives at Hankow, where the latter were asked by the revolutionaries to go on to Shanghai. It was in the British Concession in Shanghai on December 18th that these two delegations held their first meeting.

Meanwhile informal peace negotiations were taking place in Nanking. Those involved were the representatives of Tuan Ch'i-jui and Huang Hsing, Commanders-in-Chief of the two contending armies. Naturally enough, this military parley had the blessing of the political leaders on both sides. In a small bookshop, on December 20th—two days after the official negotiations began—an agreement of five articles was reached:

'1. A republican government will be established as the only government of China; 2. the Imperial House will be treated with generosity and courtesy; 3. he who overthrows the Manchu régime shall be President of the republic; 4. the soldiers of the north and south, including both Hans and Manchus, will be treated with due consideration and they will not be held responsible for the destruction during the revolutionary war; and 5. temporary administrative councils will be created in the provinces to maintain peace and order.'[1]

This agreement was the basis of the formal discussion in Shanghai.

On the morning of December 18th T'ang Shao-i, Dr Wu T'ing-fang and their fellow delegates met in the Municipal Council Building

[1] HHKM, VIII, p. 103.

to hear Dr Wu's four-point plan—the abolition of the Manchu
Government in Peking; the creation of a republican government; a
generous annuity to the Emperor after his abdication; and relief
for aged and poor Manchus. The two delegations also agreed upon
an indefinite armistice in seven provinces, including Hupei and
Kiangsu.

Three days later, at the second session, Dr. Wu insisted that a
pre-condition for any further useful negotiation was that the Northern
representatives should accept the first two points in his plan. This
was a grave demand, far beyond T'ang's authority to agree to or to
reject. T'ang thereupon asked for an adjournment and sent a telegram to his Government for instructions in which he pointed out the
perils facing the Imperial Court and put forward the suggestion
that the choice between a republic and a monarchy could be made
at a National Assembly. He also sent a personal message to Yuan,
advising him to follow in the footsteps of George Washington, for
'the fall of the dynasty is imminent'.[1] Wang Ching-wei, for his part,
telegraphed Yuan K'e-ting, his sworn brother, asking him to explain
the situation to his father, and he also advised his comrades in the
south to be patient. These personal messages undoubtedly had their
influence in shaping Yuan's policy.

On receiving them, Yuan consulted Prince Ch'ing about the
possibilities of convening a National Assembly. On the next day a
Court conference was held to deliberate on this matter. Prince
Ch'ing spoke in favour of summoning an Assembly while Yü-lang
and Duke Tsai-tse strongly opposed the proposal but failed to make
their point. Yuan and Prince Ch'ing carried the day and the Empress
Dowager Lung-yü gave her personal approval on December 28th in
an edict which J. O. P. Bland described as 'the death warrant of the
dynasty'.

The Imperial kinsmen were hopelessly divided, but in the south
morale was high, for Dr Sun Yat-sen had arrived at Shanghai from
the United States on Christmas Day. Two days later, the revolutionary representatives elected him to the first Presidency of the
Provisional Government and the inauguration ceremony was to
take place on January 1, 1912. On the day the election was held,
T'ang and Dr Wu sat down for the third time to their negotiations.
During this session T'ang, acting under Yuan's instructions, put
forward a proposal to convene a National Assembly which would

[1] HHKM, VIII, p. 118.

choose between a republic and a monarchy. Two more sessions followed on the next two days to work out the details of the composition, place and time of the Convention. It was agreed that the Assembly would be held in Shanghai on January 8th. On this harmonious note, the year drew to an end.

On January 1, 1912 Dr Sun Yat-sen was sworn in as the first President of the Provisional Government in Nanking. The oath ran:

'To overthrow the despotic Manchu Government, to consolidate the Republic of China, and to plan for the welfare of the people, I, Sun Wen, will faithfully obey the wish of the citizens, be loyal to the nation, and perform my duty in the interest of the public, until the downfall of the despotic Government, until the complete restoration of peace in this country, and until the Republic has been firmly established and duly recognized by all the nations of the world. Then, I, Sun Wen, shall relinquish the office of Provisional President. I hereby swear this before the citizens.'[1]

After the ceremony, as he had done after the election to the Presidency, Dr Sun telegraphed Yuan to explain his selfless attitude towards power and high position and to confirm his promise that, once Yuan declared his support for republicanism, he would relinquish this exalted post to him. The oath made the promise irrevocable. Yet Yuan and his officers were not to be satisfied by a mere promise, however firm it might be. Through Liang Shih-i, Yuan asked T'ang Shao-i to resign from the Imperial peace delegation, which T'ang did; Yuan also telegraphed Dr Wu T'ing-fang saying that T'ang had exceeded his power in signing the agreement on the composition and method of nomination of the proposed National Assembly. Sixty-eight military leaders of the Northern Army, such as Baron Feng Kuo-chang and Tuan Ch'i-jui, openly declared their firm support of the throne, while Chinese envoys abroad memorialized by telegram in favour of an abdication. All these happened in a single day—January 2nd, five days after Dr Sun's election.

T'ang Shao-i's resignation aroused some controversy. J. O. P. Bland thought that T'ang had betrayed the Prime Minister, for in his opinion:

[1] Based on H. F. MacNair's translation, *Modern Chinese History*, p. 719 and *Hsin-hai Ke-ming Hsien-chu Chi*, p. 249. See also LSCFKP, No. 1, 29.1.1912.

'he [Yuan] would have won if T'ang Shao-yi, as Imperial Delegate to the revolutionaries, had not betrayed his confidence, and if he had received from the British and American Governments support which he had every right to expect. For the solution of crisis in December depended essentially upon his obtaining a foreign loan. Had he obtained it, not only would public opinion in the south have given him credit for prestige abroad, but many waverers would have immediately joined themselves to him as the ultimate disperser of loaves and fishes.'[1]

Betrayal is a grave word! Bland's verdict could only be valid if Yuan's sincerity in supporting the Manchu throne was not in doubt. In fact, since his recall, Yuan had had no reason to be and had shown no definite signs of being what Bland assumed him to be. He told his close associate, Liang Shih-i, that he was in favour of a republican government; he told his son the same; and as Morrison had said in his despatch to *The Times* on December 28, 1911 'I have reason to believe that he [Yuan] would accept such a post [Presidency] if to the wishes of the Convention [National Assembly in Nanking] were added the wishes of the Manchus, whose dynasty he has served so faithfully'. Judging by Yuan's conduct before and after the Manchu abdication, this somewhat biting observation by the head of the military government of Wusung, Li Hsieh-ho, was very much to the point:

'Yuan's unreliability is no news to any of us. His past consists of nothing but duplicity. The Sino-Japanese War of 1895, the Reform of 1898, the Boxer Uprising of 1900, and the present Revolution have all been used to further his own ends. We have seen that during each of these unrests, his influence was enhanced. He is loyal to neither the people nor the throne. . . . This unscrupulous man deals with people by cunning devices, unaware that he himself is the slave of his own ingenuity. Therefore Yuan is thoroughly untrustworthy. To give him confidence, in other words, to trust his treachery, is self-deceiving. Even he does not believe in himself.'[2]

The crux of the matter was not T'ang's signature on the agreement, but Dr Sun's inauguration on January 1st. Yuan could not placidly

[1] *Recent and Present*, p. 133.
[2] *Shih-pao*, 19.1.1912.

accept Sun's Presidency and empty promise without a protest, either for his own sake or for the sake of the throne, whose continued existence now became more necessary to him as a bargaining counter against the Nanking government.

With the resignation of T'ang, Yuan personally took charge of the peace negotiations with the revolutionaries, while the amphibious Wang Ching-wei, equally at home on either side, who shared Dr Wu's temporary residence in Shanghai, did his best to make Yuan's wishes known to the revolutionaries. The negotiations themselves came to a standstill and this fact aroused considerable indignation among the southern leaders. Li Hsieh-ho put it bluntly: 'The gravest miscalculation in the past month was the agreement to negotiate peace. Since the choice between the Republic and the Empire is clear-cut and there can be no compromise, I see no point in discussing either peace or war [with the North].'[1] Ts'en Ch'un-hsuan, an erstwhile high official of the Imperial Government and now an important revolutionary, sent a telegram to Yuan, laying at his door the sole responsibility for the breakdown. Dr Sun, for his part, telegraphed the foreign Ministers, giving details of the peace negotiations and accusing Yuan of obstruction. The Provisional President said in his communication that he was willing to hand over his office to Yuan, who had already agreed to accept it. But suddenly Yuan demanded the dissolution of the Provisional Government in Nanking. This, according to the President, could not be done. The Republic would make concessions for Yuan's benefit, Dr Sun said, as long as Yuan was willing to give it his full support. In Peking, the members of an underground cell of the Revolutionary Party, under the leadership of one Chang Hsien-p'ei, were discussing ways and means of getting rid of Yuan Shih-k'ai. They had made up their mind to assassinate him as early as December 9th, but Wang Ching-wei, who was then still there, advised against it. Now, in the middle of January, while Wang was in Shanghai and Yuan was obstructing the peace talks and arresting members of the Party in T'ungchou, Chang Hsien-p'ei and his comrades reviewed the situation and decided to assassinate Yuan on January 16th.

On that day, the Prime Minister drove from his office to the Palace to present an unusually important memorial. The Party cell obtained information about his movements beforehand and planted four small groups of their supporters along the route from the

[1] *Shih-pao*, 19.1.1912.

Tung-hua Gate to the Palace, waiting for Yuan to pass. At 11.15 in the morning, the audience with the Empress Dowager was over and Yuan's carriage had just passed the Tung-hua Gate where, in a teashop, Chang Hsien-p'ei and his small group of ten were lying in wait with some home-made bombs. Four of the bombs were thrown at the carriage, all exploded, but none hit the target. One of the pair of horses drawing the carriage was killed and the other fell on the ground, pulling down the vehicle and the passengers. A dozen guards were also killed, but Yuan emerged unhurt. He was at once helped on a horse, and rode away, while his escort searched the teashop and arrested all his assailants. Three were shot and seven released later at the request of some of the foreign correspondents in Peking.

Yuan's genius lay in his ability to utilize every situation to his full benefit. He immediately telegraphed Wang Ching-wei accusing the revolutionaries of breaking their promise that during the period of the peace negotiations they would not start any 'unpleasant incident'. Wang replied that these revolutionaries were in fact bandits. On receiving this reply, Yuan ordered further arrests in and around Peking.

The attempt on his life and the arrests that followed dispelled the last vestige of distrust in the minds of his opponents in the Court, and Yuan also seized the opportunity to ask for a month's sick-leave. Through Sir John Jordan, he made known his intention of going to Tientsin, for he knew that the memorial he had presented just before the assassination would cause some unpleasant scenes in the Palace, and it was better for him to stay away from there for a while. He also knew that his retirement, however short it might be, would be fatal to the tottering régime, so the request was in fact a threat which Yuan hoped would compel the Empress Dowager and her kinsmen to agree to the proposal contained in the memorial. The Imperial lady, understanding his meaning, promptly exempted him from the obligation to attend Court conferences, but refused to grant him leave. In addition, she conferred upon him the highest honour that any Han Chinese, apart from Marquis Tseng Kuo-fan, had ever received from the Manchu throne: Yuan was made a marquis of the first class. According to tradition, he declined respectfully three times before he finally accepted the honour on January 26th.

On that same day, an important Cabinet meeting which lasted until late in the evening was held at Yuan's residence. The Chief-of-Staff, Liang-pi, who was the leader of the Manchu Cabal, was attacked by a fanatical revolutionary on his return home from the meeting. The assailant died at once and his victim on the next day. As Liang-pi had been consistently opposed to Yuan's peace policy, Yuan was thought by some to have contrived his death.

The urgent matter discussed at the Cabinet meeting was a telegram from forty-two commanding officers of Yuan's troops, including the commander of the First Army, General Tuan Ch'i-jui, but not Baron Feng Kuo-chang; this telegram requested the Manchu Emperor to abdicate. Only twenty-four days before, these same generals had pledged themselves to defend the throne to the last drop of their blood. The telegram which arrived at the time of the two outrages in Peking dealt a lethal blow to the dynasty. The Imperial kinsmen were forced to reconsider their opposition to an early abdication, not so much on the ground of high principles as on that of their own safety. At the Court Conference on the following day, the Empress hysterically screamed to Yuan's deputies, Liang Shih-i, Chao Ping-chun and Hu Wei-te: 'My own and the boy's [the Emperor's] lives are in your hands. Go and tell Yuan Shih-k'ai, tell him nicely that he must save us.'[1]

Now we must reveal the contents of the 'unusually important memorial' which Yuan presented before the attempt on his life. This historic document was a petition in the name of the Cabinet as a whole to the Empress Dowager for an early abdication. A Court Conference was held on January 17th to discuss it; Prince P'u-lun and Prince Ch'ing advocated an Imperial proclamation of a republic whereas the ex-Regent, Prince Kung and Duke Tsai-tse strongly disagreed. The Empress hugged the infant Emperor in her arms and wept. The atmosphere was heavy and sad; the sun was setting on the dynasty.

Two days later, a second conference took place in the Yang-hsin Hall in the Palace to deliberate on two main proposals. The first, raised by Yuan's deputies, Liang Shih-i and Chao Ping-chun, was in favour of setting up a provisional Government in Tientsin in addition to the Imperial Government in Peking and the Revolutionary Government in Nanking, and Yuan's intention was to kill two birds with one stone. Firstly, he would secure unity by superseding both existing Governments with a new one and also secure his own position as its head. Secondly, he hoped to obtain more favourable terms for the Imperial House after the abdication. All the princes

[1] Liang, *Nien-p'u*, p. 111.

who attended the Conference objected to this proposal. The second proposal concerned the prickly problem of financing the civil war against the revolutionaries. Yuan Shih-k'ai asked for 12 million taels, provincial governors asked for 30 million taels, and even the most loyal Baron Feng Kuo-chang wanted at least three months' expenses or, in other words, some 6 million taels, but there was no money in the Treasury. It was about this question that the princes were most despondent. Their personal wealth deposited in foreign banks amounted, according to the Japanese Minister's estimate, to several tens of millions, but none was willing to make the personal sacrifice for the preservation of the dynasty. Fourteen princes attended the Conference, yet only four spoke. Hesitation and indecision continued until after Liang-pi's death. It was then, at the final Court Conference on January 30th, that the decision to proclaim a Republic by Imperial Decree was taken by the Empress Dowager Lung-yü on her own initiative.

In England, the scoop of the year was Morrison's forecast of the abdication as early as January 10th and his despatch entitled: 'A Republic by Imperial Decree,' which was published by *The Times* on January 15th.

The deadlock in the peace negotiations was thus broken. Having accepted the first two points of Dr Wu T'ing-fang's plan—the abdication and the establishment of *a* republic—Yuan through Yang Shih-ch'i and Wu through Wang Ching-wei resumed their debate on the last two points of the plan—namely, a generous annuity to the Emperor after his abdication and a pension for aged and poor Manchus. Agreement on these points was soon reached, the details of the ceremony were worked out, and Yuan's erstwhile friend, Chang Ch'ien, was asked to draft the last edict that the Manchu sovereign was to issue.

On February 12th, the whole Cabinet was led by the Prime Minister into the Yang-hsin Hall, and there they were joined by the Imperial kinsmen and Court Officials, come to pay their last tribute to their liege and to witness the end of the rule which had lasted 267 years. Presently the Empress Dowager Lung-yü and the boy Emperor, P'u-i, arrived and ascended their thrones. The Abdication Edict was presented to Her Majesty by a eunuch for her final approval. As she was reading it, tears streamed out of her eyes and all her vassals prostrated themselves on the ground, quite overcome by grief and fear of the verdict of history. Suddenly she stopped, wept bitterly, and handed the Edict to Shih-hsü and Hsü Shih-ch'ang to be sealed with the Imperial Seal on it. Then the members of the Cabinet signed their names one by one at the end of the document. In silence and with dignity, the last Audience was adjourned; and with it, the curtain fell on another episode in the long history of China.

Later the Edict was published in the name of the Emperor. It read:

'We have to-day received from the Empress Dowager, Lung-yü an edict stating that on account of the uprising by the Army of the People, with the co-operation of the people of the provinces, the one answering to the other as the echo does the sound, the whole Empire is in turmoil and the people have endured much tribulation. We therefore specially appointed Yuan Shih-k'ai to instruct Commissioners to confer with the representatives of the Army of the People for the convening of a National Assembly at which the future of the government should be decided. For the past two months there has been wide divergence of opinion between the north and the south, each strongly maintaining its own views, and the general consequence has been the stagnation of trade and deployment of troops. As long as the form of government remains undecided, so long will the disturbed condition of the country continue. It is clear that the minds of the majority of the people are in favour of the establishment of a republican form of government, the southern and central provinces first holding this view, and the officers in the north lately adopting the same sentiments. The universal desire clearly expressed the Will of Heaven, and it is not for us to oppose the desires and incur the disapproval of the millions of the people merely for the sake of the privileges and powers of a single House. It is right that this general situation should be considered and due deference given to the opinion of the people. We, with the Emperor at our side, hereby hand over the sovereignty to the people as a whole, and declare that the constitution shall henceforth be republican, wishing to satisfy the demands of those within the confines of the country, hating disorder and desiring peace, and anxious to follow the teaching of the sages, according to which the country is the the possession of the people.

'Yuan Shih-k'ai, having been elected Prime Minister some time ago by the Political Consultative Council, is therefore able at this time of change to unite the north and the south—*let him then with*

I

full powers so to do, organize *a* provisional republican government, conferring therein with the representatives of the Army of the People, that peace may be assured to the people while the complete integrity of the territories of the five races, Hans, Manchus, Mongols, Muhammadans and Tibetans, is at the same time maintained, making together a great state under the title of the Republic of China. We, the Empress Dowager and the Emperor, will retire into a life of leisure, free from public duties, spending our years pleasantly and enjoying the courteous treatment accorded to us by the people, and watching with satisfaction the glorious establishment and consummation of the perfect government.

IMPERIAL SEAL

Signatures:
Prime Minister Yuan Shih-k'ai
Acting Minister of Foreign Affairs Hu Wei-te
Minister of the Interior Chao Ping-chun
Acting Minister of Finance Shao-ying
Minister of Education T'ang Ching-ch'ung
Minister for the Army Wang Shih-chen
Minister for the Navy T'an Hsüeh-heng
Minister of Justice Shen Chia-pen
Minister of Agriculture, Industry and Commerce Hsi-yen
Minister of Communications Liang Shih-i
Minister of Suzerainty Ta-shou.'[1]

This lamentable document was far from an unconditional surrender of Peking to Nanking. In fact, it did not recognize the existence of the Nanking Government. Instead, it instructed Yuan Shih-k'ai '*with full powers*' to organize *a* provisional republican government in order to unify the north and the south. This, in essence, was Yuan's original proposal for establishing a provisional government in Tientsin. Furthermore, the phrase, 'let him then with full powers so to do', was, according to both Chang Ch'ien's and Liang Shih-i's biographies, inserted by Yuan himself, so it was Yuan, rather than the Nanking Government, who inherited the Will of Heaven.

[1] Based on the translation in *China Mission Year Book*, 1912, app. C, p. 16 and collated with R. Johnston, *Twilight*, p. 87, Kent, *Passing of the Manchus*, p. 314, Feng Tzu-yu, *Ke-ming I-shih*, II, p. 329, and ʜʜᴋᴍ, VIII, p. 183. Author's italics.

Whatever he was to do was not done as a usurper. Legitimacy, he hoped, was on his side.

As soon as the abdication was announced, Yuan telegraphed a lengthy message under the odd title of the Plenipotentiary (ch'üan-ch'üan, *with full powers*) to provincial governors:

'For three years I had been convalescing from an illness, and the idea of resuming my political career never entered my mind. Then His Majesty repeatedly commanded me to render my humble serivce once more and my refusal was not accepted. I therefore undertook a trip to the front to inspect the troops and then came back to the Imperial Capital with the preservation of the Empire as my sole duty. Yet the general situation deteriorated so rapidly, and meanwhile pressure was applied upon me from both within and without the capital. The areas in the south-east were lost and the north-west provinces showed from time to time signs of unrest. The Political Consultative Council, the provincial political councils and people of all walks of life were opposed to military suppression. Furthermore, the Treasury had very little in reserve and was unable to borrow from abroad. There was no possibility either of purchasing ammunition or of expanding the army. Consequently the recovery of Hankow was followed by the mutiny of the navy and the conquest of Hanyang by the loss of Nanking, which put the financial resources of Kiangsu and Shanghai out of the Government's reach. In spite of all these events, I tried to preserve the *esprit de corps* of my officers and men and succeeded in persuading Shantung and Shansi to renounce independence and in stabilizing the situation in Shensi, Honan and the adjacent areas of Tat'ung. The north is for the time being out of danger.

'Nevertheless, the tide continued to rise everywhere else. Members of the People's Party hid in Peking and Tientsin awaiting their chance and bandits roamed and buzzed like wasps. There were not enough troops at my disposal for me to take every precautionary step. In addition, six countries came forward to mediate, to appeal for a truce in the name of the people. The Imperial Commissioners were sent out and the edict was issue as an attempt to secure a negotiated settlement on the question of the form of a central government. After lengthy discussions, no agreement had been reached, and the situation worsened as the problem remained unsettled. Foreigners complained about the loss of their trade and the Government's inability to honour its indemnity promises, and brigands went on plundering and ravaging the countryside. These circumstances prevented the Government from taking rigorous measures to maintain peace and order. Lately, Urga, Ili and Hulun declared independence and Tibet was restive. Such internal problems might have provided an excuse for foreign intervention. The Army of the People attempted to drive northward, and there were urgent reports from Shantung and Honan; reinforcements failed to reach Hsüchou and the Yin River area. The Government could not pay the enormous military expenses incurred. Unless additional millions of taels could be found, there was no way of making ends meet till the year was out. The ebbing morale of the fighting troops has undoubtedly had its effect on the political situation. If affairs continue to go this way, when the spring comes and the weather turns warm the Army of the People will advance further north. The Government will find itself on the horns of a dilemma between war and peace. Not only will the people have to endure further tribulation, but the Capital will be threatened and I shall find myself unable to protect the Imperial Court, Temples, and Mausolea, nor shall I be able to ensure the safety of the Imperial House and the Bannermen. At this critical moment, I have prayed for death and begged for permission to relinquish my duties, yet both were in vain. I and my colleagues have been in deep anxiety and have often wept together.

'Recently our envoys abroad, chambers of commerce, provincial councils, military units and governors have sent me telegrams saying that, since the people generally favoured a republican régime, the situation was extremely grave. Instead of a surrender forced by defeat, with all its undesirable consequences, it would be better for Their Majesties to show their benevolence by declaring the establishment of a republic. If this is done, according to these telegrams, the throne will be able to uphold its dignity and the people will be grateful and willing to repay its kindness. All of them advised against taking the risk of embarking on a war which may endanger Their Majesties as well as the possessions of the people of the north. Her Majesty the Empress Dowager and the members of the Imperial House, fully aware of the changing situation and the people's wish, likewise spoke against a war at several Court Conferences. Her Majesty also instructed me and my colleagues to give full consideration to the Temples and Mausolea and her own and the Emperor's safety. Her Majesty was particularly determined to avoid a terrible conflict between the two races. I, trembling, accepted her orders, fearing that my competence might fall short of her expectations. Exhausted in both energy and wits as I was, I could not but give my foremost consideration to the interests of the country, the safety of Their Majesties, and the well-being and the wishes of their subjects. Having received Her Majesty's gracious command, my Commissioners at once began to work with the representatives of the Army of the People on terms for favourable treatment of the members of the Imperial clan. They also endeavoured to decide on fair treatment of the Manchus, Mongols, Muslims and Tibetans. From the Government's point of view, this was to choose the lesser of two evils. If an agreement could be obtained and peace could be concluded, the Imperial House would be able to enjoy a dignity and honour unheard of in previous dynasties, and the nobility of the Manchus, Mongols, Muslims and Tibetans as well as all the Bannermen would continue to draw their allowances. There could be no comparison between this and a war and its sufferings. After careful deliberations, the Court came to the present conclusion.

'Gentlemen, you have fervently hoped for peace and order and, sagacious as you are, you are sure to agree with this. I and my colleagues are not certain whether you have been informed of the processes by which the decision was reached and we have hereby reported to you in detail.'[1]

A second message from Yuan Shih-k'ai on the same day, February 12th, was addressed to Dr Sun Yat-sen, the President of the Nanking Government. In this, Yuan confirmed his support for republicanism, and went on:

'Henceforth we shall exert our utmost strength to move forward in progress until we reach perfection. *Never shall we allow monarchical Government in our China.* [Author's italics]. At present the work of consolidation is most difficult and complicated. I shall be most happy to come to the south to listen to your counsels in our conference as to the methods of procedure. None the less, on account of the difficulty of maintaining order in the north, the existence of a large army requiring control, and the division of the popular mind in the north and east, the slightest disturbance would affect the whole

[1] *Hsin-hai Ke-ming Shih-liao*, III, pp. 319-20.

country. All of you, who thoroughly understand the situation, will realize my difficult position. . . . I beg you to inform me as to the way of co-operation in the work of consolidation.'[1]

The request at the end of the message reminded Dr Sun to keep his promise handing over the Presidency to Yuan, who had also made it abundantly clear that he had no intention of taking up office in Nanking, lest he should place himself at the mercy of disobedient revolutionaries. Dr Sun, for his part, protested against the Abdication Edict on the ground that a republic could never be created by an Imperial Decree. However, being a man of honour and a true revolutionary, who put the welfare of the people before his personal interests, he tendered his resignation on February 13th in a message to the Provisional Senate in Nanking. Attached to it, were these conditions:

'1. The Provisional Government of the Republic of China, as has been decided by the representatives of the provinces, is and will be situated in Nanking and should not be transferred elsewhere.

2. Although the President and his Cabinet have resigned, they will continue to discharge their duties until the new Provisional President is elected by the Senate and sworn in.

3. The new President must obey the Provisional Republican Constitution adopted by the Senate; and the legislation which has been adopted by it will remain in force unless revised by the Senate itself.'[2]

At the same time, Dr Sun nominated Yuan Shih-k'ai as the new Provisional President of the Republic, and the Senate, having praised Dr Sun's self-abnegation, accepted both his resignation and the nomination. Yuan thus became President of China on February 15th.

The vote for Yuan in the Senate was unanimous, and so was that for the election of General Li Yuan-hung to the Vice-Presidency on February 22nd. The inevitable congratulatory telegrams from the civil and military leaders of the provinces flooded into both Peking and Hankow, expressing a wide approval of these choices. These facts seemed to indicate that the search for a political system which

---

[1] Based on H. F. MacNair, *Modern Chinese History*, p. 726, and collated with *Hsin-Hai Ke-ming Hsien-chu Chi*, p. 276. Author's italics.

[2] *Hsin-hai Ke-ming Hsien-chu Chi*, p. 277, and LSCFKP, No. 17, 20.2.1912.

had been going on since the Shimonoseki Treaty of 1895 had come to an end, and that a chance of peaceful reconstruction in unity was at last in sight. But, confronting the newly established régime with its head in Peking and its legislature in Nanking, was the question: Would republicans work in a country whose monarchical tradition had been so long and where the general standard of education among the people was so lamentably low? No one, except Dr Sun Yat-sen, seemed to care whether the Republic was created by an Imperial Edict or by popular demand, whether the Manchu Emperor abdicated or was overthrown by the Revolution, or whether the Abdication referred to the throne of China or to that of the Ch'ing Empire. All the common people knew was that the title 'Ta Ch'ing' (Great Ch'ing) was now changed into 'Min-kuo' (Republic) and that they had to cut off their queues. Indeed, even among the great intellectuals of the time, Chang T'ai-yen was in favour of the election of a President, but opposed to the convening of a parliament; and Yen Fu, in an anonymous letter in English to Dr Morrison of *The Times*, published on November 28, 1911, maintained: 'China . . . is unfit for a totally different new form of Government such as the Republic of America. . . . A Republic has been strongly advocated by some hare-brained revolutionists such as Sun Yat-sen himself and others; but it is opposed by everybody who possesses some common sense.'

The Revolution was mainly racialistic. Once the Manchu Emperor was removed, the arrow had no further target. The wrangles between Peking and Nanking made no sense to the man in the street.

The first quarrel was about the location of the capital of the Republic. In his telegram to Dr Sun on February 12th, Yuan clearly expressed his unwillingness to go to Nanking, while the Senate there insisted that the capital should not be situated elsewhere.

The influence of the location of the Chinese capital on her history has never been properly analysed, therefore it is necessary to digress a little at this juncture. From the unification of China in 221 BC to the fall of the T'ang dynasty in AD 907 the political centre of the Empire had always been in Ch'angan (the present-day Sian) where the rulers found the most fertile land to the north and to the south; this was necessary for the support of a large metropolitan population and a sizeable army to defend China's north-west frontiers. In those times, her north-west regions were often harassed by tribes of nomads. With the climatic and geographical changes which occurred towards the end of the ninth century, the strength of the nomads in the north-west declined and the land in Shensi became less productive; meanwhile the tribes in the north-east grew to be a serious menace. As a result, the capital had to be transferred to Peking. The underlying reason was that China, to defend herself against strong neighbouring peoples, required a large army which, if not under the direct command of the Emperor, must be entrusted to an able general. Where there was a strong army, there was power; and that power could be harnessed for defence against foreigners or used by the able general (ability and ambition often go hand in hand) to challenge the Emperor. The Northern Sung dynasty (960-1126) experimented with the compromise of situating its capital in K'aifeng. This was a typical decision of a transitional period which inevitably caused a weakening of its defence forces along both the north-western and the north-eastern frontiers. It was a weak dynasty, followed by a still weaker one. The Mongols did not hesitate to make Peking their capital in China; but, later, the founder Emperor of the Ming dynasty (1368-1643), ignorant of the change in the situation, located his capital in Nanking, and, at the same time, sent his ablest son to command a large army in Peking. When this Emperor died and another son was chosen to succeed the throne, there was a revolt in Peking which ended in Peking's triumph over Nanking. From 1403 onwards, the capital of China had remained at Peking until the dispute between Yuan Shih-k'ai and the revolutionaries broke out.

At the time of the dispute, north-east China was obviously in danger of being swallowed up by Japan or by Russia, yet no one attached sufficient importance to analysing the question of the location of the capital as an element in long-term strategy. So we cannot be sure whether both sides wished to avoid the issue or simply considered such an approach fruitless, since China had no defences in any case; neither are we sure what would have become of China had Yuan heeded the revolutionaries by going to Nanking. With regard to the latter question, we have only Chiang Kai-shek's experience to throw some light on what might possibly have happened some twenty years earlier.

Yuan's arguments in favour of Peking were that the combined menace of the latent danger from Japan and Russia and the divided opinions in the north was too great to ignore; that the transfer from Peking to Nanking would cause a great deal of inconvenience to the diplomatic missions; and that the border regions such as Hei-lungkiang and Outer Mongolia might fall into the waiting hands of the neighbouring powers. The revolutionaries, on the other hand, regarded Peking as the symbol of all the evil customs of the Manchu bureaucracy—a view best put by a non-revolutionary, Liang Ch'i-ch'ao:

'The capital, Peking, has become the hotbed of all evils. Not only has the land lost its auspicious features and the water its sweet taste, but a thousand crimes, a myriad scandals, weird carbuncles and chronic diseases of this sinful world are also concentrated there. If the political centre stays there, China will never see a single day of clean government.'[1]

Both sides were insistent, and Yuan threatened them in these words: 'Instead of President Sun resigning, I had better retire from public life altogether.'[2] Seeing no result could be achieved by sending telegrams to and fro, Dr Sun and the Provisional Senate decided to send a delegation to welcome Yuan to the south. This was intended to stop further argument by courtesy, and the delegation included such famous men as Ts'ai Yuan-p'ei, Sung Chiao-jen, Liu Kuan-hsiung, Wang Cheng-t'ing and Wang Ching-wei. Yuan was equally courteous; he agreed to come to the south and send people to welcome the welcoming delegation. Yet to the revolutionaries in the north, the inclusion of Wang Ching-wei clearly indicated that Yuan would never leave Peking, and the arrival of the delegates was preceded by scores of telegrams from the northern leaders, exhorting Yuan not to abandon Peking.

The delegation was housed near the International Hotel, to the north of the Legation Quarter. Four days after its arrival, the situation underwent a startling change. In the night of February 29th, Yuan's most trusted Third Division, under the command of one of his most dependable officers, Ts'ao K'un, mutinied in the west of the city and attacked, looted and burned various places around Hatamen and the Foreign Ministry. They shouted slogans against Yuan's departure and against the delegation. Ts'ai, Wang and others, caught unprepared, hurriedly fled in their nightshirts to safety into the International Hotel. The timing and the units

[1] *Yin-ping-shih-ho-chi*, ch. 25, p. 196.
[2] *Shih-pao*, 21.2.1912.

involved in the mutiny suggested that the whole incident was
staged for the benefit of the delegates, in order to back up Yuan's
expression of fear that the situation in the north was unstable.

Forty-eight hours after the Peking incident, troops in Tientsin,
Paoting and Shihchiachuang also mutinied. Like the Third Division,
these were all Yuan's troops led by reliable lieutenants. The mutinies
were soon put down without much fighting and none of the
commanding officers of the disobedient units was punished afterwards. Instead, the master blamed himself in a public notice for his
lack of control over them.

These events convinced the delegation of the necessity of Yuan's
remaining permanently in Peking, and they mediated in the reaching
of a compromise between Yuan and the Senate, completed on March
6th. The delegation also published a message explaining why the
capital should be Peking. The Nanking Senate later decided to come
to Yuan, since he would not come to it, and, to safeguard the newly
created Republic, it imposed three conditions on the President-elect
in return for its acceptance of Peking as the capital: 1. The President
must take an oath of loyalty to the Republic; 2. the nomination of
his Cabinet must be approved by the Provisional Senate; and 3. the
Provisional President, Sun Yat-sen, and the Provisional Government
in Nanking would cease to perform their duties when the new
Government was formed in Nanking.

These were not really conditions, but normal procedures through
which a President of a Republic took up his office and carried out his
work. The Senate, however, believed that Yuan's power could be
effectively limited by the Provisional Republican Constitution which
the Senate had been working on since February 8th, but which still
remained shapeless when the compromise was reached. Therefore
Yuan asked the Senate: 'What is the Constitution?'[1] after he had
taken the oath to obey it. It was only then that the Provisional
Constitution was proclaimed by the out-going President Sun. This
important document, in seven chapters, made clear that ' . . . the
Ministers of State, and ambassadors and ministers accredited by
foreign powers, should be approved by the National Assembly,'[2] but
did not say whether the Cabinet was responsible to the President or
to the Assembly.[3] It was full of loopholes, yet the Senate hoped to

---

[1] LSKP, 11.3.1912.
[2] Ch.4, articles 34.
[3] Ch. 5, article 44. See H. F. MacNair, *Modern Chinese History*, pp. 729-734.

use it to restrict the ambitious Yuan Shih-k'ai. Yuan was shrewd enough to assess the exact weight of the sheets of paper on which these articles were written, and accepted them without a murmur. On March 10th the ceremony of his installation was held and he was sworn in as the second Provisional President of the Republic of China. Within a stone's throw of the hall where the ceremony took place, in the Imperial Palaces, the Ch'ing Emperor, who had retained his title, was spending an ordinary quiet day.

CHAPTER VIII

The President 1912-1913

YUAN'S investiture on March 10th and the Senate's decision to reassemble in Peking on April 29th ostensibly patched up the split between the north and the south, and the co-existence of two governments gave way to unification. The new President at once embarked upon the urgent task of Cabinet-making. There was at one time a suggestion that Dr Sun Yat-sen should be appointed the first Premier of the Republic, but this did not materialize. Instead, Tang Shao-i, Yuan's old friend and a new member of the Revolutionary Party, was designated pending the Senate's approval; this was readily given on March 13th. At the same time Liang Shih-i was appointed Secretary-General and Feng Kuo-chang Chief of the Military Department on the President's personal staff.

The list of China's first and T'ang's only Cabinet was completed and approved by the Senate in Nanking at the end of March. Yuan's erstwhile teacher, Chang Ch'ien, was asked to take up a ministerial post, which honour he refused on these grounds:

'I am nearly seventy.... My self-respect permits me neither to tread on the floors of an office nor to accept the exalted position of a Minister.'[1]

Earlier he had declined to join Yuan's 1911 Cabinet and also the Revolutionary Government in Nanking. By living contentedly in the political wilderness and dedicating himself to industrial development and local welfare, this grand old man, like Weng T'ung-ho (his and Emperor Kuang-hsü's tutor and the Grand Secretary at the time of the 1898 Reform) and Dr Sun Yat-sen, became one of a handful of famous men in the post-1895 period who emerged with their integrity unblemished in spite of the infamy of his period.

[1] *Chi-chih Hsien-sheng Chuan-chi*, p. 161.

T'ang's Cabinet included two professional diplomats, Lu Cheng-hsiang as Minister of Foreign Affairs and Shih Chao-chi as the Minister of Communications; a monarchist, Hsiung Hsi-ling, as Minister of Finance; two confidants of the President, General Tuan Ch'i-jui as Minister for the Army and Chao Ping-chun as Minister of the Interior, and five revolutionaries, Ts'ai Yuan-p'ei as Minister of Education, Wang Ch'ung-hui as Minister of Justice, Sung Chiao-jen as Minister of Agriculture and Forestry, Ch'en Ch'i-mei as Minister of Industry and Commerce and Liu Kuan-hsiung as Minister for the Navy. Ostensibly the five avowed revolutionaries counter-balanced the five others, while the Premier himself was at once Yuan's close friend and a member of the Revolutionary Party; but to make a more realistic assessment one must not lose sight of two facts: 1. the so-called professional diplomats and the monarchist were actually Yuan's men in one disguise or another, and Liu Kuan-hsiung, as we shall see presently, was no more revolutionary than Yuan himself; and 2. all the important Ministries such as those of Foreign Affairs, the Interior (which also controlled the police), Finance and the lucrative Communications, went to Yuan's lieutenants. The Revolutionary Party which had created the Republic was now playing second fiddle in this Coalition Government.

Cabinet-making was only a part of Yuan's work in forming a Central Government. The rest consisted of the election of a National Assembly of two chambers—the Senate and the House of Representatives—and the election of a permanent President. The procedure for all these was based on the stipulations of the Provisional Constitution which were by definition temporary in nature, and so a more permanent Constitution had also to be drafted.

During the adjournment from April 2nd to 29th, the Senate had only thirty-eight members, while, according to the Provisional Constitution, the number should have been 121.[1] The difference provided Yuan with an opportunity to break the Revolutionary Party's monopoly in that legislative body and also to transform it. At once he ordered the provincial councils to nominate new Senators; this was speedily done and so, at the time the Senate reconvened in Peking, some sixty-eight members were present at the Opening Ceremony. Afterwards, more Senators arrived from more remote

[1] Ch. 3, article 18.

districts, but, as the records show, the number present at a meeting never exceeded a hundred.

Most of the seats in the new Senate went to the two major parties —the Republicans under the leadership of Vice-President Li Yuan-hung, Chang Ch'ien, Dr Wu T'ing-fang and others, and the Revolutionary Party, which changed its name to Kuomintang in August 1912, under the leadership of Dr Sun Yat-sen, Huang Hsing, Sung Chiao-jen, and so on. The former oddly enough had a slender lead over the latter. The Republican policies were the maintenance of national unity, national progress under the guidance of a strong Central Government, and a peaceful foreign policy, with emphasis firmly laid on the power of the State. In contrast to this, the Kuomintang's political programme stressed the democratic rights of the people. By this time, the Party had become more conciliatory, as it had already abandoned such extremist measures as the public ownership of land and equality between the sexes, but it still insisted on giving a liberal share of administrative power to the provincial governments, equal partnership among the different races in the country, and the promotion of the people's economic welfare. Since they stressed the power of the State, the Republicans inevitably supported the President, while the Kuomintang aimed at restraining his loosely defined powers. The instrument by which the Kuomintang hoped to achieve this was a Constitution.

The slender lead of the Republicans over the Kuomintang in both the Senate and the provincial councils gave rise to a number of small parties which, in the hope of making full use of the stalemate and of being able to tip the balance between the two major parties, now formed a united front with Liang Ch'i-ch'ao, T'ang Hua-lung, Wu Ching-lien, Ts'ai O, and others as its leaders. Indeed, this small force proved to be of some importance; for instance, Wu Ching-lien was elected Speaker of the Senate.

Prior to the opening of the National Assembly, the Provisional Senate was the only legislative body of the country and its main task, apart from routine enactments, was to draft the regulations for the organization and election of the Assembly. In this as in many other matters, opinions were divided among the parties in the Senate, and consequently heated debates were often made warmer still by exchanges of invective across the floor, and they sometimes developed into fist fights. Yuan benignly watched this development, aware of its advantages to him, and, at times, intervened as an umpire or as a mediator. Twice he issued instructions to the Senators and the provincial councillors, admonishing them to give up their partisan and personal feuds in the interests of the nation. This paternal advice brought its result in August, when the Senate at length passed the bills concerning the organization and the election of the National Assembly. The President signed and promulgated them on August 10th. They provided that the future Senate should have 274 members and the House of Representatives, 596—all to be elected by a small class of voters in the provinces.

The first of such elections were held at the end of 1912 and the beginning of 1913, and in them the Kuomintang, under the energetic leadership of the youthful Sung Chiao-jen, scored a resounding victory, winning 269 seats in the House and 123 in the Senate, while the Republicans' share was only 120 and 55 respectively. The Kuomintang was indisputably the master of both chambers and there was a suggestion that Sung Chiao-jen should be appointed the next Premier. Yuan shuddered to think of Sung as his Prime Minister, and, at once, began a more severe suppression of the Kuomintang. To him, the only comforting result of the 1913 elections was that in both chambers there was a large number of members who held more than one party card. Such people amounted to 147 in the House and 38 in the Senate. In this he saw his opportunity.

However, Yuan's main hope of crushing the Kuomintang opposition lay in his army and the army's control over the provinces. On April 25, 1912, he decreed that henceforth the old titles of viceroy and governor were to be abolished and the head of a provincial government was to be called the Military Governor. In that period of martial law and military rule, it was no surprise that all the twenty-two Military Governors were commanders, having fighting forces of their own, and half of them were either members or supporters of the Kuomintang. Ostensibly half of the country was in the hands of that Party, yet, in fact, only three of the eleven—Hu Han-min of Kuang-tung, Po Wen-wei of Anhwei and Li Lieh-chun of Kiangsi—could be reckoned as its faithful followers. But the influence of the parties was more prominent in the provincial councils, which were designed to restrict the powers of the military heads, and, to a lesser extent, on the staffs of local newspapers. Both Kuomintang elements were naturally viewed with a mixed feeling of resentment and apprehension by the commanders, who were either illiterate or had no knowledge, or experience, of democracy. The way in which the soldiers treated these men in the Councils or on the newspapers was clearly illustrated by the shooting in the provincial council of Honan on July 26th, when more than ten councillors were seriously injured, and by the killing of newspaper-men and the banning of their papers in Fukien in August. The terror and suppression which went on in the provinces made nonsense of the Kuomintang programme of local self-government. It was by military power that the country was ruled; the Assembly and the Councils were merely decorative arrangements.

What then was Yuan's military power at the beginning of the Republic? What was the Manchus' military legacy to him?

At the time of the Revolution, the Manchu Government had about half a million men under arms, of whom some 240,000 were foreign-drilled and equipped with 162 batteries of mountain and field artillery, each with six guns. The annual expenditure was estimated to be about £8,000,000, but there was neither a war budget nor sufficient money. The foreign-drilled units were under the direct control of the Central Government while other contingents were answerable either to the provincial governors or to the Tartar Generals, who were also left with the problem of paying the garrisons.

The Revolution inflated the number of armed men to the neighbourhood of 800,000, and the majority of whom were now under the command of local military leaders who had declared independence or neutrality, as philatelists called it. Thus it was the Revolution which provided an answer to the age-old problem of demobilizing the traditional Han archers—the Green Corps—by by making them into the warlords' own forces. After the Revolution, the provinces were no longer the responsibility of civil leaders appointed by the Central Government, but the domains of local autocrats recognized by the Republican Government. Yuan's own officers were no exception; they too underwent a transformation and acquired spheres of influence. Feng Kuo-chang, for instance, was in control of Chihli; Chao Ti of Honan; Chang Tso-lin and Feng Te-lin of Manchuria; Chang Hsün of the Huai River region, and so on.

For Yuan, as much as for anyone else, the work of unification was far from complete, in view of the state of affairs in the provinces. To strengthen his position as the supreme leader of a constellation of warlords he had to weaken the local forces under the influence of the

Kuomintang, to prevent the warlords from forming a united front against him, and to increase his own military power.

His first step towards fulfilling these aims was to disband the Revolutionary troops in Nanking under the command of Huang Hsing while leaving those under Li Yuan-hung temporarily intact. Huang was incidentally asked to become the Chief-of-Staff of the Army, which post he declined; eventually it went to a promising young officer by the name of Ch'en Huan. Huang preferred to stay on in Nanking to carry out the work of demobilization. His Party agreed to disband its forces for two reasons: firstly, for the sake of unification and, secondly, because it was unable to feed and clothe them.

Yuan's second step was to recruit thirty corps of new troops after the February and March mutinies, on the pretext of strengthening the defence of the north. Nanking of course objected strongly to this strange performance of simultaneous recruitment and demobilization, and Huang Hsing, embarrassed by having too little money to demobilize many soldiers, suggested that the Revolutionary forces in the south should be sent to the north instead, but the protests and suggestion came too late, for, in the meantime, the work of recruitment had been accomplished with astounding speed.

The third step was to attempt to unify the command of all the fighting forces by a decree issued on March 31st, which had little result, and to forbid them to take part in politics. In response to the latter order, Liu Kuan-hsiung, the 'Kuomintang' Minister for the Navy, and his deputy at once announced their withdrawal from the Party on September 1st. Furthermore, local commanders were not allowed to borrow any more money from abroad.

All these measures could be explained by Western theories or supported by Western examples. In that age of unbounded admiration for the West, contradictory theories and precedents of European origin were quoted to further or to suit one's aim, without carefully examining whether the conditions in China were congenial to their application. One could also ask what exactly were the 'conditions in China?' No one seemed to know for sure and everyone, Chinese or foreign, agreed that China was a riddle. Only the Chinese were too bashful to admit it. Any theory was apparently suitable for the premises could be neither proved nor disproved. There was no right or wrong, but matters of opinion. As opinions differed, confusion arose.

K

But in one diagnosis all opinions united: The newly established Central Government was in dire financial difficulty. The Manchus left Yuan with an empty treasury, and funds had now stopped coming to him from the warlords, who were collecting taxes, normally in excessive amounts, to pay their own troops and line their pockets; the taxes directly under the control of the Central Government, such as the maritime customs and part of the inland tariff, were either mortgaged as security against indemnities or loans or in a chaotic state like the Salt Gabelle and the *likin* (excise). Yuan therefore had to find ways and means to pay his officials and troops and to discharge the Government's obligations to repay foreign loans or their interest. The sums required were about 3, 15, and 5 million yuan respectively each month. J. O. P. Bland was of the opinion that little change had taken place in the revenues after the Revolution. He quoted from Yuan's own report that the Government's income from various sources after the Revolution was roughly:

	million yuan
Land tax	46
Salt and tea tax	46
Customs revenue	42
Sundry taxes	26
Likin	44
Income from Government property	37
Sundry income	19

Total 260 million yuan[1].

This gives us a monthly income of some 22 million yuan, which should have been just enough to provide shoe-strings for the Government. In fact, according to H. G. W. Woodhead,[2] 'not a single province to-day remits the land tax collection to Peking'; and, according to Hsiung Hsi-ling's report to the Senate, only 2·6 million yuan was received from the provinces from January to October 1912. With the customs entirely and the Gabelle and *likin* largely out of the Government's reach, Bland's monthly income of 22 million should be reduced to the more realistic figure of a meagre 8 million or less. Thus the monthly deficit was about 13 million which, in a country of

---

[1] *Recent and Present*, p. 378.
[2] *The Truth about the Chinese Republic*, pp. 124-125.

no adequate monetary or financial structure, could hardly be met by borrowing at home alone.

Yuan did try to float loans at home. The first was announced on January 8, 1912, aiming at 100 million yuan, but in fact only 7·37 million's worth of it was sold. He then turned to foreign lenders, from whom he obtained 9·35 million yuan before the troublesome Belgian loan agreement of March 14th. These small amounts helped to tide him over, but the fundamental question was far from being solved. For some time to come, the Chinese Government had to rely on loans to keep going, a situation which was as clear to Yuan as it was to foreign money-lenders. The Government's credit was poor, and loan negotiations were arduous.

By this time, the great financial interests of Britain, France, Germany, and the United States had merged themselves into a consortium in order to eliminate rivalry amongst themselves, to strike the best bargain with the Chinese Government, and to deal with other competitors. The consortium consisted of the Hongkong and Shanghai Banking Corporation, the French *Banque de l'Indo-chine*, the *Deutsche-Asiatische Bank*, and the American group represented by W. D. Straight. Although the credit of the Chinese Government was poor, the terms it was willing to offer were extremely attractive. The consortium was therefore anxious to monopolize the supply of funds to the Chinese Government and, at the same time, hoped to obtain the safest possible guarantee for a loan. On March 12th, in return for a sum of 2 million Shanghai taels (in fact only 1·1 million was paid out) and a promise to provide money for the Government in April, May, June, and possibly July and August, the consortium succeeded in inducing Yuan to write:

'in consideration of the assistance rendered by the Groups [the consortium] to China in the present emergency and of their services in supporting her credit on the foreign markets, the Chinese Government assures to the Groups (provided their terms are equally advantageous with those otherwise obtainable) the firm option of undertaking the comprehensive loan for general reorganization purposes already proposed to them, to be floated as soon as possible. . . .'[1]

The General Reorganization Loan indicated in this letter was an

[1] Yuan to the consortium, quoted from Kent, *Passing of the Manchus*, pp. 348-349.

enormous undertaking which we shall presently discuss. The assurance which Yuan had given seemed to give the consortium first priority in any future borrowing. This however was not so, at least in Yuan's view; on the next day, March 13th, the new Premier, T'ang Shao-i, in urgent need of money, signed a loan contract with the *Banque Sino-Belge* for £1 million (or 10 million yuan), at a 3 per cent discount, bearing a 5 per cent interest rate. This amount fell short of what T'ang originally visualized—some £10 million, not to mention the sum of £60 million he had first proposed to the consortium. Still, the Government could well do with the money and the *Banque* did not ask to supervise the way it was to be spent. All T'ang needed to offer was the Peking-Kalgan railway as security and a guarantee that if any future loan was to be raised by China and the terms offered by the *Banque* were the same as those of the others, the Government of China would ask the *Banque* to undertake the loan.

The money was borrowed to finance the demobilization of the troops in Nanking, but before it was paid over the consortium and the diplomatic representatives of the four powers concerned lodged strong protests on two realistic grounds—the consortium could hardly tolerate the *Banque Sino-Belge's* attempt to break its monopolistic position, and, although described as a Belgian loan, it was in fact a Russian affair, for the syndicate which the *Banque* represented was identical with that formed by Russia to participate in the six-nation consortium a few months later.

The protests from the representatives of the four powers which had not yet established diplomatic relations with the new Government produced the results expected, but also one that was not. Yuan disingenuously denied any knowledge of the Belgian loan, leaving his betrayed friend the Premier to make pitiful trips to the Legation Quarter to offer apologies and explanations. The powers thereupon demanded that the loan contract should be cancelled, that Japan and Russia should be excluded from any future loan negotiation with China, that the Chinese Government should send a copy of its annual budget to each of the four Ministers for reference, and that the Government should extend a formal apology. Purse strings, if long enough, can become apron strings. Furthermore, Yuan badly wanted diplomatic recognition from these four powers. He therefore complied with their demands and jettisoned one who was both his friend and an eminent member of the Cantonese Communication Clique.

There were other reasons for Yuan's duplicity towards T'ang Shao-i. Taking literally every word in the Provisional Constitution, T'ang regarded himself as the leader of a responsible government, and was therefore constantly at loggerheads with the President. The President had no love for a responsible government; nor had the Minister of the Interior, Chao Ping-chun, who had never attended T'ang's Cabinet meetings or discussed any matter with his chief before reporting directly to the President. During the three months from March to June, T'ang and Yuan became more and more estranged; the northern warlords, too, disliked the Premier for his respect towards the Constitution and the Senate. In June, another incident occurred. The council of Chihli province chose a Kuomintang officer, Wang Chih-hsiang, as commander of the troops in that province, and the nomination was approved by both the Cabinet and the President. But when the commander-elect arrived at Peking from Nanking Chihli soldiers issued a statement opposing his appointment. Once more Yuan gave way and sent Wang Chih-hsiang to the south to inspect troops. This was the last straw; the long-standing but much strained friendship was broken. The Premier left a letter for the President announcing his resignation of his post on the grounds of ill-health and left for Tientsin without saying goodbye. It was then twenty-six years since Yuan and T'ang had met in Seoul, on that eventful evening of the Post Office Banquet, when Yuan was only twenty-four and T'ang a year younger. Then they had gone through the long years in Seoul, Hsiaochan, Shantung, Chihli and Peking together, T'ang giving Yuan unflinching support and earning the reputation of being 'his chief henchman and adviser'.[1] Now in the face of strong opposition—first from the four powers and then from the warlords—the friendship had become expendable, but not conspicuously so. Another henchman, Liang Shih-i, was at once despatched to Tientsin to try, as Liang himself put it, 'to persuade the Premier to change his mind'.[2] But T'ang told him:

'You know very well my relationship with Hsiangcheng (Yuan). To my mind he is the only man who can unify the country, provided he will co-operate sincerely with the Revolutionary Party. But judging by what has happened in the past three months, I fear that disillusionment may come in the end. Therefore I have to think

[1] *The Times*, 2.4.1907.
[2] Liang, *Nien-p'u*, p. 122.

again about the future. This is a matter of great national importance. How can I continue to discharge my public duties in a correct manner, simply because I am his friend?'

After these words of farewell conveyed by Liang Shih-i, the friends were never to see each other again.

In the first instance, Yuan permitted T'ang Shao-i to take five days' sick-leave and then Foreign Minister, Lu Cheng-hsiang, was appointed acting Premier. Five other members of the Cabinet resigned with their chief, all Kuomintang members, but the rest carried on as usual. T'ang's resignation was accepted on June 26th and those of the other five on July 14th. The Senate must have observed the unlawful action taken by the President in the matter of Wang Chih-hsiang's appointment, yet it did not utter a murmur of protest. So much for the restraining power of the Constitution upon Yuan Shih-k'ai.

Before he accepted T'ang's resignation Yuan was already busy consulting the parties about the next Cabinet. The Republican Party was opposed to a one-party government while the Revolutionary Party insisted on either a one-party or a non-party one. The President himself laid emphasis on finding the right man for the right job; he was against any change in the general principles of Cabinet-making, 'because the foundation of the Republic was not yet firm'.[1] The result of the consultations was that the Premier was to continue to be non-partisan, presiding over a coalition Cabinet.

Lu Cheng-hsiang was nominated by the President and approved by the Senate as the Premier-designate, and was instructed to commence forming a government. On July 18th, he presented to the Senate the list of his Cabinet. It consisted of Lu himself, concurrently Minister of Foreign Affairs, Chou Tzu-ch'i as Minister of Finance, Hu Wei-te as Minister of Communications, Chang Tsun-hsiang as Minister of Justice, Chao Ping-chun as Minister of the Interior, Tuan Ch'i-jui as Minister for the Army, and Liu Kuan-hsiung as Minister for the Navy. All these men were Yuan's confidants. The Ministries of Education and Agriculture went to two wavering members of the Revolutionary Party and that of Industry to an ex-Mandarin. This predominantly pro-Yuan Cabinet was firmly rejected by the Senate. The situation took a sharp turn in the following week when the garrisons and police of Peking telegraphed

---

[1] CFKP, 20.6.1912, a Presidential statement.

to the leaders of the provinces denouncing the Senate in the foulest
terms; echoing them, the military leaders of some southern provinces
then telegraphed Peking upbraiding the Senators in equally abusive
language. On July 24th, public notices in the name of 'Chinese
Soldiers' went up everywhere in Peking, charging the Senators with a
long list of crimes. Meanwhile anonymous placards also appeared
offering rewards for the august senatorial heads. On the same day
one hundred and three Senators received a letter each, threatening
bomb-attacks upon them; on the next day, some of Yuan's officers,
such as Generals Chiang Kuei-t'i, Tuan Chih-kuei, Ma Chin-hsü,
and Lu Chien-chang who was the head of the Military Court—
which Putnam Weale described as 'an engine of judicial assassination'[1]—called a press conference at which they menacingly said: 'If
the Senate rejects the second list tomorrow, we shall execute its
members!'[2] On July 26th, Lu Cheng-hsiang duly presented his
second list of only six Ministers—Chou Hsüeh-hsi for Finance, Hsü
Shih-ying for Justice, Chu Ch'i-ch'ien for Communications, Fan
Yuan-lien for Education, Ch'en Chen-hsien for Agriculture and
Forestry, and Chiang Tso-pin for Industry and Commerce, the rest
of the Cabinet remaining unchanged—which list was duly approved,
except for Chiang Tso-pin, who was replaced by Liu K'uei-i.
Somehow this ramshackle Cabinet had been put together, but no
one expected it to last long and everyone was sure that in the process
of making it the Provisional Constitution had died.

The supreme duty of this hand-picked and so-called non-party
Cabinet was to complete the loan negotiations with the four-nation
consortium which had commenced in February. The amount
originally proposed by T'ang Shao-i was £60 million, to be paid to
China in five instalments. The negotiations were very arduous, for
China was unwilling to agree to the security terms and the supervision
over the spending of the loan demanded by the group. However, the
powers knew that 'money was urgently needed if the country was to
be freed from the danger of collapse, and the powers have rightly
resolved to entrust the loan to President Yuan and his advisers, who
seem best qualified to produce order and stability'.[3] The continued
existence of Yuan's Government and 'order and security' were what
the powers desired; as a result they also provided Yuan with the only

---

[1] *Fight*, p. 202.
[2] Li Chien-nung, *Chung-kuo Chin Pai-nien Cheng-chih Shih*, p. 378.
[3] *The Times*, 22.5.1913.

trump card in his hand. On the day before the Peking mutiny the consortium advanced 2 million taels and the second advance of 1,015,000 taels was handed over just before the Presidential Investiture.

The negotiations went on. In the Oriental eyes of Yuan and T'ang, the Western bankers were striking a very hard bargain which had been the reason for the monopsonist's attempt to break through the monopolist's encirclement by signing the Belgian loan contract in March. After that, the loan discussions had come to a standstill for a while. May brought the news of an agreement reached in Peking for another advance of 12 million taels. Meanwhile both sides had been doing some heart-searching in the light of the Belgian loan episode. On the Chinese side, T'ang Shao-i had been forced to resign and had been replaced by the suave and more pliable Lu Cheng-hsiang, whose Finance Minister, Chou Hsüeh-hsi, was a relative of Yuan's; on the bankers' side, a conference had been called in Paris from June to July to seek for unity among the financiers themselves. The Japanese and Russian groups were this time invited to take part and the six powers eventually resolved to set up a new consortium by which the sum of 600 million taels was to be lent to China on the condition that its use should be supervised and that the Salt Gabelle should be collected on China's behalf by the agents of the consortium.

In order to strengthen his position in the loan negotiations Yuan tried to dress up China as a united country by inviting several important leaders of the Revolutionary Party to Peking for consultation. The first to arrive was General Chang Chen-wu from Hankow. At the time of the Wuch'ang uprising, General Chang had played a courageous role, a fact of which he was later rather proud. He had not only led his troops to revolt against the Manchu Government, but also literally made General Li Yuan-hung do the same. Subsequently Li became the leader of the Hupei group; in Chang's eyes, however, he was no more than a pusillanimous opportunist. Friction between these two generals was frequently reported, and, at the beginning of August, Li seized the chance of Chang's visit to Peking to request Yuan to execute this arrogant and disobedient subordinate. Having an array of murderous weapons at his disposal, the idea of using one of them on behalf of Li Yuan-hung did not bother Yuan's conscience, especially since when the deed was done Li would become easier for him to handle. On August 15th General Chang was summarily executed, after having been lavishly dined and wined.

The Senate, shocked by this killing of a well-known leader of the Revolution, demanded an explanation from the Government. It wanted to know why Chang had not been tried by a court of law. Tuan Ch'i-jui, the Minister for the Army, was sent to face a barrage of angry questions, to which he promised to give an answer on the following day. When the time came, the Senators waited and waited, and there was no Tuan Ch'i-jui. In Tuan's stead, Yuan sent a message saying that the Senate had no power to deal with the execution of a soldier, and at the same time published General Li's telegrams. This outraged the Senate, which rejected his message and demanded a satisfactory explanation. On August 22nd, Yuan despatched a second message, alleging no less than fourteen crimes against the dead man. The oddity of the day was that it was announced to the Senate that the Government intended to publish the charges against Chang after making further inquiries from General Li. The man had been dead a week already, yet his executioners still needed two more weeks to make up their minds about his crimes. The Senate, quite rightly refusing to allow tragi-comedy in State affairs, proceeded to censure the Government and to demand Li's impeachment. But at this critical moment, when the Senate's integrity was at stake, a commotion broke out in the chamber, so the debate was adjourned before a decision could be reached. Thereafter, many Senators refrained from attending further meetings on this question and the Government Publishing House stopped issuing daily bulletins of the Senate's proceedings. Soon the storm was over and the matter was forgotten.

Before the dust had settled, Dr Sun Yat-sen arrived at Peking at the invitation of the President. This event was followed about a fortnight later by the arrival of yet another eminent member of the Revolutionary Party, General Huang Hsing. General Li Yuan-hung was invited also, but, on account of the unpleasantness of the Chang Chen-wu case, he declined the honour of taking part in the so-called Big Four Conference. The Big Three however reviewed the general situation and the basic policies of the Government. Dr Sun hoped to persuade Yuan Shih-k'ai into becoming the leader of the Kuomintang, observing the fundamental principles of a responsible government, and moving the Capital to Nanking. As a *quid pro quo* Sun was prepared to stand down from the forthcoming presidential election and to guarantee Yuan's incumbency for the next ten years. Yuan preferred his Olympian status, and so Dr Sun's solicitude came to nothing. However, the politically naïve General Huang Hsing succeeded in recruiting Chao Ping-chun, the head of Yuan's police, into the ranks of the Kuomintang.

The host and his guests sat through thirteen meetings, some of which lasted until the small hours of the morning, in a cordial agreement on some points, among which the most noteworthy was support of an open-door policy with regard to foreign investment. This policy and the show of unity that had been made were the real points of Sun's visit as his host saw it. In order to prove his sincerity towards Dr Sun, Yuan appointed him on September 9th to take full charge of the planning of railway construction. Dr Sun stayed in Peking for about a month, at the end of which, when bidding Yuan farewell, he advised him to train a million soldiers, while he himself would try to build some twenty thousand *li* of railway.

Amid the pomp and joviality of Dr Sun's visit, a totally new loan negotiation was afoot, for the discussions with the six-nation consortium had once more run aground. In June 1912 contact had been made between the Chinese Government and a British firm, Charles Birch Crisp's Corporation of 11 Angel Court, London, and an agreement was signed in August 1912. The contract was to provide China with a loan of £10 million, at 98, bearing an interest of 5 per cent, and secured on the full surplus of the Salt Gabelle. The firm also undertook to advance a clear £500,000 on short-dated Treasury Bills of which £100,000 was remitted immediately through the Chartered Bank of India, Australia, and China. This loan kept the Chinese Government financially afloat, for the Mid-Autumn Festival was not far away (September 25th) and the officials and soldiers had to be paid. It however put the British Government in a very awkward position—it was 'disingenuous, to say the least'[1]— for it was at Britain's suggestion that the discussions with the con- sortium had been suspended for the second time; yet, when they were resumed in September, the unfinished business between China and Mr Birch Crisp continued without any interruption. Crisp was an Englishman and Yuan's political adviser, Dr G. E. Morrison of *The Times*, was also a British subject. Under such circumstances, Sir John Jordan, the British Minister, whose Government had not yet recognized the Chinese Government, nor of course the Crisp loan, could only protest against what was in his eyes a flagrant breach of good faith. To this, Yuan's reply was that Hsiung Hsi-ling, a

[1] *The Times*, 20.9.1912.

Chinese negotiator, had already (on August 5th) notified the six powers of China's intention to seek a loan in other quarters, and now nothing could be done towards cancelling the contract with Crisp. Jordan and his colleagues denied any knowledge of such notification. On October 25th the six powers, none of whom recognized Yuan's Government, sent a joint protest and, four days later, the eleven powers of the Peace Protocol of 1901 reminded the Government that the Salt Gabelle, having been allocated as security against the payments of the Boxer Indemnity, could not be used to pay the Crisp loan. In London, Birch Crisp worked fervently to obtain a *fait accompli* in spite of the Foreign Office's strenuous disapproval of his conduct. First, he obtained the backing of Lloyds Bank at the beginning of September, and, before the month was out, his loan prospectuses were selling like hot cakes in the City. The first batch disappeared in a single day, and, on the next day, September 28th, the subscription list had to be closed! The credit of the prospectuses was further strengthened by a message of Yuan's to Crisp saying that 'The President, the Cabinet, and the whole Chinese nation are deeply grateful to its [the loan's] supporters',[1] and by Crisp's own statement to the press that 'as the Foreign Office possessed no means of enforcing its views upon me, [he] was free to act as [he] thought fit'.[2]

The successful negotiation of the Crisp loan coincided with the collapse of Lu Cheng-hsiang's Cabinet. As the country was preparing to go to the polls for the election of the first National Assembly, the people were no more stirred by a change in the Cabinet than were the French under the Third Republic. Chao Ping-chun's appointment as Lu's successor did not arouse much opposition in the outgoing Provisional Senate. The new Cabinet was constituted on September 30th with Chao himself concurrently Minister of the Interior, Liang Hao-ju as Minister of Foreign Affairs, and Tuan Ch'i-jui, Chou Hsüeh-hsi, Chu Ch'i-ch'ien, and Liu Kuan-hsiung keeping their old portfolios.

The new Cabinet found itself dealing with three foreign loan negotiations at once—the unfinished business of the Crisp loan, the long-drawn-out six-nation loan, and the newly started Belgian railway loan. The six-nation consortium had the greatest financial strength, being the only body which could provide sufficient funds to

[1] *The Times*, 28.9.1912.
[2] *The Times*, 27.9.1912.

get Yuan's Government out of its present plight, and was thus in the most favourable position for bargaining. After repeated protests from the consortium, the Crisp loan fizzled out at the end of 1912, when its second issue was stopped, and the Belgian railway loan was abortive. China, having once nearly broken through the consortium's encirclement, was now compelled by her urgent need of money to come back into their net.

The time was opportune, as Sir John Jordan adjudged in his communication to the Foreign Office on December 6, 1912. European rivals in lending money to Yuan had been repelled, and inside China the military governors, who opposed the loan, were silenced by the President's pertinent question: 'If you, as provincial governors, could provide the funds, would I shamelessly beg others to help?'[1] The Provisional Senate was eventually convinced that the loan was necessary and gave its sanction on December 27th in a private session.[2] The outline of what was to be known as the Reorganization Loan was settled on December 12th; the principles and the details of foreign supervision, especially of China's Salt Gabelle, were agreed upon by mid-December, and the preliminary agreement was concluded on January 1, 1913.

The official reasons for contracting this loan of £25 million were the need for reorganization of the administrative system, the improvement of the Salt Gabelle collecting machine, the promotion of industrial and handicraft production and the preservation of peace by maintaining a balance of foreign interests in the country. In fact, the main object was to save Yuan's Government from total collapse.

The path towards final agreement with the Chinese Government on the loan was at long last swept clear as outside China, the diplomatic position had been eased by the peaceful resolution of the question raised by the Turks over Adrianople. Optimism prevailed in all the financial centres of Europe and America. The consortium was confident of issuing the loan at an early date, but its high hopes were 'unfortunately . . . shared by its financial rivals and there is now danger of the Chinese finding money elsewhere. . . .'[3]

Sir Walter Langley's fears proved to be correct. Birch Crisp inquired in February whether for reasons of state the British Foreign

---

[1] *Jung-yen*, I, Vol. I, No. 13, p. 12.
[2] Yuan to the Military Governors, CFKP, 10.5.1913.
[3] Langley to Jordan, 22.1.1913.

Office still objected to the issue of the second part of his loan. 'Of course we do but we shall have to frame our answer very carefully as we do not know how he stands with the Chinese Government and have no mind of being accused of instigating him to break his contract.'[1] Crisp's reviving hope was however short-lived.

The major difference between his and the consortium's loan terms lay in the latter's insistence on supervising China's fiscal revenue and expenditure. Woodrow Wilson, the new American President, also took issue with the consortium on exactly this point. On March 19, 1913, he announced:

'The conditions include not only the pledging of particular taxes . . . to secure the loan, but also the administration of those taxes by foreign agents. The responsibility on the part of our Government implied in the encouragement of a loan thus secured and administered is plain enough, and is obnoxious to the principles upon which the Government of our people rests.'[2]

Five days later, the American group withdrew from the consortium to propose a loan to China of some £2 million on a short term and another of £20 million or more on a longer term basis. Coming after the experience of the Belgian and Crisp loans and at the eleventh hour, the American offer failed to get any response from the Chinese. The details of the final agreement with the consortium were soon hammered out, but the newly constituted National Assembly was not even given a chance to discuss the propriety of raising such an enormous sum.

On the eve of the signing of the agreement the leaders of the Assembly called upon Yuan Shih-k'ai, who refused to see them. Eventually they discovered from the President's Secretary-General, Liang Shih-i, that the decision was already irrevocable and the signing was to take place shortly in the Peking office of the Hongkong and Shanghai Banking Corporation, so they hurriedly sent pickets thither to prevent the Chinese representatives from entering the building, while they themselves went to see 'certain of the foreign Ministers in Peking'. They 'had almost gone down on their knees . . . in a vain attempt to persuade them to delay—as they could very well

[1] Langley to Jordan, 13.2.1913.
[2] *The Times*, 19.3.1913.

have done—the signature of this vital agreement for forty-eight hours so that it could be formally passed by the National Assembly, and thus save the vital portion of the sovereignty of the country from passing under the heels of one man.'[1] Their and their pickets' efforts did not stop the signature, which took place in the Corporation's building in the small hours of April 27, 1913; the Chinese deputies entered and left through the backdoor. Before the signatories had begun their nocturnal errands, Finance Minister, Chou Hsüeh-hsi, slipped away to Tientsin where he found sanctuary in the foreign concessions. The Kuomintang members of the Assembly at the same time appointed Tsou Lu to draft a motion censuring the Government and condemning the loan.

The loan, £25 million, bearing an interest of 5 per cent, was actually paid at 84; in other words, only 21 million actually changed hands. Its uses were specified in the agreement as follows:

Liabilities due from the Chinese Government £4,317,778
Repayment of provincial loans   £2,870,000
Liabilities of the Chinese Government shortly
    maturing   £3,592,263
Reorganization of the Salt administration   £2,000,000
Current expenses of the Chinese Government
    (April to September 1913)   £5,500,000

The title, the Reorganization Loan, could only be justified on the strength of the smallest of these items; and, taking that and the first three items away, the Chinese Government was left with the meagre sum of £8·5 million. There were other expenses to be reckoned up too: the loan was to be floated at a 10 per cent discount and the commission for selling the bonds was 6 per cent. The Chinese Government's net benefit from this huge undertaking was no more than £8·2 million, but their total liability, when and if the loan was repaid in forty-seven years' time, would amount to £42,850,809 18s 3d! The Salt Gabelle, a part of the maritime customs and the local taxes directly under the control of the Central Government in Chihli, Shantung, Honan and Kiangsu were pledged as security against the loan. Therefore an Englishman, Sir Richard Dane, was appointed Co-Inspector General of the Salt Gabelle. To supervise

[1] Putnam Weale, *Fight*, p. 39.

the expenditure of the Chinese Government, M. Konavaloff and M. Padoux were planted as co-advisers on accounting in the newly created Audit Department in the Government, and, to control the loan, Herr Romp was first nominated for the Audit post, but had to take up the less important directorship because of France's determined objection to him. Under this arrangement, in which Russia and Japan more or less played the part of sleeping partners, if, say, the Ministry of Education needed money to pay its daily expenses, it would first of all have to request both the Audit and the Loan Departments for their approval; then the endorsed request would be sent to the Ministry of Finance, which drew out a cheque, as well as issued a payment order, giving the reasons for the request and approving it; finally, the cheque was presented to one of the five banks of the consortium which had to decide whether the amount demanded exceeded the Ministry's budget or not before paying cash. In spite of this humiliating strait-jacket, the system somehow worked. But how can one wonder that it had to be decided on in secret in the small hours of the morning, when all good people should have been sound asleep? The terms of the agreement also eloquently explained why the leaders of the National Assembly ran hither and thither trying to stop or to delay the signing of the agreement, and why the Finance Minister had to flee for his life.

Did the loan really lift Yuan's fiscal difficulties? Temporarily yes; but only very temporarily. The first advance of £1·5 million, for instance, was immediately swallowed up by these expenses:

	million yuan
Allowance to the Manchu Emperor	2·5
Ministry of the Interior and Police	1·5
Peking garrison	0·8
Bannermen and infantry	1·0
Presidential Office and the Cabinet	0·6
National Assembly	0·17
Disbandment of Troops in Hupei	2·5
Foreign Ministry	0·4
Navy	0·4
Other administrative expenses	0·8

Total 10·67 million yuan, or, in other words, £1·067 million.

The signing of this infamous agreement was, to say the least, inopportune at a time when the relationship between Yuan and the Kuomintang was at its worst. The five powers, by giving money to Yuan, actually encouraged him to intensify his campaign of intimidation against the Party. The loan agreement was signed soon after the cold-blooded murder of the leader of the Kuomintang, Sung Chiao-jen, by Yuan Shih-k'ai's henchmen.

The Kuomintang, founded in August 1912, was the successor to the Revolutionary Party of the 1911 Revolution, and had been expanding rapidly under Sung's brilliant leadership. In the new National Assembly the Party had 269 Representatives and 123 Senators, and, in the country as a whole, it controlled six rich provinces in the south. To consolidate his own power, Yuan had to tackle this growing force.

Yuan's honeymoon with the Party had ended almost as soon as Dr Sun Yat-sen left Peking, for on September 29, 1912, the President issued an order banning local 'secret organizations'. This was aimed at the Kuomintang, not at the secret societies as such. The following winter Dr Sun went to Japan and Sung Chiao-jen became the chairman of the Party's executive committee, so he was constantly travelling between Peking and Shanghai. Once when Sung was in the Capital, Yuan offered him a book of blank cheques as a contribution to his political activities, but he was alert enough to return it with proper courtesy. After the Party's victory in the Assembly election, he was widely tipped as the next Premier, and he himself was interested in this idea, but would not think of taking office unless his Government was to be a responsible one. Yuan, who had overthrown the Manchu regime as the head of a responsible Cabinet, could hardly agree to this. Consequently the young man remained in the political wilderness as the leader of a strong opposition. Yuan hated him.

On March 20, 1913, Sung Chiao-jen was to take a train from Shanghai to Peking. For him, it was a regular affair; only a few close friends, including Huang Hsing, Liao Chung-k'ai and Yü Yu-jen, came to the North Station to see him off. Suddenly a short man in black emerged from the crowd on the platform and shot him. The bullet passed through his stomach. There was naturally a panic in which the assassin managed to get away. The victim was taken to a hospital where he died in the morning of the 22nd; he was only thirty-one years old. Before breathing his last, he asked for pen and paper and wrote down this valediction:

'I hope the President will rule our country with sincerity and justice and strive to protect the rights of the people. In so doing, he will help the Assembly to make a permanent Constitution. If that can be done, my death will not have been in vain.'[1]

All the members of the Party put on mourning, Dr Sun at once returned home to deliver a speech at the funeral and Yuan Shih-k'ai was obliged to issue a warrant for the assassin's arrest.

On the day after Sung's death, an antique-dealer walked into a Shanghai police-station and made this statement:

'Ten days ago I delivered some antiques to Mr Ying Kuei-hsing at his home in Wen-yuan Fang. He has been a customer of mine for some time. He then showed me a photograph of a man and asked me to kill him at a certain place and a certain time. He also promised to give me a thousand dollars for the job. I am, as you can see, merely a businessman, and have never killed anyone, so I refused. This morning, I saw the same photograph in the papers. . . .'[2]

Acting on this clue, the police arrested Ying Kuei-hsing in a private brothel at 228, Ying-ch'un Fang, Hupei Road, Shanghai; the next day a search was made at Ying's home, where the police found a revolver with only two bullets left in the chamber, three copies of the secret code used by the Cabinet and a large amount of telegrams in the same code between Ying and the Premier's confidential secretary, Hung Shu-tsu, and between Ying and one Wu Shih-ying. Soon Wu Shih-ying was captured and the sensational trial of both Ying and Wu began on April 16th in a court in the International Settlement. Wu pleaded guilty, saying that he alone was responsible for the assassination, whereupon Ying pleaded not guilty.

During the hearings, the following evidence was adduced:

February 1st, telegram, Hung to Ying: 'For big subject, style must be forceful.'

February 2nd, telegram, Hung to Ying: 'Reported subject and style. You should telegraph Chao asking for an amount.'

February 21st, telegram, Hung to Ying: 'Ask for money when Sung case is done.'

[1] PYCFTCSCSH, I, p. 156.
[2] ibid, I, p. 156.

L

February 22nd, telegram, Hung to Ying: 'Pay after delivery, not more than three hundred thousand.'

March 13th, telegram, Hung to Ying, confidential: 'Destroy Sung; will be rewarded with medal.'

March 20th, at 2.30 a.m., telegram, Ying to Hung, confidential: 'Urgent order of 24.10 received.'

March 21st, telegram, Ying to Hung, confidential: 'Bandit leader destroyed; no casualties; please report.'

Undated letter, Chao Ping-chun to Hung: 'Mr Ying asks for money. Will you please deal with him directly and pay him when I have obtained the President's permission?'

Both Wu and Ying were kept in custody after the trial, but, about a week later, Wu was found dead in his cell and on July 25th, Ying was freed by a group of Shanghai gangsters who broke into the gaol, released him, and sent him to Tsingtao.

The Shanghai trial and the warrant issued by the court for the Premier to give evidence caused great indignation throughout the whole country. Yuan and Chao had a thorny task to clear themselves of the responsibility for this bloody deed. At first, an announcement was issued in the name of the Government stating that there was an illegal body existing in Shanghai which had made statements about crimes committed by Sung Chiao-jen, Liang Ch'i-ch'ao, Yuan Shih-k'ai, and Chao Ping-chun and had also announced its intention of executing Sung.[1] This fiction did not still the public clamour, so on April 3rd Chao Ping-chun, in an interview with a correspondent of the Peking paper *Hsin Chi-yuan*, described his cordial friendship with Sung Chiao-jen and explained that Hung Shu-tsu was not *his* man. His 'frankness' and 'innocence' merely aroused more suspicion, so he had to appear in the Assembly to answer questions. It was then that he admitted giving 50,000 yuan to Ying Kuei-hsing in return for the disbandment of Ying's party, the Kung-chin Hui, which was in fact a society of gangsters. When Ying called upon him before leaving for Shanghai, Chao admitted, a copy of the Cabinet's secret telegraph code was given to him at his own request, for Chao could not see any reason for refusing to do so. Of the correspondence between Hung and Ying, Chao denied any knowledge whatever, since the telegrams were in the secret code which he himself could not read, and, after the assassination, he could not find any such

[1] CFKP, 26.3.1913.

correspondence among the files. In order to divert public attention from this case, a mysterious body made its appearance in Peking under the melodramatic title of 'Women's Assassination Group', and a woman member, Chou Yü-ching, went to the Military Court Department—Yuan's secret police—to 'confess' that their leader was no other than the Kuomintang leader, General Huang Hsing. Next, as a counter-move to the warrant which had been issued out for Chao Ping-chun's arrest, the Military Court issued an order to Huang to come to Peking to give evidence. Huang was prepared to obey, provided Chao would also obey the writ served on him. But the latter backed out, tendered his resignation on May 1st, and went to Tientsin to take up the post of Military Governor of Chihli.

On January 19, 1914, Ying Kuei-hsing was shot dead by a couple of detectives in a first-class compartment on the Peking-Tientsin train, and about a month later Chao Ping-chun died suddenly in his Tientsin office.

Hung Shu-tsu survived them both. This dubious character began his career as a comprador in a Tientsin firm which had some dealings with Yuan when the latter was still training his troops at Hsiaochan. Later, he became Yuan's quartermaster, and on June 20, 1912, he was appointed confidential secretary to the Premier and Minister of the Interior. His sister was a favourite of the august President's. He resigned along with Chao and lived comfortably thereafter as a private citizen until May 4, 1919 when he was spotted in Shanghai by Sung Chiao-jen's son. He was arrested, charged with murder and executed.

The assassination and the loan played havoc with the country's affairs and it was plain that the Military Governors of the provinces would have to come forward to lend their support to Yuan if his Government was to survive. All of those in the north and some in the south did so. The exceptions were T'an Yen-k'ai of Hunan, Sun Tao-jen of Fukien, Ch'eng Te-ch'uan of Kiangsu, Po Wen-wei of Anhwei, Hu Han-min of Kwantung, and Li Lieh-chun of Kiangsi. These six conspicuous absentees were avowed members of the Kuomintang, but the first three were not particularly perturbed by either of these two ignoble deeds, and did not make up their minds at once. Po Wen-wei, due to his lack of military strength, was himself in a precarious position, and Hu Han-min was deeply worried by the activities of Ch'en Chiung-ming, a warlord in his own province. This left Li Lieh-chun, the only ardent supporter of Dr

Sun Yat-sen's proposal to wage a war against Yuan Shih-k'ai. The gathering storm frightened many timid hearts, and the Kuomintang's majority in the National Assembly began to be whittled away. In the classified columns of Peking papers there were announcements of members' resignation from the Party day after day. 'One advertisement, bearing six signatures, declares that the Koumintang consists "Chiefly of the lower classes of society and lewd persons of the baser sort with whom it is not worthwhile to be comrades".'[1] Money was also involved in these transactions. The price per head averaged over 10,000 yuan (or £1,000), paid out from the Reorganization Loan.[2] The renegades either joined other parties, formed new ones, or remained independent. In any case, the President paid them richly for doing so. The rest, who could muster enough courage to resist bribery or threats, were closely watched or openly bullied. For instance, Tsou Lu found his servants constantly making telephone calls to the secretariat of the Cabinet and spending money lavishly on clothes and entertainment, and on the book-stalls, copies of *Dr Sun Yat-sen's Criminal Record*, a work compiled by officials and printed in Japan, were on sale. The Parliamentary Kuomintang had obviously disintegrated and was entirely powerless to prevent Yuan from taking unlawful measures against the Party itself.

Having crippled the Party in the Assembly, Yuan at once turned the point of his spear against the three Military Governors who were loyal to the Party. Li Lieh-chun provided him with an excellent pretext by ordering 7,000 rifles from a foreign firm in Shanghai on the same day that Yuan announced the appointment of a henchman of his to take charge of finance in Kiangsi. When the rifles arrived at Kiukiang the Vice-President, Li Yuan-hung, acting on Yuan's instructions, snatched them from under the Governor's nose by sending gunboats up the river to intercept the consignment. Thereupon Li Lieh-chun ordered his troops to guard all strategic points to prevent northern forces from entering his province. Yuan insisted that Li must obey orders. The situation suddenly grew tense.

At this juncture, Ts'en Ch'un-hsuan, who had been a colleague of Yuan's under the Manchu dynasty, Wang Ching-wei, Wang Chih-hsiang and others came forward to mediate, suggesting a compromise. Yuan openly refused to listen to any such talk:

[1] *The Times*, 26.4.1913.
[2] Tsou Lu, *Hui-ku Lu*, p. 54 and *Chung-kuo Kuomintang Shih-kao*, I, pp. 160-161.

'The question is not of a compromise between the north and the south, but of a local official's failure to obey my orders. The case of Sung Chiao-jen's murder can be dealt with by the law and the Loan can be discussed by the Assembly. What Mr Ts'en and I can say about them is of no consequence whatever. . . . But with regard to Li Lieh-chun, the question is completely different. He is a local official, a part of the administrative system of our country. It is his duty to obey my orders.'[1]

Soon afterwards, he made another uncompromising statement:

'My mind is made up. Now I know Sun and Huang can do nothing beyond making themselves a nuisance. I am responsible to the four hundred million people who elected me. I will not allow anyone to make a nuisance of himself, thereby endangering the safety of my people. I believe my political and military experience and international prestige are as good as the next man's. If Sun and Huang are competent enough to replace me, I am willing to hand over my duties to them. But the present circumstances simply do not allow me to relinquish my obligations. If they dare to organize another government, I swear I shall use force to smash them!'[2]

On June 9, 1913, he appointed Li Yuan-hung concurrently acting Military Governor of Kiangsi; five days later, he transferred Hu Han-min to the post of Commissioner for Tibet and promoted Ch'en Chiung-ming to Hu's vacant Governorship, and, on the last day of the month, he sent Po Wen-wei to Kansu to attend to the defence of the frontier and appointed Sun Tuo-sen to his place. Meanwhile two armies were on their way to Kiangsi and Kiangsu. The first, commanded by Tuan Chih-kuei, consisted of the Second Division under Wang Chan-yuan and the Sixth Division under Li Ch'un; the Second, commanded by Feng Kuo-chang, consisted of troops under Chang Hsün and Lei Chen-ch'un. Their destinations were respectively Huk'ou in Kiangsi and Nanking in Kiangsu. On July 12th, the soldiers of both sides were engaged in battle, and so the Second Revolution began.

[1] Quoted from Ch'en Po-ta, *Ch'e-kuo Ta-tao Yuan Shih-k'ai*, p. 21.
[2] ibid, p. 22.

CHAPTER IX

The 'Strong Man' 1913-1915

ON January 6, 1913, the President gave a New Year banquet in honour of the diplomatic representatives in Peking at which Daniele Varé overheard this conversation:

'Vitale (Italian Chinese Secretary): "What does Your Excellency think of the situation?"
'Ijuin (Japanese Minister): "I think that something will happen".
'Vitale: "Yes. But when?"
'Ijuin: "In the future".[1]

This 'something' happened at 8.00 in the morning on July 12th, when Li Lieh-chun's troops opened fire in the face of an imminent attack from Li Ch'un's units at Huk'ou. The see-saw battle lasted until July 25th, and, in the meantime, Huang Hsing in Nanking, Po Wen-wei in Anhwei, Sun Tao-jen in Fukien, Ch'en Ch'i-mei in Shanghai, Ch'en Chiung-ming in Kuangtung, Ch'en Ch'ien in Hunan, and Hsiung K'e-wu in Szechuan all declared their independence. Under these military leaders there were several hundred thousand soldiers, and Japan seemed to be on their side. But Yuan was not worried, for the deployment of his troops had been completed and Germany was active in canvassing British and American financial backing on his behalf. The German *chargé d'affaires* wrote to his Foreign Minister in these terms:

'During the crisis, the German and the British Legations, and later the American Legation too, have been in constant contact in order to find a common policy. (Good—Kaiser Wilhelm's note). Every step has been taken after consultations between the German and the British Legations. (Splendid—[Sd.] Wilhelm, Kaiser). This subtle

[1] *Laughing Diplomat*, p. 94.

form of co-operation promoted by the Deutsche-Asiatische Bank and the Hongkong and Shanghai Banking Corporation has enabled Yuan Shih-k'ai to turn the tide in his favour.'[1]

Yuan was confident, for he had the advantage in military affairs and in diplomacy—his Government was on the eve of being recognized by all the powers. He also believed that Britain would not jettison her interests in the Yangtze areas by remaining indifferent.

As soon as the guns began to roar, Li Lieh-chun, Po Wen-wei, Huang Hsing, and Ch'en Ch'i-mei were cashiered on July 22nd, 23rd, and 24th in three successive orders from Yuan, in one of which he justified his action in the loftiest terms:

'The outlaws, in league with disobedient troops, illegally occupy parts of the country, declare their so-called "independence", rupture our national unity, and break law and order. By these acts they must be adjudged as rebels against whom the Government can take no other steps than precautionary measures according to the law and pacification with military force. Only by doing so can the Government of the Republic exercise its full constitutional powers.'[2]

The battle between the forces of Li Lieh-chun and Li Ch'un at Huk'ou ended in the defeat of the former. This was the first decisive engagement in Kiangsi; the second was the battle of Nanch'ang, the provincial capital, which fell into the hands of Li Ch'un on August 18th.

The left jaw of the pincer movement advanced with equal swiftness. Chang Hsün's pigtailed troops, driving towards Nanking, took the strategic point of Hsüchou on July 22nd, and entered and sacked Nanking at the beginning of September. The new American Minister, P. S. Reinsch, arrived at Nanking on November 4th and recorded his impression:

'The semi-barbarous troops of Chang Hsun lined its streets. They had sacked the town, ostensibly suppressing the last vestiges of the "Revolution". . . . Everywhere charred walls without roofs; the contents of houses broken and cast on the street; fragments of shrapnel on the walls—withal a depressing picture of misery.'[3]

[1] Count Maltzan to Bethmenn Hollweg, 20.7.1913.
[2] Pai Chiao, YSKYCHMK, p. 57.
[3] *An American Diplomat in China* p. 11.

With these two major defeats, the Second Revolution, ill-planned and totally lacking co-ordination, collapsed ignominously. In the meantime, Po Wen-wei was driven out of Anhwei by Ni Ssu-ch'ung, and Ch'en Chiung-ming was ejected from Kuangtung by Lung Chi-kuang; Ch'en Ch'i-mei's hopes in Shanghai were dashed as soon as they began. Although the Revolution lasted only about two months, it left a long-lasting impression on the history of China in the following thirty years. In that sense, it was as important as its predecessor of 1911.

The most obvious result of the Revolution was the breaking of the Kuomintang's control over six provinces. Li Ch'un was now the master of Kiangsi; Ni Ssu-ch'ung, of Anhwei; Chang Hsün, temporarily, of Kiangsu, and Lung Chi-kuang, of Kwangtung. Soon after these new appointments, T'ang Hsiang-ming replaced T'an Yen-k'ai as the military governor of Hunan, Liu Kuan-hsiung replaced Sun Tao-jen in Fukien, and Hsiung K'e-wu fell into oblivion in Szechuan, in spite of the fact that these vacillating Kuomintang leaders had renounced their independence before the war was over. Of all the provinces in China proper, only Chekiang, Kweichow, Hupei and Yunnan were still beyond Yuan's reach. Following up his recent success, Yuan summoned the governor of Chekiang, Chu Jui, to Peking for consultations which ended in Chu's un-conditional submission to him. The distant provinces of Yunnan and Kweichow were then respectively controlled by two young military leaders, Ts'ai O and T'ang Chi-yao, of whom Ts'ai was the less obedient, and was therefore replaced by T'ang, while Ts'ai himself went to Peking on the President's orders. An obscure figure of the name of Liu Hsien-shih temporarily took over the administration of Kweichow.

General Li Yuan-hung of Hupei however remained a hard nut to crack. During the Second Revolution, he killed more Kuomintang members than most of Yuan's trusted lieutenants and worked very hard at flattering the President. He offered no excuse to Yuan for utilizing Hupei as a military base against the insurgent troops in the adjacent provinces of Anhwei and Kiangsi. When the fighting was over, but before the year ended, Yuan sent no less important a person than Tuan Ch'i-jui to Hankow to invite the Vice-President to Peking, as Yuan thirsted for an opportunity of meeting him. Li could hardly refuse this courtesy, in view of his isolated position and also of the favour Yuan had done him in murdering Chang Chen-wu. He accepted the invitation, left Hupei, and, before arriving at Peking, was superseded by Tuan Ch'i-jui as governor of Hupei.

In Peking, Li was received with pomp and fine words. Ironically, he was housed in the lake palace where the Empress Dowager had once imprisoned the Kuanghsü Emperor, and was given a generous salary of 20,000 yuan per month—the same as had been given to Dr Sun Yat-sen during his visit about a year ago. In order to strengthen the ties between the President and his deputy, one of Yuan's sons married one of Li's daughters. The country was ostensibly *united* in every sense of the word.

But there were still weak links in the chain of Yuan's power over the provinces. The south-western provinces, Kuang-tung, Kwangsi, Szechwan, Kweichow and Yunnan, were not yet in the hands of men he could trust. If any opposition was to arise, it would begin in that corner of the country.

A second result of the Revolution was the beginning of a dispute among Yuan's own generals. The victory yielded its spoils and the sharing of them was not an easy matter. In this, Yuan Shih-k'ai showed his customary distrust of people, but with a lack of his usual dexterity. He appointed two Commissioners of Pacification in Kiangsi, holding the same rank and having the same powers, but eventually the governorship of that province went to a third man. In other disputed areas, he made the same mistake. There were two Commissioners for the Huai River regions, two for the lower reaches of the Yangtze, and five for Hunan. Having given the governorship of Hunan to T'ang Hsiang-ming, he sent Ts'ao K'un with his Third Division to be stationed at Yuehyang, and, having entrusted Kiangsu to Chang Hsün, he left a division at Sungkiang to watch the governor.

Among the old comrades-in-arms, Chang Hsün was in fact the least trusted by Yuan Shih-k'ai, for his loyalty did not go to his new master but remained with the fallen Imperial House. This was why he and his soldiers were still wearing queues. His energetic participation in the campaign against the Kuomintang was mainly due to two things: his dislike of the republicans and Yuan's promise that he would be given the governorship of the rich province of Kiangsu. Unfortunately for him, during the sack of Nanking his ill-disciplined troops killed three Japanese citizens, this caused the already discontented Japanese Government to lodge a strong protest, which resulted in an unusually large number of important personages hurrying to Nanking to convince Chang Hsün that it was necessary for him to be transferred. Eventually Chang yielded, withdrew his troops to the north of Kiangsu, and gave up the lucrative office to General Feng Kuo-chang. The loss of the governorship meant that he lost the power to collect taxes to pay his troops. Because of this, he nursed a deep grudge against both Yuan and Feng.

Chang joined the campaign under the command of Feng, yet it was he, instead of Feng, who became governor in the first instance. This did not please Feng at all. As a reward for Chang's allowing himself to be transferred to the Inspectorship of the Yangtze River, Yuan promised to say nothing about the 150,000 yuan which Chang had found on his arrival in the provincial treasury of Kiangsu; instead, he gave him another 150,000 yuan as a 'transfer fee'. In addition, Chang obtained control of all the river police of Hunan, Kiangsi, Anhwei, and Kiangsu, thereby taking over the lion's share of the taxes the riverine regions yielded. With his troops and these financial resources, the titular Inspectorship became a kind of hegemony, to be viewed with awe and hate by all the warlords in those five provinces. Yet to him, this was a poor consolation.

Now let us turn our eyes to Peking where, after the Second Revolution began, Tuan Ch'i-jui was ordered by decree to form a war-time Cabinet which lasted only three weeks. Then on July 31st Hsiung Hsi-ling got together his 'Celebrity Cabinet' which included the famous Reformer of 1898, Liang Ch'i-ch'ao, as Minister of Justice. In the Government, the important Kuomintang members had all been dismissed, and in the National Assembly their comrades, though still in the majority, were scared, wavering, mute, and anxious to do the President a good turn in order to secure their lives and positions. The time was ripe for the tyrant to deal a further blow to the Assembly.

Since its opening on April 8th the Assembly had run into a great deal of stormy weather. First, there was the Five Powers' Loan, then the assassination of Sung Chiao-jen, and, finally, the war between the north and the south. The Assembly was powerless either to decide any of these issues or to censure the Government, and could only confine itself to its own internal feuds over the niceties of a permanent Constitution. At that time, the country was ruled nominally by the Provisional Constitution, but actually by the Provisional President, and Yuan was anxious to have both put on a permanent basis, so the Assembly had been engaged in the drafting of a permanent Constitution. But more often than not the deputies' factious spirit got the better of them; the more they met, the remoter were the prospect of a Constitution. The country was utterly sick of the endless jabber of the Senators and Representatives. Liang Ch'i-ch'ao, whose pen was the most powerful of his time, wrote an acrimonious attack on them under the title of *The Suicide of the National Assembly*:

'It failed to elect a Speaker in the twenty days following its Opening Ceremony and failed too to constitute a Supreme Court after almost three months. Absenteeism has been reported every day, so we have been used to intermittent suspension of its meetings. If by chance a sufficient number of members decide to attend a discussion, the result is invariably a free-for-all like a squabble among a group of fish-wives or naughty children. They have dealt with none of the important matters of state, yet each one of them is entitled to 6,000 yuan a year. . . . Their dirty and evil deeds are well known. There is no need for me to list them, nor have I the mordancy to do so.'[1]

As Yuan's effort to unify the country by force was near its completion; nineteen military governors under the leadership of Li Yuan-hung made a joint statement advocating a reversal of the constitutional procedure by drafting the Law of Presidential Election before the Constitution. This curious suggestion was accepted by the Assembly on September 5th; the Law was approved on October 4th, and the election of the Permanent President and Vice-President took place on October 6th.

For the election, the two chambers of the Assembly held a joint meeting with 759 members inside the Parliament building, with a far greater number of people, in the name of the 'Citizens' Association', outside it. The besieged were not allowed to leave until their work was done. Money, according to *The Times*,[2] was offered for the election of Yuan, yet three ballots were required before Yuan was declared elected to the Presidency with 507 votes and Li Yuan-hung, with 719 votes, to the Vice-Presidency. When the results were announced, members of the 'Citizens' Association', who had been standing outside, broke out cheering, then formed up in small columns and marched away.

All's well that ends well—at least, for the time being. The election

[1] *Jung-yen*, I, No. 15, pp. 4–5 and *Yin-ping-shih-ho-chi*, ch. 30, p. 13.
[2] 3.11.1913.

results, as planned, came in time for the celebration of the Second
Anniversary of the 1911 Revolution. On October 10th, in the Palace
Hall where the Manchu Emperors had been enthroned, the Hall of
Great Harmony, Yuan Shih-k'ai was installed as the first President
of the Republic. In the uniform of a field-marshal, with plume,
knee-length boots, and sabre, this short, stout man, fifty-three years
old and at the zenith of his personal power, ascended the marble
steps of the Hall to take the oath, to read out a lengthy and meaningless declaration and to become the first citizen of the Republic for
the next five years.

'His expressive face, his quick gestures, his powerful neck and
bullet head', recorded the American Minister, P. S. Reinsch, 'gave
him the appearance of great energy. His eyes, which were fine and
clear, alive with interest and mobile, were always brightly alert.
They fixed themselves on the visitor with keen penetration, yet never
seemed hostile; they were full always of keen interest. These eyes of
his revealed how readily he followed—or usually anticipated—the
trend of conversation, though he listened with close attention,
seemingly bringing his judgment to bear on each new detail.
Frenchmen saw in him a resemblance to Clemenceau; and this is
borne out by his portrait which appears on the Chinese dollar. In
stature, facial expression, shape of head, contour of features as well
as in the manner of wearing his moustache, he did greatly resemble
the Tiger.'[1]

Another contemporary recalled: 'He had a wonderful memory,
never forgetting a face or a thing. Therefore when a local official
was being received by him and talked about local affairs and
personalities with him, Yuan often astounded his visitor by his
superior knowledge and memory. Because of this, his subordinates
were rather afraid of him.'[2]

Yet, on this day, there was scepticism in many minds. Daniele
Varé noted in his memoirs:[3]

'Yuan Shih-k'ai himself makes no mystery of his own conviction
that the monarchic regime is the best for China. . . . None of us can
tell for certain whether the Republic has come to stay, or [is] merely
a stop-gap, an expedient to tide over difficult times.'

In spite of these doubts, most of the countries in the world had by

[1] *An American Diplomat in China*, p. 1.
[2] Huang Yen-p'ei, preface to YSKYCHMK, pp. 3-4.
[3] p. 107.

this time recognized Yuan's Government. The earliest to do so were Brazil and Peru in April; they were followed by the United States of America on May 2nd; three days before the ceremony of Yuan's inauguration, Sweden, Spain, Belgium, Russia, Denmark, France, Portugal, Japan, Holland, Britain, Austria-Hungary, Italy, and Germany did the same, and on October 8th and 9th respectively Switzerland and Norway also offered to establish formal diplomatic relations. The recognition was an expression of trust. How had Yuan achieved this?

The powers, through their dealings with the Chinese Government on the one hand and with the Chinese people on the other, were absolutely convinced of the dependability of the people but of the desirability of finding a 'Strong Man' with whom they could negotiate and by whose rule their interests could be protected. In the nineteenth century they found Li Hung-chang and now they had found Yuan Shih-k'ai. Indeed, when he took over the mandate from the Manchus, Yuan instructed his officials and troops to do their utmost to safeguard the lives and property of all the foreign nationals residing in China;[1] and, upon being sworn in as the elected President, he addressed the diplomatic corps as follows: 'The basis of my policy is to honour all the treaty obligations, to follow the same tradition set up by the previous Government, and to promote friendly relations with other countries.'[2] In addition to these pronouncements, he employed a large number of foreign advisers. Dr G. E. Morrison, for instance, was appointed his political adviser on August 2, 1912, in order to win Britain's support, and American pressmen were employed in order to 'keep American public opinion favourable to him'.[3] His expressed views about England and Englishmen were 'too flattering to repeat'—even for Sir John Jordan.[4] The mechanism by which Yuan carried his foreign policy into action was often to express his views directly through the advisers and the legations to the foreign capitals, receiving replies in similar fasion. Therefore the legations 'played in international politics much the same role that provincial capitals did in domestic politics'.[5]

He had troops, connexions, money, and the trust of foreign powers.

[1] LSKP, 22.2.1912.
[2] *Yuan Ta-tsung-t'ung Shu-tu Huei-pien*, ch. 1, p. 4.
[3] Putnam Weale, *Fight*, p. 51.
[4] Jordan to Langley, 2.10.1914.
[5] Putnam Weale, *Fight*, p. 52.

These are the necessary conditions of being a 'Strong Man' in any dependent or quasi-independent country, yet they alone were insufficient to warrant the powers' recognition of his Government.

The United States, pursuing its policy of the Open Door and Equal Opportunities, was wary of the other powers raising new and unreasonable demands, and therefore advocated early recognition; Japan, on the other hand, was in favour of unanimous action at a later date. On July 20, 1912, the United States consulted with the Governments of France, Germany, Britain, Italy, Japan and Russia about the possibility of recognition, but all the answers were unfavourable. The Russians were willing to wait until a permanent Chinese Government was constituted; France seconded this. Japan did not think that the time was opportune. In view of these cold responses, the United States Government decided to wait and see what would happen.

Soon after Wilson's term as President began this question cropped up again. On April 5, 1913, the following note was sent to the powers concerned:

'The President wishes me [Bryan, Secretary of State] to announce to you and through you to your Government that it is his purpose to recognize the Government of China on the 8th of April upon the meeting of its constituent assembly. He wishes me to say that he very earnestly desires and invites the Co-operation of your Government and its action to the same effect at the same time.'[1]

But the action to the same effect was not forthcoming. Japan was reluctant; Russia and Britain wanted China to recognize their interests in Mongolia and Tibet before they recognized her, and France supported Russia. It was in this cold atmosphere that the American Minister presented his credentials on May 2nd.

The British attitude was clearly summarized by a leader in *The Times*: 'The Chinese Republic has been plainly warned that it will not be recognized by the British Government until it undertakes to respect the autonomy of Tibet, in accordance with well-understood treaty obligations.'[2] The reason behind this bargaining was that 'if China continues to be absorbed in her own internal difficulties, and no strong central control is created in Peking for a long time to

[1] Jagow to Treutler, Berlin, 5.4.1913.
[2] 5.9.1913.

come, Tibet may remain unmolested. If, on the other hand, the Chinese Government restore their authority in their disorganized provinces, an attempt will assuredly be made to reassert their control over Tibet.'[1]

Although this argument sounds very much like a shrewd prediction today, it was only intended as a justification for Britain's bargaining with China, for the dormant problem of Tibet had sprung up again on April 21st when Yuan reaffirmed that the area was a part of Chinese territory. Britain protested and, following the Dalai Lama's return from India on July 24th, a revolt broke out. The situation became quieter in August after Sir John Jordan's Note to China, recognizing her suzerainty but denying her sovereignty over the area, had been received. The Note also protested at China's 'interference with the internal affairs of Tibet' and went on to lay Britain's cards on the table; Yuan's Government would be recognized by Britain only when he was willing to meet her demands on Tibet.[2] The Chinese Press was indignant about this Note, yet the Government was ready to discuss the matter with Britain on the basis of the maintenance of the *status quo*. The ensuing Simla Conference, which began in October 1913, was to all intents and purposes fruitless. The Convention, through drawn up, and initialled, was never signed; in other words, the recognition of Tibetan autonomy was not ratified either by the Chinese Government or by the Chinese Assembly. But there was a tricky point of timing. Yuan recognized the autonomy of both Outer Mongolia and Tibet simultaneously on October 7, 1913—the day on which Britain conferred her recognition upon Yuan's Government.

The Mongolian question was in many respects similar to that of Tibet. Like Tibet, Mongolia declared her independence in November 1911, when China was in the grip of the Revolution, on the ground that the country was a vassal state of the Manchu Empire and that since the Empire had been overthrown all its relations with Mongolia should be severed. This 'independent' country had Russian troops stationed in her capital, borrowed 2 million roubles on the understanding that Russian advisers were to be employed to supervise her finances, and established a national bank which was in fact run by Russians. China was notified of the Mongolian decision and was urged to recognize it by the Czarist Government. The Manchu

[1] *The Times*, 27.8.1912.
[2] *The Times*, 28.8.1912.

administration, not quite overthrown but pre-occupied by internal problems, had no time nor power to intervene, and when Yuan Shih-k'ai became Provisional President he could do no more than send people to Urga to talk to the Mongolian leaders in an attempt to influence then. At home, Yuan succeeded in convincing the Senate of the necessity for accepting the Russian conditions in regard to Outer Mongolia, hoping to secure the Mongol's allegiance to the Republic by making concessions to them. But all these efforts came to nothing; on November 3, 1912, Russia and Mongolia signed a protocol, giving Russia the right to train Mongolian soldiers and denying China the right to station troops there. The news of this agreement outraged Peking and forced the Chinese Foreign Minister, Liang Ju-hao, to flee to Tientsin for his own safety. Lu Cheng-hsiang was appointed to succeed him and was instructed to begin negotiations with Russia on this thorny question. After six months, a draft treaty of six articles was ready for ratification. The Cabinet and the House of Representatives gave their sanction on May 26th and July 8th respectively, but the Senate vetoed the treaty on July 11th. Meanwhile two significant things had happened: Mongolia and Tibet recognized each other as independent countries, and Khutukhta, the Mongolian leader, told Yuan that his country 'could not associate itself with China at a moment when civil war between south and north is imminent'.[1]

There was a short pause after Lu Cheng-hsiang's abortive effort to improve the position. When China and Russia picked up the threads again, the situation facing Yuan Shih-k'ai was totally different. The Second Revolution had been quelled and the National Assembly had been indefinitely adjourned due to his ruthless suppression. Sun Pao-ch'i, the Foreign Minister in the 'Celebrity Cabinet', had thus a much more comfortable task to perform. On October 7th, the same day that Russia recognized Yuan's Government, China announced her recognition of Mongolian autonomy; on November 5th, an agreement was signed in Peking to this effect; meanwhile Russia undertook to respect China's suzerainty over Outer Mongolia. What did this 'suzerainty' consist of? Indeed, what was Outer Mongolia? No one seemed to know for sure.

Having gained so much through the 1895 War and being hated so much by the Chinese, Japan remained unusually content to leave China to herself in the first two years of the Republic. On the

[1] *The Times*, 21.1.1913

question of recognition, she had only two demands: that the powers should act in unison and that the British and Japanese Ministers 'should arrange with the Chinese the terms of a voluntary declaration on the subject [about Treaty Rights] which they should make before recognition'.[1] In Yuan's view, these stipulations were not unreasonable, but the incident in Nanking when three Japanese were killed by Chang Hsün's ill-disciplined soldiers had marred the otherwise tranquil relations between Yuan and Japan. Chang Hsün apologized. and, on Japan's insistence, was removed from the Military Governorship of Kiangsu. Still, to make absolutely sure of Japan's recognition, Yuan sent Sun Pao-ch'i, the Foreign Minister, to Japan, nominally to request the Imperial Government to suppress the unwelcome activities of the Kuomintang refugees in that country. This opportunity, presented on a silver salver, was naturally taken, and the result was a promise to borrow Japanese money for the construction of five railways in Manchuria and Inner Mongolia. The instruments of this agreement were exchanged on the day before Japan conferred her recognition upon Yuan's Government.

Having thus obtained the backing of the major powers, having pacified and to some extent unified the country, and having installed himself as President, Yuan Shih-k'ai was now ready to turn his attention to the legislature and the political parties which stood between him and absolute power. Before his installation, he had needed an assembly to elect him, but after it, he found this law-making body a nuisance. On October 25th he asked for five important amendments to the Provisional Constitution in order to give him a free hand to change the composition of the Government, to appoint or dismiss officials of all ranks, to declare war, make peace or sign treaties, to make valid laws on his own authority when the Assembly was in recess, and to adopt urgent financial measures without the Assembly's sanction. The odd thing about these demands was that they were raised when the draft of the Permanent Constitution had already reached its third reading in the Assembly, and that they were addressed not to the Assembly but to the provincial leaders, for the preamble said: 'The Drafting Committee of the Constitution is under the control of the Kuomintang, and the draft itself encroaches on the prerogatives of the Government and endeavours to destroy executive independence as well as to create a parliamentary dictatorship.'[2]

[1] Langley to Jordan, 6.5.1913.
[2] CFKP, 25.10.1913.

M

The warlords in the provinces, such as Ni Ssu-ch'ung, Chang Hsün and Chiang Kuei-t'i, applauded Yuan's proposals and moreover piled upon the Draft Constitution and the Assembly a whole dictionary full of epithets which were not permissble for use in public. The words, crude as they were, were not entirely libellous. Encouraged by this, Yuan outlawed the Kuomintang on November 4, 1913 and beseiged the party's headquarters in Peking with his troops and police, who also searched the houses of the Kuomintang members of the Assembly. 438 party cards were taken away from these members, who were thereby deprived of the right to attend Parliament. On the second day of this *coup d'état*, the agreement with Russia conceding autonomy to Outer Mongolia was signed, and, a week later, the Speakers of the two chambers of the Assembly announced the adjournment of Parliament for an indefinite period. One wonders whether Yuan's admiration of Britain did not go as far back as Cromwell's time. The National Assembly was no more respectable or powerful than the Long Parliament, and on January 10, 1914, it met with the same fate as its British prototype in 1653. 'Hereafter', as a leading journal of that time, *Jung-yen*, commented: 'nothing can possibly hinder him.'[1]

During the adjournment of the Assembly Yuan ordered the convocation of a Political Council which comprised ten members appointed by the President and four by the Cabinet, one from each Ministry and two from each province. All sixty-nine were hand-picked, and a former Viceroy of Yunnan and Kweichow under the Imperial Government, Li Ching-hsi, was made Speaker. By definition, the Council was a consultative body which, apart from making suggestions, had no legislative power, and the second suggestion which it ever made was for the dissolution of the National Assembly, in response to a joint petition to the President signed by no less than nineteen military leaders, headed by Li Yuan-hung.

The Political Council was convened for two main purposes—to draft another permanent constitution and to give a democratic cloak to Yuan's *de facto* dictatorship. But even these hand-picked men were reluctant to accept the grave responsibility of amending the Constitution; instead, they proposed the creation of an *ad hoc* legislative body for this task. This body was to be named the Constitutional Compact Conference and to consist of sixty-six elected members from the Capital and the provinces. An elector of

[1] Vol. II, Nos. 1-2, p. 2.

the Conference must either have held a high post in the past or obtained the second degree under the Imperial examination system or a high school diploma, and must also have a personal estate of at least 10,000 yuan. A defector from the Kuomintang, Sun Yüeh-yün, was elected Speaker on February 18th, when the Conference met for the first time. Among its members there was not a single Kuomintang representative, and all the decisions taken by the Conference throughout its lifetime were unanimous. 'The members . . . were nothing more than the instruments of the Government.'[1]

Two days after its opening, the President handed the Conference seven outline amendments to the Provisional Constitution: 1. complete control of diplomatic relations by the President; 2. complete control of the administrative system and its discipline, and the appointment of members of the Cabinet and diplomatic delegations by the President; 3. adoption of a presidential system of government; 4. the drafting by the President and a Council of State of a permanent constitution to be adopted by a National Convention and promulgated by the President; 5. the free exercise of the power to deprive or to restore the rights of a citizen by the President; 6. the granting of power to issue emergency ordinances to the President, and 7. the granting of power to take emergency financial measures to the President.[2] These proposals were all included in the Constitutional Compact which was codified by the Conference and announced by Yuan on May 1st and which replaced the Provisional Constitution. After a reign of just over two years the tattered piece of paper known as the Provisional Constitution had been put aside; it proved to have been the longest lived constitution of the period before the 1949 Revolution.

Under the new dispensation the President, as head of the Government, was to be assisted by a Minister of State instead of a Premier, and the Cabinet was to be superseded by a Board of Political Affairs, whose members, headed by the Minister of State, belonged to the President's personal staff. The legislative body of the government was a Legislative Assembly whose constitution was announced on December 27, 1914 but which was never convoked, and the consultative body was a Council of State, which came into being on June 20th. Of this new arrangement Yuan had the pluck to say

---

[1] Wang Shih-chieh and Ch'ien Tuan-sheng, *Pi-chiao Hsien-fa*, Vol. II, p. 154.
[2] CFKP, 1.5.1914.

that it reduced his power while enchancing his responsibility![1]

As soon as the Compact was announced, Yuan abolished the Caretaker Cabinet which had succeeded the 'Celebrity Cabinet' on February 12th. On the same day his old friend and sworn brother Hsü Shih-ch'ang, who had been living in retirement in Tsingtao, on the honourable grounds of having received extraordinary favours from the Ch'ing Emperors, and therefore being unable to render his services to the Republic, was appointed the first Minister of State. To him this was an honorary post, for he still refused to accept a single penny of salary from the Republican Government; under him, there were two Deputy Ministers, of the Left and the Right; these posts were given to Yang Shih-ch'i and Ch'ien Neng-hsün respectively. The Foreign Office was entrusted to Sun Pao-ch'i, Home Affairs to Chu Ch'i-ch'ien, Finance to Chou Tzu-ch'i, the Army to Tuan Ch'i-jui, the Navy to Liu Kuan-hsiung, Justice to Chang Tsung-hsiang, Communications to Liang Tun-yen, Education to T'ang Hua-lung, and, last but not least, Agriculture and Commerce to the venerable Chang Ch'ien, who never actually took up this office.

The Board of Political Affairs was housed in the Presidential Palace, the Hall of Benevolence. Being under the guidance of a staunch Monarchist, the Board revived many an archaic custom. In terms of address, for instance, 'Mr' (Hsien-sheng) was replaced by 'Master' (Ta-jen) or Your Honour' (Lao-yeh), and one's official career under the Imperial Government became a weighty factor in securing a post or a promotion. As the head of a Republic, Yuan displayed his puissance at his 1914 New Year reception at the Lake palace (where the Kuang-hsü Emperor had been put under surveillance) when twenty generals in sky-blue uniforms with acres of gold lace across their chests unrolled a carpet for him to tread on as he entered the Palace Hall.[2] His Minister of State, on May 29th, the Tuan-wu Festival, put on the Manchu official robe and headgear to which he was once entitled in the capacity of Grand Tutor to the deposed Emperor, P'u-i, to attend the Palace banquet. Indeed, he was a minister, not a premier, so he ought to have an emperor. These were trivial things, yet they indicated what was in store.

Now let us turn to the financial aspect of Yuan's Government. The two budgets, one for the year 1913 and the other for 1914, and

[1] CFKP, 1.5.1914.
[2] Daniele Varé, *Laughing Diplomat*, p. 109.

the financial returns of 1915 may help to gauge the dire straits China was in (even though the figures are about as reliable as an

	Total Revenue	Total Expenditure
	yuan	yuan
1913	412,666,695	497,872,605
1914	254,740,533	229,263,375
1915	130,678,127	139,036,454

astrologer's prediction).[1] Take the budget for 1913 for example; it was not announced until 1914, and it put the amount of the grant-in-aid from the provinces to the Government as high as 32,418,530 yuan, while the amount of subsidy to the frontier areas was estimated at 29,137,707 yuan; in fact, they were merely 5,600,000 yuan and 2,800,000 yuan respectively. According to the Finance Ministry's message to the provinces at the end of 1913[2] the Government received from the provinces a meagre 2·6 million yuan while it gave them more than 90 million. The nominal unification of the country after the Second Revolution improved the situation a little, but a complete restoration of the financial relationship between the Central Government and the provinces during the Manchu dynasty was still a long way off. On both sides of the 1913 budget, the largest single item was public loans, domestic or foreign, but more foreign than domestic. Out of the total revenue of 412 million yuan, 223 million was borrowed money; out of the total expenditure of 497 million, 380 million went to loan services. As the Government went on borrowing the last-named item naturally increased in size. This alone was sufficient to invalidate the budget figures for both 1914 and 1915, and no more proof is required of the financial insecurity of Yuan Shih-k'ai's Government. The Reorganization Loan was used up by April 1914. Sir John Jordan reported to Langley on April 6, 1914:

'Here is the last instance of reorganization loans at actual work. About 10 days ago an appropriation of Tls. 1,000,000 from the last Reorganization Loan was sent to Hankow for the disbandment of troops in Szechwan. The usual mass of vouchers, worked out to the fraction of a cent, was sent up to Peking, but not a farthing of the

---

[1] Chia Shih-i, *Min-kuo Ts'ai-cheng Shih*, pp. 47–54.
[2] CFKP, 2.11.1913.

money even went to Szechwan. It was remitted back to the Government here via Shanghai and other devious routes to cover up the transactions and hoodwink the Bankers.'

There was nothing to do but go on borrowing as long as willing money-lenders could be found. Before the storm over the Reorganization Loan had died down the Austrian Loan negotiations were under way. This was even more absurd, for the amount contracted for was £3,200,000 but the actual payment after discount was only £1,413,000! The interest was 6 per cent and the security was the newly introduced land transfer tax, which promised to yield about a million sterling a year.[1] The Austrian loan was followed by a host of others. In 1913, there were the (British) Canton-Kowloon Railway loan of £50,000, the French-Belgian Railway loan of £10,000,000, the French loan of Fr. 150,000,000, the (British) Hsinyang Railway loan of £3,000,000 and the Japanese loan of 9,000,000 yen.

From this list we may deduce one of Yuan's principles in selecting creditors: he preferred Europeans to Japanese. This was hardly surprising, for, since his term of office in Korea Yuan had never been *persona grata* with the Japanese Government, and his general policy towards Japan since he became the head of the Chinese Government had been cool and indifferent. As all the European countries and the United States were willing to support Yuan, Japan had to be content with a period of impassive diplomacy. Then came 1914 and the World War, and the situation rapidly changed.

In the dark abyss of Yuan's financial problems there were nevertheless three gleams of hope—the improvement in the Salt Gabelle administration under Sir Richard Dane, Liang Shih-i's considerable success in floating domestic loans, and the monetary reform after the Second Revolution.

At the beginning of 1913, Yuan described the Salt Gabelle as 'chaotic'.[2] The total proceeds from it for that year were under 11 million yuan, and the Government obtained nothing from it. In 1914, the total yield leapt to nearly 60·5 million, and in the following year, rose again to 70 million, out of which the Government reaped a net income of over 31 million in 1914 and 27·5 million in 1915[3].

---

[1] *The Times*, 13.5.1913.
[2] *Jung-yen*, I, No. 5, p. 1.
[3] Enclosure in Jordan to Langley, 16.4.1916.

The rapid improvement should be attributed to two main causes:
1. After the Reorganization Loan had been obtained, the Gabelle
was administered by foreign inspectors, notably Sir Richard Dane
and a Dane by the name of Oiesen; and 2. at the end of 1913 Yuan
issued a decree forbidding all provincial officials to interfere with its
collection.[1] Without the foreign inspectors, his decree could not have
been effective.

Yuan's resorting to domestic loans was in itself a desperate
measure, for the European War had pushed foreign financial
resources out of his reach. At an all-night discussion with his close
adviser, Liang Shih-i, who was the leader of the Communication
Clique and the Director-General of the Banks of Communications,
he decided to float loans in the home market and gave Liang full
power to arrange this. Liang's plan was, first of all, to win the
support of Chinese and foreign banks in order to strengthen the
credit of the proposed loans, and then to deposit a sinking fund in
foreign banks so as to guarantee the repayment of the principal and
regular payments of the interest. Sir Francis A. Aglen, Sir Robert
Hart's successor, and M. P. Sellier, a French banker, were included
in the Board of Directors of the Loans Bureau which was set up in
August 1914. In the same month, 16 million yuan in loan bonds was
issued, bearing an interest of 6 per cent. This was so successful that,
soon afterwards, an additional 8 million was issued. In the spring of
the next year the Treasury showed a deficit of nearly 50 million yuan,
so a new issue became necessary. This time the target was fixed at
24 million, at 10 per cent discount, still bearing an interest of 6 per
cent. To strengthen the Government's credit a sum of 1,440,000
yuan was deposited in foreign banks for the payment of interest and a
promise was given by the Customs Inspector's Office to allocate
H. K. Tls. 4·9 million as a guarantee for the repayment of the
principal. Three months later, sales reached the unexpected figure
of 25,434,480 yuan. On the surface this was again a success. Yet, in
fact, the Government depended too heavily upon the banks'
underwriting and, because their need of money was so urgent,
had to pay unusually high rates of interest and discount which in
many cases ate up 50 or 60 per cent of the total. Nonetheless, the
loans produced some 26 million yuan to meet the Treasury's
demands.

Previously issued loans had never been as remunerative as this,

[1] CFKP, 12.11.1913.

due chiefly to the lack of capital, credit, and a well-organized money market. Liang Shih-i's achievement, under such circumstances, is a thing to marvel at. The credit of the loans stood at its highest when, at the beginning of 1915, the Government made an effort to repay the principal of the 1914 loan. Soon, however, they let this credit fall, first by stopping further deposits in foreign banks and then by incorporating the Loans Bureau into the Ministry of Finance. Later issues met with an extremely cool reception; at one time a bond of the denomination of 100 yuan only commanded a price of 27 yuan on the market.[1]

At the end of the Second Revolution, the amount of fiat money issued either by proper banks or by provincial military leaders reached the staggering height of 163 million yuan. The notes had no silver reserve behind them, and were sometimes devalued, in terms of coins, to only half their face value. Side by side with all this paper, there circulated more than ten kinds of silver coins of both foreign and provincial origin and of different denominations and fineness. There were also some 30 million copper coins in circulation as token money; these too were of different denominations and fineness. 'The root of all monetary problems' as the financial experts of that time pointed out, 'was the lack of a monetary standard'.[2] In January 1914 a conference attended by more than forty experts including Hsiung Hsi-ling, Liang Ch'i-ch'ao, Dr Morrison, Dr F. Goodnow and so on, was held in Peking with Liang Shih-i in the chair. Three weeks later the experts agreed on a programme to reform the Chinese monetary system. They admitted that the silver standard was not ideal, but, having carefully examined the merits and demerits of gold-silver bi-metallism, the gold standard and the gold-exchange standard, they came to the conclusion that the silver standard was the only practicable system for China. They recommended that the standard currency in future should be a coin weighing 0·72 taels with a silver content of 90 per cent, its face value being 1 yuan, and the token pieces of 50, 20 and 10 cents should weigh *pro rata* to the standard money and be of the same fineness. The mints in Peking and in Shanghai then began to coin silver dollars to these specifications; they bore the profile of the President. The new coins were warmly welcomed by the people, and step by step they replaced nearly 300 million Dragon Dollars

[1] *Yin-hang Yueh-k'an*, III, p. 2.
[2] Liang, *Nien-p'u*, p. 169.

and more than 400 million foreign dollars which were then circulating or being hoarded in the country.

The issue of Yuan Shih-k'ai dollars killed two birds with one stone: It eased the financial difficulties of the Treasury and gave China a standard currency. But it did not solve the problem of the irredeemable banknotes. To do this, Yuan had to obtain another sizeable foreign loan. Indeed, he asked the five nation consortium[1] for another £25,000,000, and but for the war in Europe he might have obtained it.

Foreign loans, the issue of domestic loans, and improvements in the tax and monetary systems enabled Yuan Shih-k'ai to remain solvent. On the eve of the 1914-18 War his financial situation was noticeably better than it had been a year before.

The war itself had both good and bad effects on the Chinese economy. The demand for raw materials and food-stuffs in Europe increased, so China's exports of vegetable oil, cotton, iron, tin, copper, antimony and wolfram all rose considerably; Chinese light industries, particularly the textile and food processing industries were also having a prosperous time. On the other hand, part of the increase in exports was swallowed up by the rise in the price of gold in terms of silver, which put China at a disadvantage in her overseas trade. The sterling rate of the H.K. tael, for instance, stood at an average of 3s ¼d in 1913, but fell to 2s 8¾d in 1914 and to 2s 7⅛d in 1915.[2] The most serious thing of all was that the war curtailed the supply of foreign loans to the President.

The President decided to remain neutral in the war, but Japan did not; the thing which Yuan had most dreaded soon became a reality. On August 15th, Japan issued an ultimatum to the German Government demanding the withdrawal of all German vessels from Japanese and Chinese waters and the surrender to Japan of the entire leased territory of Kiaochow within a month 'without condition or compensation' but 'with a view to the eventual restoration of the same to China'.[3] Germany's counter-move was a proposal to return the whole of Kiaochow Bay to China immediately.

Japan now regarded herself as the legitimate heir to all the German interests in China, and warned China not to accept the German suggestion. In her view, this matter no longer concerned the

[1] *The Times*, 6.4.1914.
[2] Remer, *Trade*, p. 250.
[3] H. F. MacNair, *Modern Chinese History*, p. 753.

Chinese Government, which should, in its own interests, remain absolutely passive. The Imperial Government also informed the Chinese Minister in Tokyo that although Japan had no territorial ambitions, military necessity obliged her to place troops along the entire railway from Tsingtao to Chinan. Quoting the 1905 War between Japan and Russia, which was fought in Chinese territory, as a precedent, Japan proceeded to discuss a 'free war zone', to be established in China in case military conflict between Japan and Germany became unavoidable. The zone demanded by the Japanese Government was a strip of land a hundred li wide along the length of the railway. China put up some half-hearted resistance, but eventually gave way, on August 31st, and gave permission for Japanese soldiers to take free action in the Kiaochow, Laichow, and Lungkow districts; on the next day Japanese troops moved in.

The agreed areas did not include Weihsien, nor Chinan, yet Japanese troops marched into these places on September 25th and October 7th respectively, on the grounds that both places were on the railway line and had to be occupied if Japan was to take control of the railway. China protested, but none the less withdrew her own garrison.

At this time it became apparent that Yuan Shih-k'ai intended to found a new imperial dynasty; he knew that without Japan's support this ambition would be doomed to failure, and was therefore anxious to obtain her favour. At the end of 1913, he sent Lu Tsung-yu, who was pro-Japanese, to Tokyo as the Chinese Minister, and in May 1914 special envoys were despatched to join mourning the death of the Mikado. Flirtation, however, is no substitute for diplomacy. On November 13, 1914 the Japanese Foreign Minister, Kato, recalled Hioki, his Minister to Peking, for consultations; on December 3rd, he gave Hioki the text of the notorious Twenty-one Demands, and on December 21st Hioki returned to Peking. The preparations for what was perhaps the most surreptitious diplomatic onslaught in history were complete; at 3 p.m. on January 18, 1915 Hioki presented this historic document, which was written on paper watermarked with dreadnoughts and machine-guns, not to the Chinese Foreign Office, but to Yuan Shih-k'ai himself. Hioki also impressed upon Yuan that the whole affair must be kept absolutely secret.

Peking was not a good place for keeping secrets, and it had no reason to be so with regard to matters of this kind. The American

Minister, Reinsch, learnt the real nature of the Demands on January 22nd, and soon this sensational news was generally known among diplomats and newspaper correspondents in Peking. Sir John Jordan recorded:

'They [the Chinese] consulted me today and asked me if our Government had been consulted. I said I had no information but told them to be conciliatory and run no risks.'[1]

No doubt he remembered that Japan was at that time Britain's ally.

Although the Demands were feverishly discussed in Chinese papers, *The Times*, the Associated Press and other leading papers and agencies in Europe and America withheld the news for two weeks. Their reticence could be interpreted as caution, for on January 27th it was given out 'on the highest authority' both at Tokyo and by the Japanese embassy in Washington, that current information purporting to outline the basis of negotiations was 'absolutely without foundation'.[2] Furthermore, on February 14, 1915 the Imperial Government of Japan, at the repeated requests of other powers, released an official version of the Demands. As an instructive exercise, let us collate this with the text delivered to China on January 18th. We shall call the former the 'released version' and the latter the 'genuine version'.

The genuine version consisted of twenty-one demands in five groups; the released version, only eleven in four groups. The first group of four articles concerned Shantung province; both versions of these tallied. China was required to assent 'to all matters upon which the Japanese Government may hereafter agree with the German Government relating to the disposition of all rights, interests and concessions'; to cede no territory or island along the coast to a third power 'under any pretext'; 'to Japan's building a railway from Chefoo or Lungkow to join the Kiachow-Chinan Railway'; and 'to open by herself [i.e. China] as soon as possible certain important cities and towns in the province . . . as commercial ports'.

The second group of seven articles dealt with southern Manchuria and eastern Inner Mongolia. There the difference between the two versions was astonishing. The first article in the genuine version read:

[1] Jordan to Langley, 26.1.1915.
[2] Reinsch, *An American Diplomat in China*, p. 132.

'The two contracting parties mutually agree that the term of lease of Port Arthur and Dairen and the term of lease of the South Manchurian Railway and the Antung-Mukden Railway shall be extended to the period of 99 years';

while the other version was vaguely phrased thus:

'Extension of the terms of the lease of Kwantung, the South Manchuria Railway, and the Antung-Mukden Railway'.

The second article was:

'Japanese subjects in South Manchuria and Eastern Inner Mongolia shall have the right to lease or own land required either for erecting suitable buildings for trade and manufacture or for farming';

the third:

'Japanese subjects shall be free to reside and travel in South Manchuria and Eastern Inner Mongolia and to engage in business and in manufacture of any kind whatsoever;

and the fourth:

'The Chinese Government agrees to grant to Japanese subjects the right of opening the mines in South Manchuria. As regards what mines are to be opened, they shall be decided upon jointly.'

These three became one, the second, article in the released version, which read:

'(A) Acquisition by the Japanese of the right of residence and ownership of land. (B) Grant to Japan of the mining rights of mines specified by Japan.'

The fifth article required China to seek Japan's consent before granting permission to any subject of a third power to build a railway or to make a loan for the purpose of building a railway in southern Manchuria and eastern Inner Mongolia, and to pledge the local taxes of those areas as security against a loan from a third power. In the released version, this was the third article of the second group. The sixth article asked the Chinese Government to consult Japan before employing 'political, financial or military advisers or instructors' in the same areas, and the seventh demanded that the control and management of the Kirin-Ch'angch'un Railway be transferred to Japan. These last two formed the substance of the fourth and fifth articles of the released version.

Details of these first two groups were communicated to other powers, because Manchuria and eastern Inner Mongolia had been recognized as Japan's sphere of influence for sometime and Shantung, at the end of 1914, had unquestionably become a new Japanese domain. They were unlikely to arouse much adverse criticism in Europe or in the United States. The contents of the other three groups were either phrased in an extremely ambiguous way or kept dark.

In the genuine version the third group contained two articles which tackled the question of China's biggest coal and steel works in P'inghsiang and Hanyang, the Hanyehp'ing Company, stating that at an opportune time it 'shall be made a joint concern of the two nations and they further agree that without the previous consent of Japan, China shall not by her own act dispose of the rights and property of whatsoever nature of the said Company nor cause the said Company to dispose freely of the same'. Furthermore, in the second article, it was made clear that 'The Chinese Government agrees that no mines in the neighbourhood of those owned by the Hanyehp'ing Company shall be permitted, without the consent of the said Company, to be worked by other persons outside of the said Company; and further agrees that if it is desired to carry out any understanding which, it is apprehended, may directly or indirectly affect the interest of the said Company, the consent of the said Company shall first be obtained'.

As this Company was situated right in the centre of the British sphere of influence, the Yangtze Valley, Japan's desire to fish in troubled waters was veiled by these words:

'Agreement in principle that, at an opportune moment in the future, the Hanyehp'ing Company should be placed under Japanese and Chinese co-operation.'

As an attempt to please the Americans by bowing to their Open Door policy, a fourth group was attached, which appeared in the released version as one article, the last. It was phrased most finely:

'The Japanese Government and the Chinese Government with the

object of effectively preserving the territorial integrity of China agree
to the following special article:—

The Chinese Government engages not to cede or lease to a third
power any harbour or bay or island along the coast of China.'

The last, but by no means the least, group, which comprised
seven articles, seven poisoned daggers—simply did not appear in the
released version. The articles were:

'1. The Chinese Central Government shall employ influential Japanese as advisers in political, financial and military affairs.
2. Japanese hospitals, churches, and schools in the interior of China
shall be granted the right to own land.
3. Inasmuch as the Japanese Government and the Chinese Government have had many cases of dispute between Japanese and Chinese
police to settle cases, which have caused no little misunderstanding,
it is for this reason necessary that the police departments of important
places (in China) shall be jointly administered by Japanese and
Chinese or that the police departments of these places shall employ
numerous Japanese, so that they may at the same time help to plan
for the improvement of the Chinese Police Service.
4. China shall putchase from Japan a fixed quantity of munitions of
war (say 50 per cent or more of what is needed by the Chinese
Government) or there shall be established in China a Sino-Japanese
jointly-worked arsenal. Japanese technical experts are to be employed
and Japanese material to be purchased.
5. China agrees to grant to Japan the right to construct a railway
connecting Wuch'ang with Kiukiang and Nanch'ang, and another
between Nanch'ang and Chaochou.
6. If China needs foreign capital to work mines, build railways and
construct harbour-works (including dockyards) in the Province of
Fukien, Japan shall first be consulted.
7. China agrees that Japanese subjects shall have the right of
missionary propaganda in China.'[1]

The Demands, worse than many presented by a victor to his
vanquished enemy, virtually put southern Manchuria, eastern
Inner Mongolia, and Shantung province under the jurisdiction of

[1] Both versions based on MacNair's translations, *Modern Chinese History*, pp.
768-771.

Japan, reduced China to the status of a Japanese 'satellite' and greatly encroached upon the British interests in the Yangtze Valley, yet the preamble hypocritically said: 'The Japanese Government and the Chinese Government being desirous of maintaining the general peace in Eastern Asia and further strengthening the *friendly relations and good neighbourliness* existing between the two nations agree to the following articles.'

Even more amusing were the European comments on the Demands. *The Times* leader of February 13th had this to say:

'We are told that they [the Demands] have caused a great commotion in Peking. There is nothing unusual about that. Commotion, genuine or feigned, is the ordinary result of all applications to Chinese authorities.

. . . these terms do not look harmful or unreasonable in principle. . . . They do not in any way threaten the integrity of China, nor do they appear to violate the doctrines of "equality of opportunity" and of the "open door" as hitherto accepted by other powers.'

The British Foreign Secretary simply refused to have the Demands discussed in the House on May 4th, and Reuter made the apparently sagacious observation:

'The real root of the trouble with China is the fact that she still looks down upon Japan and cannot bring herself to regard the small neighbouring country as the equal of herself, much less of the Great Powers.'[1]

Jordan, being on the spot, raised a lone dissenting voice:

'There is no reasoning with a highwayman well armed and Japan's action towards China is worse than that of Germany in the case of Belgium.'[2]

His sympathy was perhaps the only reward Yuan got for his pro-British policy.

In the United States, the Press was generally indignant, but the Government was cautious. The State Department at first sounded

[1] *The Times*, 7.5.1915.
[2] Jordan to Alston, 6.5.1915.

out other powers in an attempt to agree on a concerted action in favour of maintaining China's integrity. This being fruitless, it agreed to make informal inquiries about the discrepancies between the genuine and the released version, after the Chinese Minister of Foreign Affairs had drawn its attention to them. President Wilson's instructions to Reinsch were:

'I have had the feeling that any direct advice to China, or direct intervention on her behalf in the present negotiations, would really do her more harm than good, inasmuch as it would very likely provoke the jealousy and excite the hostility of Japan, which would first be manifested against China herself.'[1]

To the indignation of America, Japan offered the hackneyed answer that, as it was impossible for the Japanese to settle in America, the USA could not in fairness object if Japan tried to widen her activities and influence on the Asian Continent. This bare-fisted logic was uttered through the mouth of Hioki, who went on:

'The present crisis throughout the world virtually forces my Government to take far-reaching action. When there is a fire in a jeweller's shop, the neighbours cannot be expected to refrain from helping themselves.'[2]

The actual negotiations on the Demands began on February 2nd; the Chinese representatives were the Foreign Minister, Lu Cheng-hsiang, and his deputy, Ts'ao Ju-lin, and the Japanese Minister Hioki, and his Counsellor, Obata. Behind the scenes was Yuan Shih-k'ai, upon whom the final responsibility for the agreement must lie. He studied the text with great care, made detailed margin notes in the Vermilion Pencil on the copy delivered to China, which was published later by Wang Yün-sheng,[3] and instructed his negotiators to try to cancel the fifth group of articles. He also sent the Vice-Minister of Agriculture and Commerce, Chin Pang-p'ing, and his Japanese political adviser, Dr Ariga to Tokyo to parley with Japanese elder statesmen, who were believed to be opposed to the Demands in general and to the fifth group in particular. Having

---

[1] *An American Diplomat in China*, p. 137.
[2] ibid, p. 135.
[3] LSNLCKYUP, VI, pp. 283 seq.

failed to arouse British and American interest in this issue, he still hoped that the world would see the truth and judge for itself. He also heeded Reinsch's advice to try to discuss the individual demands one by one, granting only the least objectionable and gaining time, in the hope that other nations would come to realize what was at stake.

Japan's tactics were of course different. To begin with, Hioki demanded that the entire corpus of the proposals should be discussed at once. After some wrangling this was done, and the negotiations entered their second stage, which lasted from February 22nd to April 17th, during which the details of each article were examined. Finally, from April 17th to May 9th, the comparatively amiable atmosphere was swept away by new demands and threats culminating in the Japanese ultimatum on May 7th and the Chinese surrender on May 9th.

After twenty-four conferences during which some minor alterations had been made, China found the fifth group unsuitable for negotiation, for all the articles in it 'infringe China's sovereignty, the treaty rights of other powers, and the principle of equal opportunity'.[1] Although, at that stage, there were still some points in dispute, China had already indicated her acceptance of the bulk of the Demands. Yet, at 3 p.m. on May 7th, Hioki delivered his Government's ultimatum, compelling China to accept all the Demands except the fifth group which the Imperial Government 'will undertake to detach . . . from the present negotiations and discuss separately in the future'. The ultimatum went on to say:

'It is hereby declared that if no satisfactory reply is received before or at the designated time [6 p.m. on the 9th day of May], the Imperial Government will take any steps she may deem necessary.'

Simultaneously, the Japanese Government ordered a general mobilization in Manchuria, declared martial law in southern Manchuria, and advised all Japanese in China to leave the country. Washington, at this juncture, expressed a hope that the negotiations might still 'be concluded in a manner satisfactory to both nations';[2] Jordan told the Chinese Foreign Minister that the best thing to do

---

[1] Memorandum read to Hioki at a conference held at the Chinese Foreign Office, May 1, 1915.
[2] *The Times*, 8.5.1915.

was to accept the Demands;[1] but J. O. P. Bland, with all his wisdom
and incisiveness long after the event, commented:

'After four months of tedious negotiations at Peking (in which
German intrigues played an important role by means of a systematic
propaganda of falsehood in the Chinese Press) the Japanese Government presented an ultimatum to China (May 6th). . . .

'In declining the finally modified demands of the Japanese
Government on May 3rd, the Chinese Foreign Office expressed
itself in a distinctly unconciliatory manner, revealing most in-
opportunely the traditional Mandarin arrogance and contempt for
Japan's claims to be treated as a Great Power'.[2]

'China is virtually being put up for auction', as Jordan had earlier
remarked,[3] yet Bland blamed the party whose property was being
forcibly sold for arrogance and slowness.

On May 8th Yuan called a meeting of the Board of Political
Affairs at which he told his Ministers of Jordan's advice. Since
China had not the military strength to resist Japan, the only
alternative was to accept the ultimatum and the demands embodied
in it. 'This is both sad and humiliating. . . .' Yuan said in a grave
tone, 'but let us all remember it and do our best to wipe out this
disgrace.'[4] Immediately after the conference Hsü Shih-ch'ang, the
Minister of State, produced a list of names and handed it to the
Minister of Finance, asking him to find jobs for these men. Every
one in the company was flabbergasted by this insensitive gesture,
yet the Minister of State was smiling broadly. On leaving the
chamber Liang Shih-i whispered to the Minister of Finance:
'That must be due to the Twenty-one Demands!'[5]

On the same day China announced her acceptance of the
ultimatum in a lengthy reply in which she stated: 'The Chinese
Government with a view to preserving the peace of the Far East,
hereby accepts, with the exception of those [revised] five articles of
Group V postponed for later negotiation, all the articles of Groups
I, II, III, and IV. . . .' The reference to the fifth group was considered
by Reinsch to be a serious tactical mistake;[6] in fact, Hioki, through

[1] Liang, *Nien-p'u*, p. 256.
[2] *China, Japan, Korea*, pp. 44–45.
[3] Jordan to Langley, 23.2.1914.
[4] Liang, *Nien-p'u*, p. 257.
[5] Liang, ibid, p. 258.
[6] *An American Diplomat in China*, pp. 147–148.

Ts'ao Ju-lin, had come to know the contents of the reply before it was published, and objected to the original phrasing which ran 'with the exception of those five articles of Group V'. He insisted that the words 'postponed for later negotiation' should be added.[1] Ts'ao duly included those words without consulting his superiors. On May 25th, signatures were attached to the treaties, agreements, notes and declarations and, on June 8th, ratifications of the treaties were exchanged, thus concluding the first and the darkest episode in the diplomatic history of the Republic of China.

Coming as it did after the anti-foreign Boxer Uprising and the brief glimpse of freedom of the 1911 Revolution, the Chinese people's reaction to this episode was unprecedented in its sharpness, Money was donated by shopkeepers, rickshaw boys, students, coolies and overseas Chinese to finance a military resistance against Japan; mass rallies were organized in the big cities, calling on the Government to reject the Demands; strikes and boycotts of Japanese goods were also organized in such places as Shanghai, Chefoo, Amoy and Hankow. Nineteen of Yuan's own generals, under the leadership of Feng Kuo-chang, publicly declared their resolution to fight for China. All these signs of an awakening nationalism were ignored by Yuan and his Government. Instead of giving them encouragement or at least recognition, Yuan thwarted, even ruthlessly suppressed, them. A man with his long memory could not possibly have forgotten the lessons of 1895 and the downfall of Li Hung-chang, or of 1900 and the ruin of Jung-lu. His army was *built up* for defence, not to be *used for* defence.

[1] PYCFTCSCSH, II, p. 62.

CHAPTER X

The Emperor 1915-1916

A SIGNIFICANT anecdote gained circulation in 1915 among Yuan's officers.

'Yuan had a habit of taking a short nap after lunch and having a cup of tea immediately afterwards. A boy was given the job of looking after the tea.

'One day when the boy went into the bed-chamber with the tea in an exquisite jade cup, he saw, not his master, but a huge toad crouching on the couch. He was stunned and dropped the cup on the floor. Fortunately the noise did not disturb the sleeping President.

'The boy tiptoed out of the chamber and then ran to an elderly servant who treated him as his own son. He told the old man what had happened and tearfully begged him to make up some kind of a story that he could tell Yuan, hoping that he would be spared from punishment for breaking the valuable vessel. The old man pondered a while and told the child what to say, should his master ask any questions.

'Presently Yuan woke up and saw his tea in a porcelain beaker. He at once summoned the boy and asked him where the jade cup was. The boy answered truthfully.

' "Broken?" Yuan's tone was severe. But the boy calmly explained: "Yes, sir, because I have seen something very strange."

' "What's strange?" demanded the master, visibly annoyed.

' "When I came in here a moment ago with a cup of tea, I did not see you, sir, on the couch, but. . . ."

' "But what? You liar!"

' "But a five-clawed golden dragon."

' "Rubbish!" the master shouted, but his anger suddenly left him. He opened a drawer, taking our a hundred-dollar note and thrusting it into the boy's hand. He cautioned him not to mention a word of what he had just seen to anyone else.'[1]

The story, apart from reflecting a widely held belief that Yuan was about to try to found a dynasty, and ridiculing his faith in superstition, contains an allusion to a well-known Chinese saying applied to ambitious men: 'Just like a toad wanting to eat swan meat'. So it was equally widely believed that Yuan would not succeed in putting himself on the throne. But the most significant part of the tale was that it was told among his military following.

Since his investiture the President had not been able to concentrate on the training and control of his army. Political, economic, and diplomatic affairs all demanded his time and energy, and perforce he had to delegate this, the most important aspect of his rule to his trusted lieutenants. Wang Shih-chen, one of the three leaders of the Northern Army, retired from public life soon after the 1911 Revolution; after the Second Revolution, Feng Kuo-chang was stationed in Nanking to take care of the south-east. In the Central Government, General Tuan Ch'i-jui had held the post of Minister for the Army uninterruptedly since 1912; he had sole and complete control over the entire Northern Army. What had once been a triumvirate of Feng, Tuan, and Wang was now a dictatorship, and what had once been Yuan's army now threatened to become Tuan's. Having thus enhanced his power, it was inconceivable that Tuan should remain as obedient to his chief as in the past. Friction between them was inevitable, and it came, first over minor issues such as the appointment of the principal of the Paoting Military Academy and later over such major problems as the creation of the Central Command to replace the Military Department in the Presidential Office in May 1914.

The Command consisted of the Minister for the Army and the Minister for the Navy, the Chief-of-Staff, and a number of high-ranking officers; Wang Shih-chen, who had been persuaded to come out from his retirement by Yuan Shih-k'ai's eldest son K'e-ting, was in full charge of it, with the assistance of General Yin-ch'ang and Admiral Sa Chen-ping. Having no troops of his own, Wang was no more than the President's puppet, and this was exactly what Yuan wanted. The establishment of the Command however greatly reduced the power of the Ministry for the Army.

To attribute the settling up of the Command entirely to the

[1] PYCFTCSCSH, II, pp. 100–101.

personal wrangles between Yuan and Tuan would be an over-simplification. Another important factor in this decision was Tuan's clumsiness in handling the White Wolf bandits, who began their activities in Honan, Yuan's native province, in the autumn of 1913, waged hit-and-run warfare against the Northern Army under Tuan's personal command in Honan, Anhwei, Hupei, Shensi and Kansu, and eventually came back to Honan where they were at last wiped out by nearly ten divisions of the Government troops in the autumn of 1914. Whatever prestige the Army had gained through defeating the Kuomintang military forces in the 1913 Revolution was now completely lost. White Wolf (Pai-lang)—the bandit leader—and his men put the Northern Army through their severest test yet, and helped to prove that these awe-inspiring modern soldiers were in fact 'toothless'. It was mainly because of this revelation that Yuan dwelt upon the idea of reorganizing his entire military system.

Soon after the end of the White Wolf operations Tuan conveniently fell ill, and had to stay in the Western Hills on the outskirts of Peking to convalesce. At first Yuan allowed him sick-leave and gave him large sums of money for medical treatment, but he finally replaced him with Wang Shih-chen in May 1915. The first thing that Wang did on taking over the Ministry for the Army was to remove Tuan's most trusted deputy, General Hsü Shu-cheng, on a charge of embezzlement.

The discarding of a faithful associate like Tuan Ch'i-jui could not help to rally the support of the Northern Military leaders, neither could it help to raise their deteriorating morale. However General Tuan's dismissal was not to be the worst blow their loyalty to Yuan received. In October 1914, at Yuan K'e-ting's suggestion, the President organized a new army, called the Standard Regiments, under his personal command. The private soldiers were recruited from the non-commissioned officers of the Northern Army and the non-commissioned officers of the new units from the military academies. All of them, before joining up, had to take the oath of allegiance to Yuan. However busy he might be, Yuan was never absent from the weekly inspections of his new troops until his son K'e-ting took over the command in 1915. By the spring of 1915 there were four such infantry regiments, one artillery battalion, and one machine-gun corps. This was a small beginning, but Yuan's ultimate aim was to train ten divisions of new troops to replace the ineffective

Northern Army, and this plan naturally alienated the Army.

The training programme was carried out simultaneously with the reorganization of the provincial governments; this circumstance made both measures look more suspicious from the point of view of local warlords. Yuan's original idea was to abolish the province as an administrative district, so uprooting the fundamental cause of disunity. Commendable as it might be, this plan could not conceivably be carried out without encountering resolute resistance from local military leaders. Therefore his first step was to change the title of 'Military Governor' into that of 'General', at the same time making it very clear that a general's powers would be the same as those of a military governor. On June 30, 1914 he announced a list of twenty-two generals with the character 'Wu' (Martial) in their titles, signifying that they were actually in control of provinces. There was another list of generals whose titles had the character 'Wei' (awe-inspiring), indicating that they were generals who had neither their own troops nor 'sphere of influence'. All of them were however generals and could therefore replace each other. In the Capital itself, a Generals' Headquarters was set up, with the indisposed General Tuan Ch'i-jui at its head. The purpose of this change, it was announced, was 'to put an end to disunity and to begin a new era of peace.'[1]

On the same day Yuan also announced a list of provincial governors whose duties were exclusively civilian. This was evidently an attempt to deprive the warlords of their administrative power, but it failed completely, for the last word always lays with those who had soldiers and guns, and the newly appointed governors invariably became the mouthpieces of the generals. By the dismissal of General Tuan Ch'i-jui from the Ministry for the Army, the creation of the Standard Regiments and the attempt at cutting down the warlords' power in provincial affairs, Yuan Shih-k'ai had managed to antagonize his military men, perhaps in the belief that an empire could only be conquered by soldiers but never to be ruled by them.

The change in the officers' titles was soon followed by a similar step with regard to civilian ranks. Government officials, according to a decree,[2] were to be classified into nine grades—three grades of Lords President (*Ch'ing*), three of Secretaries of State (*Ta-fu*), and three of Honourable Companions (*Shih*). These quaint titles were not the only antique customs and rituals being revived in Yuan's

[1] CFKP, 30.6.1914.
[2] CFKP, 28.7.1914.

Republic. On March 4th, Yuan had issued an Audience Act and had from then on regularly given audience to his subjects. On September 25th he announced his decision to worship Confucius, and preparations were being made for him to worship Heaven, following a similar ceremonial pattern used by the Emperors before him in past centuries. In November he assumed the role of protector of the faith by ordering his people to follow the canons of loyalty, filial piety, fidelity and rectitude. The man directing the preparations was Yuan's Home Minister, Chu Ch'i-ch'ien.

The worship of Heaven was an Imperial prerogative, for only the Emperor, the son of Heaven, might intercede with Heaven for his people. But Chou ingeniously found a new meaning for it, he tried to explain the significance of Yuan's performing such a ceremony to the American Minister Reinsch in this way: 'It would be dangerous for the republican government to neglect the worship of Heaven. . . . Should there follow a leanness or entire failure of crops, the Government would surely be held responsible by the farmers throughout the land.' 'Of course,' he added, smilingly, 'the worship will not guarantee good crops, but at any rate it will relieve the Government of responsibility.' Chu also assured the Minister: 'In the ritual, we shall introduce some changes appropriate to republicanism.'[1]

At the winter solstice, December 23rd, at the crack of dawn, the President drove in an armoured car to the magnificent Altar of Heaven, on the southern outskirts of Peking. The entire route was covered with yellow sand—a necessary detail for an Imperial drive—and lined three-deep with soldiers who had been stationed there the evening before. When the retinue arrived at the gate south of the Altar, the President changed to a vermilion coach which carried him to the immediate vicinity of the Altar, whence he was carried in a sedan-chair up into the temple. There he was helped up the marble steps by Generals Yin-ch'ang and Lu Chin, and then changed out of his Field-marshal's uniform into the sacrificial robe and headgear. The robe was royal purple, adorned with twelve circular dragon designs, and the headgear was of the ancient Imperial design but without the nine strings of beads. This omission, the armoured motor-car, the purple colour and the address—'I, Yuan Shih-k'ai, representing the Republic of China' instead of 'Your son and vassal'—in the prayers were the changes 'appropriate to republicanism'

[1] *An American Diplomat in China*, pp. 24-25.

referred to in Chu Ch'i-ch'ien's conversation with Reinsch. Ninety minutes later, the ceremony was over and the President was swiftly driven back to the Forbidden City. This was one of his only two excursions out of the City between 1912 and 1914.

About two months after this comedy Yuan was seen at the ceremony dedicated to the immortal memory of Confucius, which took place at four o'clock one morning. Reinsch was again an eyewitness, and among the lofty porticoes, immemorial ilex trees, gorgeous costumes and an array of primeval musical instruments which no one quite knew how to play, he perceived some kind of 'sound instinct' by which the dignitaries refused 'to cast off entirely such traditions'.[1]

A Chinese, however, would interpret the revival of these antiquated rites in a different way. He would know that it was a prelude to the restoration of the monarchical system, and would therefore watch its development with a mixture of misgiving and self-indulgent nonchalance. Yuan's own statements did not help to make the future more assured. In 1913 the President had praised republicanism as 'the best political system' and had pledged to Heaven and Earth that he would not live to see the restoration of a monarchy in China.[2] Four months later, at the height of the Second Revolution, he once more assured the nation of his lack of interest in personal power, for, according to him, 'an old man of sixty had no ambition'.[3] He was actually only fifty-three. In the following year Dr Morrison, Yuan's political adviser, on a tour of Europe, categorically denied that his employer had any intention of founding a family dynasty.[4] But Sir John Jordan was less certain. In his report to Langley, he said: 'There seems no reason why he should seek the throne when he has all the power that any occupant of it could wish for.'[5]

Indeed, Yuan's personal power was not only widened but also prolonged after the outbreak of the war in Europe. On August 18th the obedient Council of State endorsed a suggestion that the Presidential Election Law should be amended, and the Constitutional Compact Conference duly revised it on December 28th. Under the new law the President's term of office was to be prolonged from five to ten years, with the privilege of being re-elected any number of

[1] ibid, p. 27.
[2] CFKP, 19.3.1913.
[3] CFKP, 21.7.1913.
[4] *The Times*, 25.6.1914.
[5] 8.2.1914.

times. If the Council of State deemed it justified, the President could
stay in office continuously without going through the procedure of a
re-election. It also stipulated that at each election the President was
to nominate three candidates, whose names were to be written on a
gold plate which was to be locked up in a gold casket and the keys
kept by the President, the Minister of State, and the Speaker of the
Council of State. No other candidates were to be considered apart
from the ones nominated on the gold plate.[1] By these arrangements
Yuan was assured of the Presidency for life, with the prospect that
one of his sons might succeed him. For any ordinary aspirant this
should have been quite sufficient, but Yuan was anything but
ordinary. His declared indifference to personal power was no more
credible than his pretence of being an old man of sixty. Very few
took him literally.

In February 1914 Liang Ch'i-ch'ao, the Minister of Justice, was
invited to dinner by Yuan K'e-ting; the other guests included the
President's adviser, Yang Tu. The company discussed the problem
of republicanism versus monarchy, and it became obvious to Liang
that his host was deeply interested in becoming the crown-prince of
a new dynasty. Soon after this Liang resigned his post and went to
live in Tientsin. In his farewell letter to the President, he quoted
from an ancient classic to remind him: 'Rites, justice, incorruptibility
and a sense of shame are the basic principles of an administration
without which the government will perish.'[2] But Yuan was too
obsessed with his dreams of imperial glory to be enlightened.

In June 1915 the signs of a dynasty in the making became increasingly evident. In addition to the new grading of civil servants and
the revival of antique rites, Yuan decided to honour his meritorious
officials and generals with five noble ranks. General Feng Kuo-chang,
anxious to find out Yuan's true intentions, took Liang Ch'i-ch'ao
with him to Peking. The fact that Liang went with him suggested
that Feng was planning to dissuade Yuan from this adventure, and
was therefore against the founding of a new imperial dynasty. In
Peking the general had several talks with the President, who
denounced the rumours about a revival of the monarchy as
completely groundless, and made it clear that, since his power as
President was almost limitless, there was no reason for him to
transform the political system. Yuan went on:

[1] Chou I-ping and Lo Chih-yüan, *Chung-kuo-hsien-cheng-fa-chan-shih*, 1944, p. 119.
[2] *Yin-ping-shih-ho-chi*, ch. 33, p. 22.

'I am certainly not stupid enough to try it on behalf of my sons and grandsons. People began to suspect this because I had restored the five noble ranks for the Han Chinese. This I consider as absolutely necessary, for in this multi-racial country of ours it is only the Han Chinese who are not eligible for such distinction. I fail to see why a Han Chinese cannot be granted a noble title. After all, the Draft Constitution does not forbid me to do so.

'However I have postponed the award of such ranks for the moment because of people's suspicious feeling. I shall definitely do it in future, but without the slightest suggestion that I shall, at the same time, revive the monarchical system.

'Some people seem to think that they have no time to lose [in their effort to nip the monarchical movement in the bud]. If they press me too hard I shall leave China to settle in England, where I have bought some land as my home.'[1]

In another interview with General Feng, Yuan reasoned thus:

'The only possible difference [between a president and an emperor] lies in the succession. But my eldest son, K'e-ting, is suffering from a chronic disease; the second, K'e-wen, wishes to lead a secluded life; the third is quite unsuitable for government duties, and the others are still very young. I would hesitate to make any of them a lieutenant, not to speak of entrusting to them the heavy duties of a state. Furthermore, since time immemorial the offspring of kings and emperors have been put on the throne only to fall victims to various kinds of disasters. I certainly have no heart to impose such hazards on my children.'[2]

After these assurances, Feng returned satisfied to the south. But his companion, Liang Ch'i-ch'ao, remained in the north.

In Peking the monarchical movement went from strength to strength. Soon after General Feng's departure, Dr F. J. Goodnow presented Yuan with a memorandum on governmental systems which was published in a newspaper—Yuan's mouthpiece, *the Asia* —and was reported in Tokyo papers on August 11th and in *The Times* on September 9th. Dr Goodnow had been a student of constitutional law in Germany. His appointment was a result of Charles William Eliot's visit to China in 1913, when Chinese

---

[1] Feng's statement, *Shen-pao*, 6.7.1915.
[2] *Shen-pao*, 9.7.1915.

officials had expressed to him the wish that an American should be retained as adviser to the Chinese Government. President Eliot of Harvard suggested that the Carnegie Endowment might nominate some experts from whom the Chinese Government could make a selection. This suggestion was followed, and as a result Dr Goodnow of Columbia University, now an authority on constitutional law, came to China. The English original of the memorandum, according to Dr Goodnow himself, was not available. Below are some extracts translated back from its Chinese version:

'China is a country which has for centuries been accustomed to autocratic rule. The intelligence of the great mass of its people is not high, owing to the lack of schools. The Chinese have never been accorded much participation in the work of government. The result is that the political capacity of the Chinese people is not large. The change from autocratic to republican government made four years ago was too violent to permit the entertainment of any very strong hopes of its immediate success.

'The present arrangement cannot be regarded as satisfactory. When the present President lays down the cares of office there is great danger that the difficulties which are usually incident to the succession in countries conditioned as is China will present themselves. The attempt to solve these difficulties may lead to disorders which if long continued may seriously imperil the independence of the country.

'What under these conditions should be the attitude of those who have the welfare of China at heart? Should they advocate the continuance of the Republic or should they propose the establishment of a monarchy?'

To these questions, the author provided an answer in favour of a change to a monarchical system, provided these conditions were fulfilled: 1. that there was no strong opposition either from the Chinese people or from foreign powers (since such opposition might lead to disorder); 2. that the line of succession was to be clearly defined by legislation rather than by the monarch himself; 3. that a form of constitutional government was to be developed under the Crown.[1]

[1] H. F. MacNair, *Modern Chinese History*, pp. 743-746, also *Jung-yen*, II, Nos. 1-2, pp. 9-10.

Why such an eminent scholar should have come forward to speak in such a naïve manner for Yuan Shih-k'ai on this ticklish question still remains a historical mystery. However, the significant thing was that Dr Goodnow was a foreigner, *a citizen of a republic*, and an outstanding student of his subject, whose views should therefore be objective, and who was of the opinion that, for her own benefit, China should choose a new form of Government. The publication of the memorandum shook the whole nation.

Yang Tu, the Hunanese political opportunist, who had written a report on constitutional government for the five high officials sent abroad to study this question in 1905, who had dallied with the Revolutionary forces in 1911 as a member of the Imperial Peace Delegation, and who was still trusted by Yuan, was anxious to create political capital for himself by giving the monarchical movement his early support. In August 1915 he and five others sponsored and organized for this purpose a society under the name of 'Ch'ou An Hui' (Planning for Peace). The name implied that unless a monarchy was established China might not have peace. The five other founders of the Society were Hu Ying, Sun Yü-yun, Li Hsieh-ho, Yen Fu and Liu Shih-p'ei. The first three had been members of the Kuomintang and taken part in the revolts in and before 1911, especially Hu Ying, who had played a leading role in the Hankow uprising, and Li Hsieh-ho, who had spoken so bluntly against Yuan Shih-k'ai during the peace negotiations between the Revolutionaries and the Manchu Government. Yen Fu, trained at Greenwich as a naval cadet, had been the first to translate Adam Smith, J. S. Mill and Herbert Spencer into Chinese, and was a celebrated essayist and scholar besides, Liu Shih-p'ei too was a scholar of fame; once upon a time he had attacked the Ch'ing monarchical system, but now he came forward to speak in favour of the founding of a dynasty by Yuan. These six, of whom three were Hunanese, were known ironically as the Six Gentlemen of the Society of Planning for Peace, in contrast to the Six Gentlemen who had been executed in 1898 after the evanescent Reform. Four of them readily accepted Yang Tu's invitation to sponsor the Society and shared his anxiety to draw their dividends as early as possible. Yen Fu was hesitant, but on the evening before the announcement of the Society's foundation was published he received a note from Yang Tu, which ran:

'Let me tell you candidly that I am acting under the instructions of the highest authority, who insists that your name must be included in the list of sponsors. It would be inconvenient for you to refuse and it would be unwise to lose this opportunity. The announcement will be in the papers tomorrow. I cannot wait for your reply before attaching your name to it. Knowing you to be an understanding person, I am sure you will raise no objection.'[1]

This historic document duly appeared in the Peking papers on August 14th together with a message to the generals and governors of the provinces, requesting them to send delegates to the Capital to discuss the problem of an adequate political system for China. Having praised Dr Goodnow's 'splendid' argument in favour of a monarchical system, the announcement went on to say that the Society was merely a study group with a special interest in comparing the merits and demerits of republicanism and monarchy. On August 23rd the Society held its first meeting at which Yang and Sun were elected President and Vice-President, and the other four of the Six Gentlemen members of its executive committee. It was incredible that the 'delegates' from distant places could have come all the way for the meeting at nine days' notice. Apart from electing the executive committee, they passed a resolution in favour of China's adopting a monarchical system. The reason for this rush was that the Council of State would reassemble on September 1st and the Society was planning to present a petition to the Council asking the President to assume the exalted title of Emperor.

The Society's first announcement read:

'At the time of the 1911 Revolution, our people were so anxious to destroy the racial discrimination then in existence as to have neglected the necessary political arrangements afterwards. The adoption of a republican government was, to say the least, a rush decision, but once taken, no one dared to challenge it. The thinking people were aware that it did not promise well, but for their own safety they were prepared to be pliable. The perilous situation that faced the country and the suffering endured by our people between the Manchu Abdication and the inauguration of the Republican Government and during the transition from the Provisional to the present Government, is still in everyone's memory. If nothing is done to prevent its recurrence the nation will suffer untold harm.

[1] Chou Chen-fu, *Yen Fu Ssu-hsiang-yen-chiu*, p. 258.

'In recent times republics of Central and South America like Brazil, Argentine, Peru, Chile, Uruguay, and Venezuela all have had civil wars arising from party conflicts. Portugal adopted republicanism, which was the cause of her recent crises. The worst example was Mexico, where since the resignation of Diaz, there has not been a single day of peace. Mexican party leaders all have their own troops to fight against one another. The victorious ones occupy parts of the country and the vanquished loot, slaughter the people and set fire to houses before their retreat. Now the country is ruled by five presidents, and is in a state of lamentable anarchy. Ours is also a new republic, although it is in the East. Is Mexico to set an example for us?

'The United States of America is the oldest republic in the world. Yet its great expert in political theory, Dr Goodnow, had declared that, as a political system, monarchy is actually better than republicanism, and that China must choose the monarchy. Dr Goodnow is by no means the only one who advocates this. Scholars of many lands agree with him. He is a citizen of a republic and therefore his views on republicanism ought to carry great weight. Yet he says that conditions in China are different from those in the United States, and it is therefore arbitrary to transplant an American system to our country. Foreigners who wish us well loudly warn us [against drifting along as we have been doing], yet we ourselves give in to what is called the fate instead of seeking for a fundamental solution. Some of us, who know the perilous situation facing our country, hesitate to speak up for fear of undesirable consequences to themselves. Are they being patriotic? Can this be the right way to discharge a citizen's duties?

'We are citizens of China. The survival of our country is our own survival. How can we sit back, waiting for and watching her destruction? So we gather together to form this Society in order to plan for peace in our land. We shall study and discuss the merits and demerits of republicanism in order to find out the truth about it and to present the results to our fellow-countrymen. It will be China's fortune if our far-sighted people understand the purposes of this Society and join us in our quest.'

And its case was eloquently put forward in a lengthy article by Yang Tu, *A Defence of the Monarchical Movement*,[1] which began by posing

[1] Pai Chiao, YSKYCHMK, pp. 177-207 and Putnam Weale, *Fight*, pp. 113-127.

two sensational questions? Why is it that there is no hope of China's becoming strong? Why is it that there is no hope of China's ever becoming rich? The answer, provided by the author himself, lay in the fact that China's officials, officers and scholars were mostly corrupt. Had it not been for Yuan Shih-k'ai the country would have been in turmoil for some time. But the President was mortal like everyone else, and after his death, the author foresaw a 'deluge', for none of the three successors to him named on the gold plate was sufficiently qualified to replace him. Yang could not begin to pretend that he knew the names of the successors; that was a state secret. What he meant was that there was no one good enough to succeed Yuan Shih-k'ai.

The author then turned to a general discussion on the conditions for an effective republican government which, in his view, depended upon the people having a comparatively high level of education, some political experience, and certain political ethics. Where these did not exist, the election of Presidents would be sure to cause internal disturbances, because there were always ambitious people who would contend for the Presidency, and to many others this would be less of a crime than to contend for a throne. If by chance an able man won a struggle, law and order might prevail during his term of office; if not, the disorder arising from the contest would continue. In either case steady pursuit of a long-term policy would be impossible, as it had often been said that the success of a policy depended entirely upon the man who piloted it.

According to Yang Tu, none of these dangers would arise in a monarchy where the people and the soldiers knew to whom they owed their loyalty, and statesmen and officials, whose interests were bound up with the welfare of the Imperial family, knew how to deal with an emergency when it arose. There would then be obedience and discipline, out of which the country's wealth and strength could grow.

Yang's main point was in order to avoid the intermittent upheavals arising from the problem of succession, China should change from a republic to a constitutional empire. He insisted that a constitution was the only guarantee of the continuity of policy and an emperor the only figure who could command enough loyalty and respect to rally the nation together.

A week after the publication of Yang's article, Liang Ch'i ch'ao, in the sanctuary of the Tientsin concessions, completed his critique of it under the title *The Strange Problem of the Form of Government.*

Yuan got wind of it and sent a man to offer the author 200,000 yuan in an attempt to prevent him from publishing it. The messenger also threatened Liang with banishment, but he would not budge.

Eventually Liang's article was published, to be relished by thousands of readers. He asked 'What guarantee have those who argue in favour of a monarchical system that after the proposed change a constitution will be adopted and observed . . . ? If they have none, then all that we are left with is a monarchy without a constitution. In other words, what we may have is not a constitutional but an autocratic empire. I do not understand how can an autocracy be a better alternative to this imperfect republic.'

Liang admitted that the Presidential succession might be a cause of recurring disturbances, but he advanced this argument on the other side:

'Let us look back at the history of our Imperial Houses. It is littered with intrigue, contention, and corpses. This shows clearly that the factors which determine war and peace lie elsewhere than in the constitutional forms of a republic or a monarchy.'

Furthermore,

'A monarch depends on a kind of metaphysical power which is a product of history and custom to preserve his dignity, and his dignity has inexplicable strength by which the peace and order of a country can be maintained. This is undoubtedly the most treasured quality in a monarch. But that dignity must never be blemished. Once blemished, it ceases to be dignity.'[1]

Since the unceremonious abdication of the last emperor had taken place only a few years ago, Liang did not think that it was wise to revive monarchy in China.

Having failed to stop the publication of this essay, Yuan turned to the scholar Yen Fu for literary help, offering him 40,000 yuan if he would write a reply to Liang Ch'i-ch'ao. Yen declined. At the same time Chang Ch'ien, who had been in the Capital trying to get his Huai River conservancy project taken up and put into practice, paid his old friend the President a farewell visit during which he exhorted him to abandon his imperial ambitions. Yuan refused to do so.[2]

[1] Pai Chiao, YSKYCHMK, pp. 215-239
[2] *Chang Chi-tzu chiu lu*, ch. 4, p. 15a.

o

Instead, he publicly announced that he had no wish to interfere with whatever the people were discussing,[1] and his Government also declared that it was not going to stop the activities of the Society of Planning for Peace.[2]

Yang Tu and his fellow 'Gentlemen' were not the only politically conscious sycophants. Liang Shih-i, the leader of the Communication Clique and Yuan's wealthy lieutenant, had been convalescing in the Western Hills since June from an attack on his embezzlement of railway funds; he too was anxious to exploit the situation to secure his own return to both favour and power. Under his leadership and with his financial support, the National Petitioners' Association was formed on September 19th; its inauguration stole the limelight from Yang's Society. It was ironical that Liang should once again have put Yang Tu's nose out of joint. They had encountered each other first in 1899, when they both sat for the Metropolitan Economics Examination; Liang actually beat his rival to the second place, but the examiners noticed that Liang Shih-i was a Kwangtung man, a fellow provincial of K'ang Yu-wei and Liang Ch'i-ch'ao, the leaders of the 1898 Reform. Worse still, *Liang's* family name was the same as that of *Liang* Ch'i-ch'ao and his personal name, *I*, the same as K'ang Yu-wei's courtesy name, Tsu-*i*. These were taken as signs that he was a rebel, and consequently his name was struck off the list. This small personal grudge between Liang and Yang had never been settled and now they faced each other once more as rivals in supporting the monarchical movement.

On the very next day, September 20th, the Council of State discussed the 'people's petition' and resolved on convening a National Congress of Representatives to decide the issue. After this, swarms of petitioners assembled in the Capital in less than a month, whereas normally it took four or five months to come from places like Sinkiang, Chinghai, or Tibet. Meanwhile messages from the military leaders in all provinces including T'ang Chi-yao of Yunnan and Chang Tso-lin of Fengt'ien, but not Feng Kuo-chang or Chang Hsün, streamed into Peking, urging the President to 'rectify his title and position'.[3]

The old city suddenly became animated; preparations were busily made for the convocation of the National Congress of Representatives.

---

[1] *Shen-pao*, 17.8.1915.
[2] *Shen-pao*, 27.8.1915.
[3] CFKP, 25.12.1915.

On September 26th Sun (perhaps Sun Yü-yun) telegraphed the generals and governors of the provinces:

'Now we are pursuing another way of finding out the consensus of opinion. Please select one man from each county to form provisional citizens' congresses.'[1]

Three days later, Chu (probably Chu Ch'i-ch'ien) also telegraphed the generals and governors:

'Now we are planning to organize citizens' congresses in order to decide on this important policy as swiftly as possible. The method by which these congresses are organized will be determined by the Council of State, but the Spirit by which they are guided can only come from you. Each county must have one representative and the safest way of selecting him is to choose from your subordinates.'[2]

On October 7th, Chu again sent telegrams to the generals and governors, saying:

'The words, "Respectfully urging the present President, Yuan Shih-k'ai, to assume the title of the Emperor of the Chinese Empire", must be included in your telegrams to the President and you should also telegraph the Council of State asking it in the name of the citizens' congresses to deputize for you in this matter. The more signatures you can gather the better. Please also draft in advance the congratulatory messages on the occasion of the forthcoming enthronement.'[3]

All these telegrams were earmarked either 'Board, Confidential' or 'China, Confidential', indicating that they were secret messages from the Board of Political Affairs or from Yuan himself.'[4]

Towards the end of November the preparations were near completion. Another confidential telegram was sent out to the generals and governors:

'The following words must be included in your messages exhorting

[1] Liang Ch'i-ch'ao, *Yin-ping-shih-ho-chi*, ch. 33, p. 100.
[2] ibid, p. 100
[3] ibid, p 101.
[4] ibid, p. 104 and Pai Chiao, YSKYCHMK, pp. 270-273.

the President to accept the throne: "We, the representatives of the people, represent the true wish of the whole nation in urging the present President, Yuan Shih-k'ai, to assume the title of Emperor and in giving him the greatest possible power of an emperor. May Heaven save him. May his son and grandsons inherit this position for a myriad generations to come".'[1]

The last of the monarchists' communications read:

'No matter how careful we are, some of the communications between us may survive as permanent records. Once they are know to outsiders, we cannot hope to escape the severest criticism and attack and they will mar the opening chapter of the history of the new dynasty. After careful deliberations, the Central Government has decided that all the communications should be burnt. . . . Please supervise the destruction in person.'[2]

The cremation was carried out on March 29, 1916.[3] But long before that, the National Congress of Representatives had been convoked. The 1,993 members unanimously voted for the adoption of a monarchical system and supported Yuan's elevation to the throne. Unanimity alone was not enough; all the votes bore the very same *forty-five* characters as had been laid down in the November telegram. Chou Tzu-ch'i, a confidant of Yuan's later told Reinsch: 'We tried to get some people to vote in the negative just for appearance's sake, but they would not do it.'[4] Chou was obviously trying to impress his American listener of the people's enthusiasm towards the proposed governmental change.

The vote took place on November 21st and on December 12th the Council of State, acting in the capacity of a legislative body, which it was not, on a resolution proposed by Prince P'u-lun,[5] presented a *memorial* of three thousand words urging the President to accept the throne. It was couched in the same style as the Book of Rites and addressed the President as 'Your Holy Majesty'.[6] The President once more showed his customary modesty by refusing it. Fifteen

[1] Pai Chiao, ibid, p. 272.
[2] Pai Chiao, ibid, p. 273.
[3] Liang, *Nien-p'u*, p. 331.
[4] Reinsch, *An American Diplomat in China*, p. 179.
[5] *The Times*, 14.12.1915.
[6] CFKP, 12.12.1915.

minutes later another memorial of equal length was ready for presentation, beginning by praising Yuan Shih-k'ai's virtuous refusal and ending with the insistence that he must accept the mandate of Heaven. Yuan graciously gave his consent on December 12th.

At once his Minister of State and sworn brother Hsü Shih-ch'ang fell ill. His duties were taken over by Lu Cheng-hsiang. On December 15th, the President made General Li Yuan-hung a prince in a decree which bore the President's seal-mark,[1] but this seal-mark disappeared from his decrees two days later. Since General Li was now a prince, General Feng Kuo-chang, whose lukewarm support of the monarchy had not pleased Yuan Shih-k'ai, was ordered to leave his post in Nanking in order to be transferred to the now vacant post of Chief-of-Staff. Both Li and Feng declined to accept their new dignities, the former out of sheer courtesy and the latter trying to avoid getting involved and losing the rich province of Kiangsu, but eventually General Li succumbed.

The first heir-apparent of the Han dynasty (206 B.C. to A.D. 9) had four elderly friends on Mount Shang; and in Honan, Yuan's native province, there is the Central Sacred Mountain, Mount Sung. Therefore Yuan Shih-k'ai made Hsü Shih-ch'ang, Chao Erh-hsün, Li Ching-hsi and Chang Ch'ien, all of whom had resigned their posts since the monarchical movement began, the Four Friends of Mount Sung.[2] All his important generals were created dukes, or marquises, or earls, fulfilling his promise to give Han Chinese noble titles.

To the other Imperial Court in the same city, Yuan promised no change in the agreed treatment which had been in operation since the Manchu Abdication, except that the allowance had not been paid regularly. The relations between the two Courts were as amiable as could be expected. Yuan even succeeded in inducing Prince P'u-lun, the pretender to the throne whom Yuan had supported in 1908, to kowtow to him and call himself 'Your subject'.[3]

The ceremonial aspects of the preparations for the establishment of the new Empire were taken care of by an office set up as early as September. The new dynasty was to be named 'Hung-hsien' which, according to Yuan himself, meant a 'Grand Constitutional Era'.[4]

[1] CFKP, 15.12.1915.
[2] CFKP, 20.12.1915.
[3] R. Johnston, *Twilight*, p. 120–121.
[4] Reinsch, *An American Diplomat in China*, p. 186.

The eunuch system, according to a decree of December 22, 1915, was not to be revived; instead, the new Emperor would have women as his palace officials. Early in 1916, he sent one Kuo Pao-ch'ang to Chingtechen to supervise the manufacture of 40,000 porcelain pieces for his palace at a cost of 1·4 million yuan.[1] This, compared with other items, was a small sum. The Society of Planning for Peace cost the Emperor from two to three million yuan; the redecoration of the three main palace-halls, 2·7 million; the two Imperial robes, 800,000; the jade seal, 120,000 yuan; and the budget for the enthronement ceremony, 6 million.[2] It was estimated that the enthronement would cost the Treasury altogether nearly 30 million yuan. Whence was the money to come?

The budget of 1916 showed a deficit of nearly 89 million yuan,[3] but, according to the Finance Minister's own speech introducing the budget, the actual revenue for that year could not be expected to exceed 150 million while actual expenditure would be no less than 470 million.[4] Under such circumstances, Yuan had to rely on borrowing and issuing irredeemable banknotes to finance the founding of his empire. Liang Shih-i, now restored to favour again, was given the task of floating a loan of 20 million yuan, but even he could not manage to sell bonds for more than one third of that sum.[5] Both the Bank of China and the Bank of Communications gave Yuan their generous support. Apart from these sources, Yuan also sent a trusted official to Kwangtung ostensibly to enforce the prohibition of the opium traffic, but, in fact, to sell the right to sell the drug. This proved to be unexpectedly lucrative.

All seemed to be going well. In a cave in Ich'ang, local officials even discovered the fossil of a 'divine dragon' which news was deemed important enough to merit a government announcement on January 15, 1916, and was undoubtedly regarded as an auspicious confirmation of the Mandate of Heaven. Foreign powers however believed neither in this nor in the apparent popular demand for a change; as Sir John Jordan candidly told Liang Shih-i: 'Foreigners knew perfectly well that the whole agitation was engineered from Peking.'[6]

[1] *Ching-te-chen-t'ao-tz'u-shih-kao*, 1915, pp. 305-306.
[2] Pai Chiao, YSKYCHMK, pp. 347-348.
[3] Chia Shih-i, *Min-kuo-ts'ai-cheng-shih*, p. 76.
[4] Chia, ibid, p. 193.
[5] Liang, *Nien-p'u*, p. 331.
[6] Jordan to Langley, 23.9.1915.

By June and July, the Legations in Peking were sure that Yuan had made his decision, but the European War prevented them from taking effective steps either to support or to oppose it. Japan was in a totally different position—her commitments in the War being light and, after the success of the Twenty-one Demands, her ambitions in China almost limitless. It was her support that Yuan must now enlist, to forestall his opponents. Therefore he sent his Japanese adviser, Dr Ariga, to Tokyo, to try to explain the necessity of the proposed change to Japanese statesmen and to sway Japanese public opinion. In September the *Japan Advertiser* carried these comments from Marquis Okuma:

'If the Chinese have come to their senses, it is natural that they wish to revive the monarchy.'

and

'It is to be expected that President Yuan will become Emperor if the monarchy is revived.'[1]

Although the Prime Minister later disclaimed these widely publicized statements in the Diet, Yuan could only conclude that the Twenty-one Demands had done their work by mellowing Japan's hostility towards him. Jordan had the same impression:

'They [the Japanese] are encouraging the movement here and Count Okuma has, if the enclosed notice is authentic, publicly declared in its favour. One explanation, to which I do not attach very serious importance, is that Yuan has made his terms with the Japanese. He is to be Emperor of China Proper and the Manchu reversion of Manchuria is to go to Japan. The Japanese tell the Chinese that now is the moment to go ahead.'[2]

Meanwhile, in Peking, the absence of Minister Hioki since the summer was keenly felt, for it made the Japanese attitude towards the monarchical movement extremely difficult to gauge, especially as his deputy was the taciturn Councillor Obata.[3]

As a further expression of friendliness, Yuan appointed his Minister of Agriculture and Commerce, Chou Tzu-ch'i, and the

---

[1] Quoted from Jordan to Langley, 23.9.1915.
[2] Jordan to Langley, 23.9.1915.
[3] Jordan to Langley, 20.10.1915.

Chinese Minister to Japan, Lu Tsung-yü, his special envoys at the Mikado's enthronement, and he also announced the decision to confer upon the new Japanese monarch the highest medal of the *Republic of China*. At first Tokyo welcomed these gestures and promised to receive Yuan's representatives as *princes from a kingdom*. At this stage, Japan on the surface was inclined to regard the forthcoming change as a Chinese internal affair and to maintain the appearance of neutrality. Though her people in general and the army in particular were opposed to the proposed change, her Foreign Ministry remained reticent on the subject. In October, however, there was a reshuffle of the Japanese Cabinet and, consequently, a change in her policy. The new Foreign Minister took the view that the movement now afoot in China might disturb the peace in the Far East, in which case Japan could not remain inactive.[1] Gradually Japan's attitude crystallized; she formulated a remonstrance to the Chinese Government against the proposed monarchy. She also asked Britain, Russia and the United States to associate themselves with her in this. The United States showed no interest, while Jordan reported to Langley:

'It would be folly to ignore the Japanese diagnosis of the situation and the only safe course is to join in the advice they propose to give China.'[2]

Russia's reaction to the Japanese proposal was also favourable, but China got wind of this move, and tried to forestall it by sending to Japan on October 25th and to Britain, France, Russia and the United States on October 27th a Note of explanation which defended Yuan's intention to accept the throne as the result of deference to the people's request.[3] On October 28th, a Note of Advice in the name of Japan, Britain, and Russia was delivered to the Chinese Foreign Office, whose reply was later handed to the Legations concerned. Apart from repeating the hackneyed tune of 'popular demand for a change', it gave the additional reason that the instability of the Republican régime had discouraged foreign investment during the past four years. On November 3rd and 5th, France and Italy joined Japan. Now five countries in all had declared their

---

[1] Lu Tsung-yü to the Foreign Ministry, 15.10.1915.
[2] 20.10.1915.
[3] Wang Yun-sheng, LSNLCKYJP, VII, pp. 7-8.

opposition to Yuan's bid for the throne, so Chu Ch'i-ch'ien and other enthusiasts at once telegraphed the generals and governors urging them to show 'determination and unity, in the hope that the Japanese-sponsored advice will become meaningless', and also imploring them to treat this message as 'extremely confidential'.[1] As a result of this telegram, petitions from provincial leaders flooded into Peking, exhorting Yuan Shih-k'ai to advance the date of his accession.

Yuan was not in the least perturbed by the remonstrances. The National Congress of Representatives was convoked and the vote taken, in spite of Japan's attempts, through both her Foreign Minister and Mr Hioki, to prevent it.[2] The train of events culminated on December 12th in Yuan's acceptance of the throne, which was followed, three days later, by yet another representation from the Minister of Britain, Japan, France, Russia, and Italy. The last of Japan's remonstrances was couched in a severe tone and was delivered verbally by Mr Hioki, who expressed the powers' doubts of Yuan's ability to maintain peace and order during and after the political change and their decision to watch over the conduct of the Chinese Government.[3]

That the remonstrances were entirely Japan's idea is clearly shown in a despatch from Sir John Jordan to Sir Walter Langley:

'. . . they [the Japanese] have been making themselves and us ridiculous by all these repeated representations which have produced no effect except antagonizing the Chinese and driving them into the hands of the Germans. . . . we [Jordan and his colleagues] all feel that we are so many puppets pulled by Japanese strings'.[4]

Being a close friend of Jordan's, Yuan probably knew how much the British Minister disliked the whole idea. Though he realized the seriousness of the Japanese warning, he was ignorant of the fact that, since the outbreak of the European War, Britain's influence in the Far East had been waning as her prestige was. Therefore he remained unperturbed, and the preparations for the accession went on. On the last day of 1915 he announced that the next day

[1] Liang Ch'i-ch'ao, *Yin-ping-shih-ho-chi*, ch. 33, p. 103.
[2] Wang Yün-sheng, LSNLCKYJP, VII, pp. 17–18.
[3] Pai Chiao, YSKYCHMK, p. 298.
[4] 21.12.1915.

would be the first day of Grand Constitutional Era (Hung-hsien), but the date of accession was still to be fixed.

It was plain to everyone in China that the Emperor was now diplomatically isolated, but he still had another card to play. His Minister of Agriculture and Commerce would be going to Japan as his special envoy at the Mikado's enthronement—an opportunity to win over his powerful neighbour at the eleventh hour. The date of departure was fixed as January 17th. Shortly before that day Minister Hioki gave a lavish banquet in honour of the envoy, and a good deal of cordiality was shown, but, still before he left, Japan had second thoughts, which were expressed through the same cordial host. Since the Chinese in the south suspected that the purpose of the mission was not wholly honourable, and other powers were beginning to doubt the sincerity of Japan's objections to the change to monarchy, Hioki suggested that the Chinese envoy should delay his voyage. Japan felt that it was awkward to receive him and the Mikado did not think that the Order of a dying republic which Yuan Shih-k'ai was to give him was in any sense an honour.[1]

This happened only a day after the Government had announced the discovery of the 'divine dragon' fossil in Ich'ang. Heaven it seems had changed its mind.

[1] Liang, *Nien-p'u*, p. 299, Pai Chiao, YSKYCHMK, p. 329, and Wang Yün-sheng, LSNLCKYJP, VII, p. 33.

CHAPTER XI

The Downfall 1916

WHILE Japan was trying to isolate Yuan Shih-k'ai diplomatically, a great division among the Chinese leaders gradually became clear. Yang Tu and Liang Shih-i, both committed so deeply to the monarchical adventure and both with an eye on the first premiership of the Empire, continued to voice their support for the founding of the new dynasty. Yuan's eldest son, K'e-ting, who now had the Standard Regiments behind him, would not easily abandon the enticing glory of being a crown-prince. Tuan Chih-kuei, who had always called Yuan 'Father', and Chu Ch'i-ch'ien, who had designed all the ceremonial details of the new dynasty, had no option but to cast in their lot with their master. These people however had no military power to influence the issue. Among the generals, Yuan Shih-k'ai could count on the support of Ts'ao K'un, Chang Ching-yao, Ni Ssu-ch'ung, Ch'en Huan, Lei Chen-ch'un and T'ang Hsiang-ming, who were then stationed in Anhwei, Hunan, Hupei and Szechwan.

On the other hand, there were also influential people who either actively or passively resisted the political change. Of Yuan's old friends, Chang Ch'ien left Peking as soon as the whole agitation became open, and Hsü Shih-ch'ang retired on account of ill-health; of his old lieutenants, Tuan Ch'i-jui and Feng Kuo-chang were both 'sick' and Wang Shih-chen's attitude was equivocal. These last three were known as the Big Three of the Northern Army. There was also the Progressive Party under the leadership of Li Yuan-hung, Liang Ch'i-ch'ao, Ts'ai O and others, which through the powerful pen of Liang spoke vehemently against the prospective Emperor. The once robust Kuomintang, though outlawed and rendered ineffectual by Yuan's ruthless suppression, was waiting for its chance.

Sitting between these two groups, the military leaders in Kiangsu,

Chekiang, Shantung, Shansi and, particularly, in the south-west provinces of Yunnan, Kweichow, Kwangtung and Kwangsi were all watching events as they developed with keen interest, but remained as inscrutable as the Sphinx. The destiny of Yuan Shih-k'ai was in the balance; it was a time for caution, not for false moves.

In November 1915 a brilliant young soldier who was in charge of redrawing the provincial boundaries followed many of his distinguished colleagues in Peking in falling ill. He was Ts'ai O, a Hunanese who had received his military training in Japan and his political indoctrination from Liang Ch'i-ch'ao. He had trained many cadets in Kwangsi and Yunnan, and therefore had great influence among the soldiers there. At the time of the 1911 Revolution he was elected Military Governor of Yunnan, which post he was forced to vacate after the collapse of the Second Revolution in 1913. Since then he had been put under Yuan's surveillance in the Capital while holding titular posts of various kinds. When Yang Tu, Ts'ai's fellow-provincial, was eagerly canvassing for the Hung-hsien Empire, Ts'ai O had become acquainted with a beautiful courtesan and was apparently captivated by her. His frequent visits to the brothel made his claim of indisposition sound reasonable, so at the end of November Yuan Shih-k'ai was convinced that it was necessary for Ts'ai to go to Japan for medical treatment, and he graciously gave him permission.

Prior to Ts'ai's departure, Liang Ch'i-ch'ao tendered his resignation as a member of the Council of State, thus severing his last link with Yuan's Government. Like many others, he too made his request on the ground of indisposition. In his letter to Yuan from the Japanese Concession in Tientsin where he then lived he also asked for a passport for a proposed trip to America. He was so careful as to fill in the date for the passport, January 17th, the first year of Hung-hsien.[1]

Not surprisingly, he did not go to America at all. Instead, he left Tientsin on December 16th for Shanghai, where he stayed more than two months, discussing the pros and cons of the Anti-Monarchy campaign with no less a person than General Feng Kuo-chang. His erstwhile pupil, General Ts'ai O, did not sail for Japan either. His arrival at Kunming on December 19th was an eagerly awaited event. General T'ang Chi-yao and others at once went into conference with him, and on December 23rd an ultimatum demanding the

[1] *Liang Jen-kung Nien-p'u*, p. 463.

abrogation of the Empire and the execution of thirteen prominent monarchists was sent to the Emperor, Yuan Shih-k'ai.

The ultimatum addressed Yuan as *The President* and allowed him twenty-four hours for his reply. Yuan chose to ignore it; perhaps he did not think it important. Two days later, Yunnan declared independence. The manifesto issued on the occasion stated that Yunnan no longer recognized Yuan as the President of China, in other words: 'Since he has betrayed the Republic, Yuan Shih-k'ai naturally loses all his claims to be the head of the State.'[1] This was obviously too serious a document to be overlooked even by Yuan Shih-k'ai, but his reaction was most peculiar. In the name of the Board of Political Affairs, he asked T'ang, Ts'ai and others whether this was really issued by them or forged by others.[2] This extraordinary handling of a grave situation might be intended to provide a ladder for the insurgent generals to climb down, by giving them a chance to revoke their decision. As not a single word was taken back by the Yunnan leaders, Yuan Shih-k'ai once more telegraphed T'ang Chi-yao, reminding him of his earlier support for the monarchical movement and attributing his present change of mind to Ts'ai O's influence. T'ang indeed had supported the monarchy and his original telegram to that effect was published by the Government as evidence on December 28th,[3] but this failed to drive a wedge between Ts'ai and his comrades and, on December 29th, Yuan lost patience and cashiered the insurgent lot. An internecine war was now unavoidable and both sides began preparations.

The Anti-monarchists announced the aims of their campaign on New Year's Day 1916. They declared that 1. the Constitution of the Republic of China must be protected at any cost and, in doing so, the traitor must be eliminated; 2. the Military Junta of the Anti-monarchy Army undertook to reorganize the Central Government by reconvening the National Assembly to elect a new Head of State as the representative of the Republic; 3. all the laws which had not been approved by the National Assembly would be abrogated; 4. the principles of democratic government would be observed and the prerogatives of local councils would be respected in order to promote unity of the nation; and 5. China would become a federation of autonomous provinces whose governors would be elected by the

[1] Liang Ch'i-ch'ao, *Yin-ping-shih-ho-chi*, ch. 33, p.p 7-8.
[2] CFKP, 26.12.1915.
[3] See CFKP.

people. This announcement was signed by the Chairman of the
Military Junta, General T'ang Chi-yao, and the Commanders of its
First and Second Armies, Generals Ts'ai O and Li Lieh-chun.[1]

The Junta's plan was to capture Szechwan by force, since that
province was then under the control of Yuan's trusted general,
Ch'en Huan. By taking it, the Anti-monarchists hoped to threaten
the adjacent provinces of Hupei and Hunan and to influence the
wavering military leaders along the lower reaches of the Yangtze,
particularly Generals Feng Kuo-chang and Chang Hsün. At the
same time they would launch a political offensive against the
leaders of Kweichow, Kwangsi and Kwangtung, who were not
considered as Yuan's own men. If all went well, they expected to
complete a grand alliance south of the Yangtze in three or four
months' time and then drive northward to central China and Peking.
The plan had been determined as early as October 1915 when
Ts'ai O, Tai K'an, and Liang Ch'i-ch'ao met in Tientsin;[2] and now
at last it was being put into practice.

Ts'ai O at once led his First Army into Szechwan. According to
Liang Ch'i-ch'ao the army consisted of some 15,000 men;[3] another
report gave the figure of just over 3,000 and stated that they carried
less than two months provisions with them.[4] Facing this tiny army
were two divisions and three mixed brigades, one of which was
commanded by Brigadier Feng Yü-hsiang, later known as the
Christian General. All these units were directly controlled by
General Ch'en Huan. Yet Yuan apparently thought them insufficient; on January 5th he despatched Ts'ao K'un's Third,
Chang Ching-yao's Seventh, and Li Ch'ang-t'ai's Eighth Division
to Szechwan to reinforce Ch'en Huan, while two other divisions
and a mixed brigade were sent to Hunan. He also ordered a
Kwangtung division under the command of Lung Chin-kuang to
attack Yunnan via Kwangsi; this Lung agreed to do.

At the back of the decision to reinforce Szechwan was Yuan's
distrust of Ch'en Huan, for Ch'en was Ts'ai O's close friend.
Reinforcement created a serious problem, finding a Commander-
in-Chief who could be respected by such arrogant soldiers as Ts'ao
K'un, Chang Ching-yao and others. He asked Tuan Ch'i-jui but

[1] Pai Chiao, YSKYCHMK, pp. 312-313.
[2] *Yin-ping-shih-ho-chi*, ch. 33, p. 144.
[3] ibid, ch. 33, p. 29.
[4] Li Chien-nung, *Chung-kuo-chin-pai-nien-cheng-chih-shih*, p. 447.

found him ill; he approached Feng Kuo-chang who was also unwell; and finally he tried 'Prince' Li Yuan-hung who, having been neglected for so long, showed no interest in pulling chestnuts out of the fire for others. Therefore the Emperor himself had to direct the campaign in person, setting up the Supreme Command in his own palace. Even so, orders were issued to lower-ranking officers like Feng Yü-hsiang by Yuan in Peking, Ts'ao K'un in Chungking, and Ch'en Huan in Chengtu simultaneously. The worst of it was that the orders were not always consistent.[1]

This confusion in the higher command explains why, against such odds, Ts'ai O managed to capture Hsüfu on January 31st and hold his ground. Then he began making secret overtures to Liu Ts'un-hou's officers; in less than a fortnight, Liu took his division and joined forces with Ts'ai. On February 6th the enlarged Anti-monarchy Army occupied Luchou.

Meanwhile the political agitators of the Anti-monarchists were busily making contacts with Kweichow and Kwangsi. In the wake of Ts'ai O's victory at Hsüfu, Tai K'an arrived at Kueiyang, the capital of Kweichow, to find the whole province in a ferment. The people wanted to cut off all relations with Yuan Shih-k'ai, but Liu Hsien-shih, the military leader, was waiting for a remittance to arrive from Peking. The money, no less than 300,000 yuan, duly came on January 26th and the province made known its inde-pendence on the next day. Thereupon Tai K'an led some eight corps of Kweichow troops towards Szechwan to open the second front in that province, and by the middle of February he was threatening Chungking.

Before the Yunnan uprising it had been generally believed that Lu Jung-t'ing of Kwangsi would soon join the Anti-monarchists. Two months had elapsed, but Lu made no move. His inaction was partly due to Lung Chi-kuang's opposition. Lung, the general of Kwangtung, was related to Lu, and was, at that time, loyal to Yuan Shih-k'ai. His refusal to take the plunge weighed heavily in Lu's mind. Furthermore Lu Jung-t'ing, like Liu Hsien-shih of Kweichow, needed money and ammunition. He therefore volunteered to attack Yunnan, provided Yuan would give him a million yuan and supply him with weapons. The true aim of this move was to prevent Lung Chin-kuang from going to Yunnan through his own province. Yuan Shih-k'ai took the bait and gave him the money, but still he did

[1] Feng Yü-hsiang, *Wo-ti-sheng-huo*, II, p. 7.

nothing. Meanwhile Liang Ch'i-ch'ao wrote to him from Shanghai, urging him to take up arms against the tyrant. Lu remained cautious, for he was waiting for a lead from Feng Kuo-chang in Nanking.

Lu was not alone; T'ang Chi-yao, for instance, clearly expressed his feelings: 'The entire situation depends on the lower reaches of the Yangtze'.[1] Feng himself fully realized that this point was crucial, and he had little cause to love Yuan Shih-k'ai, the Emperor. As long as Yuan remained President, Feng, or Tuan Ch'i-jui or Hsü Shih-ch'ang, had a hope of succeeding him some day. Now this hope was cut off and worse still, when he visited Peking in the middle of 1915, Feng was assured by Yuan himself that there was not to be a new monarchy. Subsequently Yuan's bad faith revealed a tinge of distrust in Yuan's attitude to him, and since the monarchical movement had become open, Feng had referred to it from time to time in disrespectful terms which increased Yuan's dislike. In November the garrison commander of Shanghai, Admiral Cheng Ju-ch'eng, was given a secret order to assassinate Feng Kuo-chang. Cheng conveyed a warning to his proposed victim, the result being that the Admiral himself was brutally murdered on the streets in Shanghai.[2] Immediately afterwards Feng fell ill, and at the height of the battle of the southern Szechwan, he was still absent from his office on sick leave. His indisposition was reminiscent of Yuan's 'affection of the foot' in 1911. He knew that Yuan as well as the Anti-monarchists looked to him for assistance, which could only be given in his own time and according to his own convenience and interests. In a telegram in January he supported Yuan against the Yunnan leaders, while he kept up a long and frank correspondence with Liang Ch'i-ch'ao.[3] As the Anti-monarchy Army made its inroads into Szechwan, he 'stated openly that he no longer favoured the monarchy'.[4] But no one could honestly believe that he, an associate of Yuan Shih-k'ai's of such long standing, would really turn against the Emperor.

The initial successes of the Anti-monarchy Army under Ts'ai O had other political repercussions. At first Sir John Jordan did not think that the rebellion has much chance of success; he reported to

[1] T'ang to Liang Ch'i-ch'ao, 15.1.1916, *Liang Jen-kung Nien-p'u*, p. 465.
[2] Putnam Weale, *Fight*, p. 181 and CFKP, 10.11.1915.
[3] CFKP, 7.1.1916 and Liang, *Yin-ping-shih-ho-chi*, ch. 33, p. 23.
[4] Jordan to Langley, 10.2.1916.

Sir Walter Langley that 'The Yunnan movement is one of those things which have marked the beginning of all dynasties in China and is accepted as an ordinary incident in Chinese history'.[1] But, perhaps knowing Britain's inability to do much either to support or to stop the monarchical movement (being completely preoccupied in fighting Germany), his advice to the Foreign Office was forgivably vague. Apart from joining Japan in giving warnings to Yuan, he and other Ministers in Peking did very little. Japan, however, was active in opposing the Emperor. Her agents in China helped both Ts'ai and Liang Ch'i-ch'ao to reach their destinations in the south; they also expressed her willingness to give financial and military aid to the insurgents. In January Hioki, the Japanese Minister, was instructed to tell Yuan's special envoys to postpone their trip to Tokyo for the Mikado's accession, and in February, according to the *Japan Advertiser*,[2] politicians, pressmen, and others staged a demonstration at the Seiyoken Tsukiji against Yuan Shih-k'ai, demanding that the Government should grant recognition to the Military Junta in Yunnan.[3] Meanwhile, in Peking, the same five Ministers for the third time advised Yuan to give up his imperial ambitions. The Kuomintang, which had been inactive for a long time, began to show a resurgence of life. Ch'en Chiung-ming declared independence in Huichou, Kwangtung, on January 28th, and riots led by members of the Party broke out in Nanch'ang and Ch'angsha in February. These efforts were, however, all abortive. On February 23rd Yuan Shih-k'ai was forced to make his first tactical retreat by announcing the suspension of the preparations for his enthronement.

At this stage large contingents of Yuan's troops arrived in Szechwan, and a fierce battle ensued between Chang Ching-yao's Seventh Division and Ts'ai O's army of three thousand men. Casualties on both sides were heavy, and eventually Ts'ai was compelled to evacuate Nahsi, which was taken by Feng Yü-hsiang's mixed brigade at the beginning of March. For this, Feng was made a baron; never before had a brigadier been so honoured. With at least one victory to his credit, Yuan deemed the time opportune to initiate a peace offensive. A decree on March 3rd admonished the insurgents to stop this internecine war in a much milder tone than

[1] 14.1.1916.
[2] 28.2.1916.
[3] Chang I-lin, *Wu-shih-nien-kuo-shih-ts'ung-t'an*, in Shen-pao, *Tsui-chin-chih-wu-shih-nien*, p. 4; *Liang Jen-kung Nien-p'u.* 467-469; Jordan to Langley, 14.2.1916.

his previous pronouncements. At the same time he stepped up military pressure against the Anti-monarchists on all fronts. The right wing of the Anti-monarchy troops, commanded by Tai K'an, had to abandon Ch'ichiang and the Kweichow troops were defeated by Yuan's Hunan army at Mayang. Isolated on the Kwangtung-Kwangsi border, Lung Chin-kuang forced his way into Kwangsi. The tide was turning in Yuan's favour. Delighted by the good news, he rushed medals and money to the front to reward his officers and men. He also announced the issue of a loan on March 10th.

His revived hopes were evanescent. His decision to remove Lu Jung-t'ing from Kwangsi in order to make sure that that province stayed on his side was a grave mistake; so was his order to Lung Chin-kuang instructing him to launch an attack on the Kwangsi troops. Lu had hitherto been unable to decide which side to take, but these two moves by Yuan helped him to make up his mind. In a telegram dated March 11th he advised Yuan to retire from politics and, four days later, declared Kwangsi independent. This bold step coincided with General Feng Kuo-chang's sudden recovery from his prolonged illness. On the battlefront the Anti-monarchy troops, now regrouped and encouraged by the favourable political development, began a counter-attack in which they smashed Chang Ching-yao's division in a few days and retook what they had lost a fortnight before. In Kwangsi Lu Jung-t'ing also brought the weight of his forces to bear upon the invading Lung Chin-kuang, disarmed his entire army, and forced him to exhort his brother, General Lung Chi-kuang of Kwangtung, to declare independence.

These sudden reverses stunned Yuan, who at once asked his old lieutenants, Hsü Shih-ch'ang, Tuan Ch'i-jui and Feng Kuo-chang, to try to stablize the situation for him. He also asked Liang Shih-i, as a friend and a fellow provincial, to parley with Liang Ch'i-ch'ao. Yuan was trying to make the best of a desperate situation, for he had now realized that his Northern Army, without diplomatic and foreign financial backing, could not smash the southern insurgents as it had done in the Second Revolution of 1913. Furthermore, the Chinese Minister in Japan reported that the Japanese might take action under the pretext of maintaining peace in the Far East; from Tientsin, Hsü Shih-ch'ang wrote asking Yuan to seize the earliest opportunity to come to a *rapprochement* with Yunnan; from Nanking, Feng Kuo-chang and four other military leaders sent a message urging Yuan to abandon the Empire; and K'ang Yu-wei, a staunch supporter of the Manchu Imperial House, sent him a letter which contained these unkind words:

'From the point of view of the Manchu Imperial House, you are a usurper, and from the Republic's point of view, you are a traitor. Heaven's wrath and the people's discontent are omens of a calamitous ending to your present course. Instead of being forced to retire by our fellow-countrymen, you would do better to withdraw voluntarily from public life.'[1]

Dr Wu T'ing-fang, the Revolutionary peace negotiator of 1911, also telegraphed him asking what contributions he had made in his capacity as President during the past four years and why the people hated him so much. He accused him of shedding the blood of millions for his own power and glory. 'We used to say that the Manchu Government was bad. Who would have thought that the present Government would be even worse?'[2]

On March 17th Liang Shih-i went to see Yuan, who was then sitting at his desk reading these communications.

'We sat opposite each other. He dipped his finger in a cup of tea and began to draw maps on the desk, explaining to me the detailed situation and his counter-moves. He did this several times and then told me: "As things stand, I have made up my mind to abrogate the Empire. I shall first ask Hsü Shih-ch'ang and Tuan Ch'i-jui to form a Central Government and Feng Kuo-chang to stabilize Central China for me. You perhaps will telegraph Ch'en Huan, instructing him to strengthen the defence of Szechwan and, at the same time, to find a peace formula with Ts'ai O. Please also write to Liang Ch'i-ch'ao, since you know him well, asking him to pass on my decisions to Yunnan and Kwangsi. On the other hand, you should also reply to K'ang Yu-wei, see whether he can influence Liang Ch'i-ch'ao on these matters. I don't mind making any concession, as long as there are ways and means of maintaining peace and order" '.[3]

Four days after this preliminary discussion a conference attended by

---

[1] Pai Chiao, YSKYCHMK, p. 361 and Liang, *Nien-p'u*, pp. 321-329.
[2] Pai Chiao, ibid, p. 350.
[3] Liang, *Nien-p'u*, p. 321.

Hsü Shih-ch'ang, Tuan Ch'i-jui, Li Yuan-hung and others was held at Yuan's palace. It was then decided to abolish the Empire formally; to appoint Hsü Shih-ch'ang as Minister of State in succession to Lu Cheng-hsiang; and to make peace with the south, simultaneously offering Ts'ai O the Ministry for the Army, Tai Kan the Ministry of the Interior, Chang Ch'ien the Ministry of Agriculture and Commerce, T'ang Hua-lung the Ministry of Education, and Liang Ch'i-ch'ao the Ministry of Justice 'in order to satisfy the Progressive Party's demand for power'. Yuan's eldest son insisted at this conference that his father should continue to be President of the Republic after the abandonment of the Empire.

On the next day Yuan, as President of the Republic of China, decreed the abolition of the Hung-hsien Empire, thereby ending a dream which had lasted eighty-three days. In the decree, he attributed both the establishment and the abolition of the Empire to popular demand, while he painted himself as a victim of circumstances, a mere pawn in the game, an escapist who had retired from public life in 1908, given up all interest in politics, and was later urged to come out of his hermitage to take charge of the affairs of the State. In spite of all this, he blamed himself for the turmoil in which the country now found itself and stressed the point that, as the President of China, it was his sacred duty to preserve peace and order in the land. By this declaration, and by the offer of ministries to the republicans, he hoped to remove the cause of the conflict, to induce the south to agree on a peaceful settlement with him, and to divide the insurgent forces. At the same time he secretly approached the Americans for a loan, in case the peace offer was rejected. He also called the Council of State to endorse the abolition of the Empire, which they duly did with the same unanimity as they had shown eighty-six days before voting for its inauguration.

As the obedient members of the Council were saying their 'Ayes', a long letter from K'ang Yu-wei reached Yuan Shih-k'ai, accusing him of betraying the Manchu Empire and the Chinese Republic and of selling the country to foreigners. His old colleague and friend, T'ang Shao-i broke his long silence by sending him a telegram (in which he addressed him as 'Mr Yuan') saying:

'You still wish to stay on as the President of China after the abolition of your Empire. You hope people may overlook this, but, in fact, they consider this the most shameless action, unprecedented in the history of China and of every other country.'[1]

The decree of March 22nd and the Council's resolution of March 25th changed the entire nature of the civil war. As the monarchy which the south was fighting against was no longer in existence, there was no point in continuing the struggle. At the end of March Ch'en Huan managed to conclude a truce with Ts'ai O. With the war now over, Hsü Shih-ch'ang, Tuan Ch'i-jui and Li Yuan-hung proposed a peace settlement to the south, which was firmly rejected by Ts'ai O. Thereafter political contacts through various channels between the north and the south became increasingly frequent and all their discussion was centred on the one question of whether Yuan should or not retire.

Among the insurgent leaders, Ts'ai O and Liang Ch'i-ch'ao insisted that Yuan must go while T'ang Chi-yao and Lu Jung-t'ing were less resolute. There were signs, at this critical moment, that the unity of the insurgents was strained, and Liang Ch'i-ch'ao thought it necessary to telegraph T'ang and Lu imploring them to stand firm. Two events however turned the tide in Liang's favour. Ch'en Huan, the general of Szechwan, communicated with Ts'ai O at the end of March, informing him that he had decided to join forces with the insurgents. He also intimated to Ts'ai that Hupei and Kiangsi, then under the control of T'ang Hsiang-ming and Li Ch'un respectively, would act in concert with him. A week after this Lung Chi-kuang of Kwangtung saw the time ripe to show his hand; he declared independence on April 6th. His example was followed by Chu Jui of Chekiang on April 12th. With circumstances as they were, Sir John Jordan ruefully forecast Yuan's disappearance from political life 'within a measurable distance of time'.[2] A fortnight before, the question posed to the nation was Yuan's retirement; now it was his life.[3]

The rot had set in and the collapse was rapid. The commandants of the fortresses of Chiangyin and Wuchiang went over to the insurgents on April 16th and 18th, and Feng Yü-hsiang surrendered to Ts'ai O on the 20th. In Peking the Bank of China and the Bank

---

[1] T'ao Chü-yin, PYCFTCSCSH, II, p. 186 and Jordan to Langley, 5.4.1916, the enclosure was published on 27.3.1916 *Shanghai Mercury*.

[2] Jordan to Butler, 11.4.1916.

[3] *The Times*, 18.4.1916 and 21.4.1916.

of Communications, having issued too many irredeemable notes as
advances to the Government, ceased to pay silver on demand. As a
result, public confidence in their notes was badly shaken and inflation
was no longer available to the Government as a means of financing
war. As a desperate measure to rally people to his side Yuan decided
to constitute a truly responsible Government, as a sign of his sincere
desire to put democracy into practice. On April 24th Tuan Ch'i-jui
was appointed Premier, to be fully responsible for governmental
decisions; Yuan himself was thus apparently stripped of all power
except the command of a bodyguard of some twenty thousand
Honanese.

Yuan's retirement was now certain, and his life and property a
matter for discussion. A corollary to these debating points was the
question of who would succeed Yuan to the Presidency. By the
Constitution Li Yuan-hung, the Vice-President, had a legitimate
claim to the position; judging purely by military strength, Tuan
Ch'i-jui and Feng Kuo-chang were both possible candidates. With
Tuan about to become the Premier of a responsible Government
and hence a step nearer the Presidency, Feng could not remain
inactive any longer. He put out a feeler on April 17th in the shape of
a telegram, still supporting Yuan's claim to the Presidency, but
advocating a final decision on all the outstanding issues by the
National Assembly, which could be reconvened for the purpose.
These suggestions were coldly, and in some cases unfavourably,
received, so on April 26th Feng changed his tune and advised Yuan
to retire. He was the first of the northern warlords to speak openly
against his master. Close at his heels was the general of Shantung,
who made a similar pronouncement.

This was on the eve of the vitally important Nanking Conference
sponsored by Feng Kuo-chang with Yuan's approval, and there were
still other political developments taking place at the same time. The
insurgents had established a military government at Chaoch'ing in
Kwangtung with General T'ang Chi-yao at its head and Ts'en
Ch'un-hsüan—Yuan's old colleague in the closing years of the
Ch'ing dynasty and now a member of the Kuomintang—as his
deputy. Neither of them had the faintest chance of becoming President, and the fact that they had been chosen showed clearly that the
insurgents did not wish to get involved in the inevitable struggle
for the highest post after Yuan's disappearance from the field.

Indeed the struggle for the succession moved into a very delicate stage in May. Feng Kuo-chang telegraphed Liang Ch'i-ch'ao arguing that since Yuan had torn up the Constitution, the Vice-President, like the President himself, had lost his office, and consequently his claim to the higher one. Liang was strenuously opposed to this view, for the first aim of the entire Anti-monarchy campaign was to protect the Constitution at any cost, and in this he had the support of the insurgents who had previously exhorted the Diplomatic Corps in Peking to deal directly with the Vice-President instead of Yuan Shih-k'ai.[1] He sent a message to Tuan Ch'i-jui saying:

'Your position today is similar to Yuan's in 1911. Yuan could not have solved the dangerous situation then, had the Manchus refused to abdicate. Likewise, you will not succeed in your assignment if Yuan does not go'.

He also advised Tuan to support Li Yuan-hung.[2] The insurgents' opinion on the succession was thus made abundantly clear.

But Feng Kuo-chang had his own ideas. The Nanking Conference was called mainly to further his claim to the Presidency by creating a third force between the north, led by Tuan Ch'i-jui, and the south-west, led by T'ang Chi-yao; this third force, being a compromise force, might win the support of the other two, and eventually gain control of the whole country On May 18th, the Conference duly took place, attended by twenty-three deputies from five provinces other than Feng's own—Kiangsi, Anhwei, Hunan, Chekiang, and Shantung Although the south-west declined to take part, the nation waited anxiously for the result of the Conference. But it ran into some unexpectedly heavy weather at the very beginning. On the question of Yuan's retirement the representatives were divided; Shantung and Kiangsi were in favour but Anhwei was dead against it. In the end, this question had to be shelved pending a final decision by the National Assembly. The second item on the agenda, which was contrary to the spirit of the first, was the choice between a resumption of war and making peace, and there the deputies agreed that the only way to achieve an honourable peace was to prepare for a war. Thus the members went on to discuss the

---

[1] Liang Ch'i-ch'ao, *Yin-ping-shih-ho-chi*, ch. 33, pp. 11-12 and 50, and *Liang Jen-kung, Nien-p'u*, p. 477.
[2] Liang to Tuan, 4.5.1916, *Yin-ping-shih-ho-chi*, ch. 33, p. 53.

possibilities of an all-out attack on the south-west. On the question of the Presidency, the Conference resolved to invite the insurgents to take part in joint deliberations.

The resolutions, if they were honest, made little sense. No one could discuss the problem of succession while still supporting Yuan Shih-k'ai, or ask the ·south-western provinces to take part in a discussion on the succession while preparing an attack on them. The juxtaposition of these decisions was due to the lack of a united view among the deputies and Feng's naïvety as a politician. The third force was a still-birth and the Conference itself was a disappointment.

Immediately after this, Generals Chang Hsun and Ni Ssu-ch'ung issued a joint communiqué, in which they declared their loyal support of Yuan Shih-k'ai and their willingness to lead their troops to quell the rebellion in the south-west. Feng Kuo-chang too issued *his* communiqué, insisting that Yuan should retire but, in the same breath, saying that he had no interest in meddling with affairs beyond the boundaries of Kiangsu. Sitting in his parlour in Peking, Yuan Shih k'ai knew perfectly well that Feng's attempt at creating a third force had failed and that Chang Hsun had now come out to barter his support against the control of Kiangsu which he had conceded to Feng in 1913. He was willing to accept Chang's terms, but at this juncture the political situation took another sharp turn.

On May 22nd, when the Nanking Conference was still wrangling over the question of succession, Ch'en Huan of Szechwan announced his independence in a telegram which read: 'From today, Szechwan severs all its relations with Yuan Shih-k'ai.'[1] This was the lethal blow! Ch'en had always been Yuan's trusted lieutenant, and on reading his telegram 'the strong man' fainted. When he came round, there were tears in his eyes and his face was crimson. On regaining his self-possession he told Liang Shih-i: 'Now, even Ch'en Huan is like this. What is there for me to say! Please reply to him and tell him that I will retire.'[2] A week later, another reliable man of Yuan's, General T'ang Hsiang-ming of Hunan, also declared independence. On that day Yuan Shih-k'ai was already a very sick man, but he continued to attend to various problems on his sick-bed. However 'his power of quick decision has left him; he is helpless among the troublesome alternatives that confront him', reported his close associate Chou Tzu-ch'i, and went on: 'Formerly it was "yes"

[1] T'ao Chü-yin, PYCFTCSCSH, II, p. 223.
[2] Liang, *Nien-p'u*, p. 341.

or "no" in an instant to my proposals. Now he ruminates, and wavers, and changes a decision many times.'[1] Reinsch was sounded about giving Yuan a safe conduct and asylum in America, but before a decision could be made Yuan was obviously too sick to travel.

His old friend and sworn brother, Hsü Shih-ch'ang, hearing the news of Yuan's deteriorating health hurried from Weihui in Honan to Peking only to find Yuan beyond the help of doctors. It was June 5th. In a feeble murmur, the patient told him: 'It's very nice of you to come. I know I have no hope now.' Hsü tried to comfort him and also asked him what arrangements he had made. With a great effort, he uttered the word 'Constitution'!

He was suffering from uraemia of the blood induced by nervous prostration. He had from the beginning been treated by three French doctors and a number of Chinese physicians. On the first two days of June, he was considered to be in no danger, but his condition was 'subsequently worsened and complicated by the treatments applied. The French doctors' orders were often ignored'.[2]

A few minutes after ten in the morning on June 6, 1916, the great man breathed his last, after fifty-six eventful years.

On the same day his valediction was published, recommending Li Yuan-hung, the Vice-President, to act as President of China.[3] As the northern warlords were clearly divided into two rival groups under Tuan Ch'i-jui and Feng Kuo-chang, this was a wise choice, which at least helped to preserve the unity of China for a short period, for Li was a man of weak character and hence suitable for the part of a figure-head. In a quiet ceremony on June 7th, Li became President. Subsequently telegrams came in from all the provinces, including those which had declared independence, to express their unanimous support of the head of the Chinese Government.

Yuan's body, dressed in the robes which he had worn for the worship of Heaven, was enclosed in its coffin. These ceremonies, the dressing and the enclosing, took place on June 7th. Now that the nails were driven in, as the Chinese saying goes, it was time to pronounce the final judgment on the deceased. In the first announcement that Li Yuan-hung made as President, he praised Yuan Shih-k'ai's meritorious role in 1911 and 1912 in helping to found the

---

[1] Reinsch, *An American Diplomat in China*, p. 192.
[2] *The Times*, 7.6.1916.
[3] CFKP, 6.6.1916 and Putnam Weale, *Fight*, pp. 196-197.

Republic and giving peace and order to the country.[1] On a more
personal note Sir John Jordan, in a message to Langley,[2] defended
Yuan's action in dissolving the National Assembly and contracting
the Reorganization Loan and went on to say:

'I could go on indefinitely reciting acts to the credit of my dead
friend—for simply as a friend I shall always remember him—who
has crossed the border and gone down the last long vale. He fell in
an unequal struggle and to me he was greater in his adversity than
he had been even at the height of his power.'

Liang Ch'i-ch'ao was less complimentary. Before Yuan's death,
he said:

'Yuan does not know the difference between a man and a beast. All
he knows about human beings is that they fear weapons and love
gold and it is by those two things that he rules the country. For four
years there have been no politics in Peking except the ghostly
shadows of a knife and a piece of gold. . . . Day in and day out, he
has enticed people on by waving a piece of gold in front of their
eyes and threatened them with a knife at their backs. By bribery
and terror, he has enslaved our people. . . . For four years, there has
not been a moral standard among the *élite* of our country. It cannot
be denied that seven or eight out of every ten of them are now
thoroughly corrupt and rotten. Who is responsible for this? I do not
hesitate a moment in saying that it has been entirely due to Yuan
Shih-k'ai. . . . If his empire exists and continues to exist for many
years to come, good people will become fewer and fewer and
eventually perish and only bad ones will survive, to make the entire
Chinese nation lose all their values as human beings.'[3]

As some people in the North mourned Yuan's death, those in the
South joyfully celebrated it. On June 26th the commemorative
ceremony was held in the great hall of the Presidential Palace where
he used to receive his guests and officials. It was a strange mingling
of old and new. There were the traditional funeral offerings of food,
candles, and joss-sticks as well as modern weapons, tunics, and other

[1] CFKP, 7.6.1916.
[2] 13.6.1916.
[3] Liang Ch'i-ch'ao, *Yin-ping-shih-ho-chi*, ch. 33, pp. 108-109.

things which had belonged to the departed. There were lamas who conducted the ceremony, chanting the sutras and playing Mongolian musical instruments, and also a modern brass-band playing European funeral marches. There were mandarins in their robes, yellow jackets and decorations, and also diplomats and military leaders in their colourful uniforms. High up on the catafalque was Yuan himself, and below it this conglomeration of styles and men that he had left behind.

The same strange medley was seen in the funeral procession two days later, escorting the coffin out of Peking. The ultimate destination was the mausoleum in the ancestral shrine in Hsiangcheng, Honan. At the head of the procession rode twenty heralds, then followed in succession three large detachments of infantry bearing their arms reversed, the Chinese musicians playing their *sonar*, a squadron of riders in old Chinese costume carrying huge banners, a company of lancers escorting an empty state carriage, Buddhist monks beating drums and clanging cymbals, the President's military band, a long line of sacrificial vessels preceding the sedan-chair in which was set Yuan's soul-tablet, another long line of men bearing the food offerings and Yuan's personal belongings, high officials on foot in military uniforms or frock coats and top hats, the white-clad mourners, including Yuan's sons, and finally the gigantic catafalque, which was carried by a hundred men by means of a complicated arrangement of poles. Lining the route to watch the pageant were vast crowds of people, looking on with no sign of grief, but rather with mute indifference.

An Appraisal

THE preceding chapters have given us some idea about Yuan Shih-k'ai the politician, less about him as a man, and least of all about the working of his mind. This is due to the lack of reliable data, which, in turn, arises from the fact that chroniclers of the past paid only scanty attention to his private life (which, it must be confessed, was not remarkable for any well-defined purpose), and they often ignored his personal reactions to an event. We know next to nothing about him as a father, a husband, or a friend. However, judging from the steadfast support given to him by such people as Hsü Shih-ch'ang, T'ang Shao-i, Chao Ping-chun, Chu Ch'i-ch'ien, Liang Shih-i, Yang Tu, and the army leaders, he must have been a good friend and a good colleague. Indeed, Sir John Jordan, in his despatch to Sir Walter Langley on June 13, 1916, paid him this tribute after his death:

'I have a great personal liking for the man and feel both his loss and the manner of it acutely. . . . During his early life in Corea he formed friendships with a number of Englishmen . . . and to his last day he remained a firm friend of Great Britain. He could not speak a word of English, but he could repeat the names of all his British friends and often told me anecdotes of his associations with them. Almost the last time I saw him he said that he had been on very friendly terms with Englishmen since his early manhood and that he had learned to trust and like them. Of this he gave innumerable proofs by appointment of British advisers, the engagement of British teachers[1] and tutors for his children, by sending three of his sons to school in England, by contributions to British war funds, and in general by his admiration for British ideals.'

[1] Miss Bowden Smith, daughter of an Admiral and a graduate of Cambridge and Cornell, USA, was an example. See Timothy Richard, *Forty-five Years in China*, p. 353.

Although he, like many of his contemporaries, had more than one wife, Yuan had never been accused of opium-smoking or embezzling funds.[1] He was, at the same time, a ruthless man, responsible for the deaths of Sung Chiao-jen, General Chang Chen-wu, and perhaps also those of Chao Ping-chun, Admiral Cheng Ju-ch'eng. Ch'en Ch'i-mei and a host of others. There were other charges too laid against him, such as 'conceit, extravagance, lechery, and treachery' by Chang P'ei-lun,[2] and the senile Ma Hsiang-po recalled that Yuan was compelled to leave for Shantung to serve in General Wu Ch'ang-ch'ing's headquarters on account of a crime he had committed in his home town in Honan, and that Yuan often boasted of his sexual appetite and told his friends of a certain expressed wish of the Korean queen![3] These fragments of unsupported information, evidently biased and perhaps invented, do not help us greatly to form a coherent picture of the man. Our description therefore is perforce a chapter of history seen through the man; not the man in the light of history.

Biography in the modern sense did not, and still does not exist in China. This therefore is not a biography.

Yet we must make some effort to appraise him. We are by no means the first in the field; Yuan's contemporaries and many others did so, and presently we shall examine some of their views. Our predecessors seem to have erred in judging him as a man and a politician at the same time, and consequently their personal feelings have coloured their political discernment. Although some of them might justify their views by the fact that they knew Yuan personally themselves, in spite of that they give no details of the information upon which they formed their opinions. Yuan's critics have also made the mistake of confusing the *individual* politician with the *type* of politicians whom he represented. Yuan, like other political figures, was a type as well as an individual. The former was a product of the period, of the interplay of many historical factors, while the latter was the expression of his own nature and intelligence. To use a simile of the theatre, the former resembled a dramatic part while the latter the man who played it. It is therefore unjustifiable either to hold Yuan Shih-k'ai responsible for the shortcomings of his type

---

[1] 'He seemed to have been disinterested as regards money, a quality rather rare among Chinese officials of the time and he also tried to stop the opium traffic.' (Henri Cordier, *Historie Générale de la Chine*, Paris, 1921, IV, p. 295).

[2] *Vide supra*, p. 50.

[3] *I-jih i-t'an*, p. 13.

or to give him credit for its virtues. He should, however, be judged
in relation to others of the same historical category.

To avoid confusion, the type and the individual must be
differentiated and judged separately at two levels. Unfortunately
all opinions about Yuan have hitherto been simultaneously at a
number of levels. To take a few examples.

K'ang Yu-wei, the leader of the 1898 Reform, wrote to Yuan
in 1916:

'You single-handedly revised the Constitution, dissoved the National
Assembly, created your own "legislative bodies", prolonged your
own term of office to ten years, underwrote the sale of our territories
to strong neighbours, and finally founded a monarchy. What law is
there under your rule?

'You think that since it was created by you, the Republic can now
be cancelled by you. You are the conjuror who regards all the rest of
us as ants and termites completely at your disposal. The changes in
recent years have left no impression on your conscience whatever.'[1]

While K'ang was trying to dissuade him from carrying on with his
monarchical adventure, Dr Sun Yat-sen gave this message to his
nation:

'Yuan has torn up the Constitution, dissolved the National Assembly,
cancelled regional autonomy, and altered the judicial system, so
that he can have absolute power to kill and to confiscate as he
wishes. His spies infest the cities and bandits roam the countryside.
Heavy penalties and summary executions are used to reinforce
the heavy taxation which alone does not seem to satisfy his greed.
He has sold mining rights and thus the Treasury becomes empty;
he has massacred members of the Kuomintang, so the nation is
weakened. The Republic which the Revolutionary Government
created with such difficulties has been entirely destroyed by him.
The traitor has surely done enough!'[2]

K'ang and Sun wrote the above just before Yuan's death, and the
following two, both by famous scholars, were composed immediately
after it:

---

[1] *A letter to the President*, see Pai Chiao, YSHYCHMK, p. 366.
[2] ibid, p. 372.

Dr Ting Wen-chiang: 'He began his career as China's political agent in Korea and was more than anyone else responsible for the Sino-Japanese war of 1894. By betraying the Emperor Kuang-hsü, who was endeavouring to reform the political system in 1898, he became the favourite of the infamous empress-dowager, and was entrusted with the formation of China's new army, from which had been drawn almost all the present military governors who are by common consent China's greatest curse. During the republican revolution of 1911 he betrayed the Manchu dynasty, to which he was premier, to become president of the republic, which position he retained by first bribing then dissolving parliament. There are at least two murders of his political opponents proved against him, and finally he worked his own ruin by trying to create a monarchy by fraud. He died a miserable failure and unblessed.'[1]

Huang Yen-p'ei: '1. Virtues never fail.
2. But wicked forces always do.
3. Actions against the will of the people can only lead to ruin.
4. A ruler whose knowledge does not justify his position will invariably be overthrown.
5. Extreme turpitude is extreme stupidity.
6. The desire to subjugate the whole nation under one man can only end in the whole nation opposing him.
7. Falsehood can never deceive all people just as brute force can never humble them all.
8. By luring people to do evil one will inadvertently lure oneself to the same to one's own ultimate destruction.
9. By trying to destroy a moral standard one will in effect help to prove its indestructibility.'[2]

Ten years later, Lu-chiao-k'e (a pseudonym) looked back to the monarchical episode and remarked:

'By uniting and making full use of the Northern warlords, Yuan achieved everything that he wished for, and paved the way for

[1] R. Johnston, *Twilight*, p. 130.
[2] Pai Chiao, ibid, pp. 4-5.

the warlords' control of the provinces. He bribed his generals with money and positions to slaughter members of the Kuomintang, who had helped to found the Republic. The Party members also had themselves to blame. Their own mistakes and corruption gave Yuan an opportunity to defeat them. Nevertheless Yuan had no thoughts for his country and paid no notice to the unity of the nation. His merciless suppression of his opponents led to endless internal strifes. His sins were beyond forgiveness.'[1]

And nearly forty years later, Chang Ch'i-yun commented:

'In short, all of Yuan's crimes came from his self-centred idea that the country was his. In addition to cruelty and despotism, he resorted to bribery, deceit and other covert means. As a result, he met his doom.'[2]

All the above quoted opinions were expressed by non-communist statesmen and scholars, none of whom spoke a word of praise, as if Yuan was a villain of a melodrama who had no commendable qualities whatsoever. K'ang and Sun, writing from political motivation, attacked Yuan on all three levels—as a type of politician, an individual politician, and as a man, by bringing into their consideration his policies and his ways of handling political problems, as well as his ethics; Ting and Huang also criticized him at all three levels with emphasis particularly on his lack of moral sentiments. We do not know the basis of Ting's accusation of Yuan being responsible more than anyone else for the 1894 war. There is evidence to show that Yuan was bellicose towards Japan then, but he was in none of the policy-making bodies, nor was he important enough to determine the course of events in that crucial year. The issue of war or peace was, according to all records, decided by the Imperial Court, the Grand Council, and the redoubtable Li Hung-chang, not by a mere political agent holding the rank of a senior prefect. Ting made much play with the word 'betray', while Huang did the same with 'virtue'. Their opinions were largely an expression of their own moral indignation. Writing ten years and forty years respectively after Yuan's death, Lu-Chiao-k'e and Chang Ch'i-yun both failed to advance our understanding of the man an inch; if

[1] *Shen-pao*, 10.10.1926.
[2] Chang Ch'i-yun, *Chung-hua min-kuo shih-kang*, Taipeh, 1954, I, p. 204.

anything, they hopelessly over-simplified the whole issue. Clearly neither of them had given much thought to what they were actually writing. From the high moral tone of all the above quoted opinions, we can safely conclude that Yuan was judged by them first and foremost on *ethical* grounds. His policies and ways of handling politics were bad, because the man himself was depraved. This approach was common among all non-communist critics of Yuan Shih-k'ai.

Sir John Jordan used the same method and made the same mistake, only in a different way. He liked Yuan personally, so he defended his policies.[1] However, he had the grace to admit that his opinion was not a balanced one.[2] But the influence of his view survived in England, as is shown in the introduction to the Foreign Office Documents on China 1929-1931, published in 1960, which still described Yuan as 'sagacious'.[3] Another Englishman, Sir Reginald Johnston, who was Emperor Hsün-t'ung's tutor, disliked Yuan, and therefore his comment on him was not at all complimentary:

'If Yuan had been content to remain in the great position he had (by dubious means) achieved for himself—which was practically that of a life-dictator with power to nominate his own son as his successor —*he might have succeeded in leading his country into the way of peace and ordered progress* (author's italics), and in spite of his faults of character his name might have been recorded in history as that of a great man who deserved to be remembered by his country with gratitude. That he had, in his prime of life, great energy and ability cannot be doubted. It is equally true that his ambition was of a thoroughly selfish type and that he was crafty and treacherous.'[4]

and

'Yuan Shih-k'ai—who betrayed his sovereign, betrayed the throne and betrayed the republic—was neither a chun-tzŭ nor a gentleman.'[5]

He made no secret of his personal feelings, so he too cannot be considered as fair.

[1] *Vide supra*, p. 336.

[2] 'As to Yuan Shih-k'ai, you will not expect a balanced opinion from me at this moment.' (Jordan to Langley, 13.6.1916.)

[3] Second Series, VIII, p. 2.

[4] R. Johnston, *Twilight*, p. 129.

[5] ibid, p. 130. *Chun-tzŭ* is the Chinese idea of a gentleman.

The place of moral indignation was taken by class hatred in the verdicts of Yuan's communist critics. Li Ta-chao, writing shortly after Yuan's death, regarded the man's downfall as a watershed in Chinese history and looked forward to the reconstruction of China in the near future.[1] But Li's class consciousness was not as pronounced as alleged, and his hope was not to be fulfilled. Li Shu, in his book on the political situation before and after the 1911 Revolution,[2] points out:

'He [Yuan] was the favourite of the feudal and the comprador classes and of the imperialists.'

But for a more comprehensive view of Yuan Shih-k'ai, we must consult Ch'en Po-ta's book—*Yuan Shih-k'ai the Usurper*. Ch'en, an important theoretician and historian, published his book in 1945 in the wake of the Japanese surrender and at the height of Chiang Kai-shek's popularity and power, and evidently used Yuan as Chiang's silhouette. He writes:

'Yuan Shih-k'ai—a political phenomenon, a dark shadow in the semi-colonial and semi-feudal society of modern China—was no ordinary mandarin. Yuan the politician flourished in a period of struggle between reformers and conservatives, revolutionaries and reactionaries during which the reactionary elements of the landlord and comprador classes selected and trained this extraordinary man, Yuan Shih-k'ai, in the hope that he could wield the power of the state in his hands to strangle the future of China.'[3]

Why was Yuan selected and how did he succeed? Ch'en Po-ta replies: 'Because, representing the landlords and compradors in the struggle against progress and the people, he had unusual intelligence and stratagem. Moreover, under his control there was an armed force whose special task was to suppress the people.'[4] What was Yuan's stratagem? Here the author's answer is a simple 'duplicity'.[5] With the newly created army as the basis and duplicity as the application of his power, Yuan gained step by step the support

[1] *Hsin-ch'ing-nien*, II, No. 1.
[2] Li Shu, *Hsin-hai ke-ming ch'ien-hou ti Chung-kuo cheng-chih*, 1954, p. 167.
[3] Ch'en, *Ch'e-kuo ta-tao Yuan Shih-k'ai*, p. 1.
[4] ibid, p. 2.
[5] ibid, p. 3.

of both Chinese and foreign reactionaries, and became the *first* usurper in modern China.[1] He identified the country with himself— 'I am the State'. Yet he failed miserably. Why? Ch'en poses the same question thus:

'This feudal, compradorial, and unpopular dictator, relying upon the assistance of foreign reactionaries, armed forces, intrigues, money, deception and fraud, abused his powers by slaughtering the people and strangling their freedoms as well as by other extreme cruelties. Yuan Shih-k'ai thought that no one could possibly harm him. But where is he now?'

And he immediately adds: 'Only *the people* will go on living forever',[2] implying that it was *the people* who overthrew Yuan Shih-k'ai.

For Ch'en, Li Shu and other communist historians, Yuan represented a type or a class of people—landlords and compradors— in their struggle against *the people*; he was bad since the type itself was obnoxious. These authors were also indignant, theirs was a *class* indignation. Once the indignation—be it moral or class—is deemed just and necessary, other considerations become secondary in importance or sheerly apologetic, however authentic in feeling and realistic in the light of historical facts they may be.

For two reasons the above quoted views fall short of being convincing. In the first place, none of these authors have defined their criteria of judgment. It may be answered that the non-communist historians use the Confucian moral standards to appraise Yuan Shih-k'ai whereas the communists simply apply their Marxian yardsticks. But it may pertinently be asked: Can such criteria be justifiably applied in that particular period and against a specific background? In other words, should one judge a historical figure according to contemporaneous or present-day standards? In the second place, none of them has taken the trouble to demonstrate Yuan's mistakes by pointing out a better, wiser, and, at the same time, more realistic alternative. Without this, criticism becomes purely destructive and is as unconvincing as the resort to indignation.

It is therefore necessary for us to re-examine and to analyse the period before judging the man.

---

[1] ibid, pp. 4-5. Author's italics. The *second*, according to Ch'en Po-ta, is Chiang Kai-shek.

[2] ibid, pp. 64-65. Author's italics.

Although it is generally accepted that the sorry history of *modern* China began with the Sino-British War of 1839, the real point of departure from her traditional ways was not until after the Anglo-French Expedition of 1859. The former war was waged on the periphery of China, whereas the latter drove right into the Imperial Capital and compelled the Manchu Emperor to flee in a panic. After the 1859-60 ordeal, the Ch'ing Government re-examined its policies, looked to its own weakness, and came to these conclusions:

'Before the defeat at Taku, we had the choice of either fighting against the foreigners or making peace with them; and after it we can only appease them. At a time when foreign troops occupy the Imperial Capital, we are certainly not in a position to fight, not even for our own defence. Both fighting and appeasing are to our disadvantage. The inevitable conclusions are therefore that we must, on the one hand, adopt appeasement as a short-term measure, and, on the other, prepare for our defence as a long-term policy.'[1]

So, in the next quarter of a century, the Chinese Government maintained peaceful relations with European powers while, internally, concentrating on suppressing the T'aip'ing, the Nien, and other rebels as well as on strengthening itself. The policy became known as the Self-strengthening Movement,[2] and, to pilot it, there were Li Hung-chang, and, of lesser importance, Chang Chih-tung. To begin with, Li equated the 'strength of a state' with its 'military power'. As he said in a memorial: 'China's civil and military systems are superior to their Western counterparts, with the single exception of modern arms and their manufacture.'[3] Even as late as 1870 he still maintained:

'Western arms are being improved day after day at immense cost. They have become the best in the world and enabled the countries that possess them to dominate distant places. If China does not follow this example, she has no hope of ever becoming a strong state.'[4]

---

[1] Prince Kung, Wen-hsiang, and Kuei-liang, *A Rehabilitation Programme, Ch'ou-pan i-wu shih-mo*, 24.1.1861, Hsien-feng, ch. 72, pp. 17b-18a.

[2] Also called 'Chinese Conservatism' by Professor M. C. Wright in her book, *The Last Stand of Chinese Conservatism*, 1957; see also my doctoral thesis, *The State Economic Policies of the Ch'ing Government 1840-1895*, 1956.

[3] *Ch'ou-pan i-wu shih-mo*, 2.6.1864, T'ung-chih, ch. 25, p. 9b.

[4] ibid, 20.11.1870, T'ung-chih, ch. 78, p. 39b.

The growing strength of Japan, however, made him reconsider these somewhat narrow views; and it was during the Formosan dispute with Japan in 1874, when China could not adopt a firm policy, that he realized the inadequancies of his and his country's strengthening policy. Thereafter he modified his position, and, in 1876, he wrote to a colleague of his:

'China's weakness lies in her poverty.'[1]

This changed view was shared by Chang Chih-tung, who proposed the production of coal and iron, the making of modern arms, and the training of a technical staff, for 'Only a good technical staff can perfect weapons; only coal and iron mines can make weapons plentiful, and only the mines and the arsenals can fully utilize a good technical staff'.[2]

Based on this estimate of the situation, the Self-strengthening policy was carried out in the period between 1862 and 1885 and continued until 1895. It changed China's defence and economic structure to a considerable extent, but her administrative system remained intact. Indeed, none of the leaders of this policy had ever questioned the efficacy of the Government and the civil service. In other words, the policy was purely economic and military, aiming at wealth and strength of the State through the expansion of trade and the use of the armed forces.

In many ways, this policy resembled the mercantilism of Europe. This may sound stranger than it actually was. At this time, the only industrialized power was Britain which was understood to have achieved this enviable status through mercantilism and a navy. She was China's only example and therefore China decided to copy her, quite unaware of the difference between their political, economic and social backgrounds.

The policy produced some meagre results; at any rate, it afforded China nearly a generation of peace. In 1885, the Sino-French War for the first time seriously tested its promised results and China was defeated; then, in 1894, the Sino-Japanese War sounded its death knell. The total collapse of China's army and navy in the latter conflict opened a new epoch in her modern history. It was the most important turning-point in the century before the Chinese Communist Revolution of 1949.

[1] *Li Wen-chung-kung ch'uan-shu*, letters, 13.10.1876, ch. 16, p. 25b.
[2] *Chang Wen-hsiang-kung ch'uan-chi*, memorials, 27.7.1885, ch. 11, pp. 22a-22b.

The 1894 war destroyed China's defence, impoverished her economy, discredited her archaic administration, and erased the last vestiges of her self-confidence. Li Hung-chang, the pillar of the Self-strengthening policy, the strong man of the 19th century China, was out of the running, and Chang Chih-tung, in a desperate attempt to rescue the policy, produced his famous essay, *Exhortation to Study*,[1] in which he carefully drew the distinction between the 't'i' (the body or the essentials) and the 'yung' (the use or the application). The manufacturing industries, for instance, were the 'body' while commerce the 'application'; or, in other words, the Chinese traditional doctrines on administration, justice and ethics were the 'body' and the foreign technological knowledge the application. According to him, China should adopt Western technology and, at the same time, retain *in toto* her traditional systems. Despite its persuasive style, the essay was coldly received. Yen Fu ridiculed it in these words:

'The *use* of the *body* of an ox is to carry heavy burdens; the *use* of the *body* of a horse is to run fast. I have never known of an ox's body being used to perform the function of a horse. . . . Chinese doctrines have their body and use, just as Western knowledge has. As long as we keep the two [Chinese doctrine and Western knowledge] strictly apart, they will both function and live; once we arbitrarily mix them together and let the body of one do the work of the other, both will become useless and inert.'[2]

Liang Ch'i-ch'ao acrimoniously remarked: 'In less than thirty years, it [the essay] will become dust and ashes. When the dust is scattered by wind, the passers-by will have to cover their noses.'[3]

The vanished 'strong man' needed replacement; so did his discredited policy. In 1895 the former was an urgent task and the latter, a matter for long deliberation. To replace Li Hung-chang as leader of the nation, Yuan Shih-k'ai was chosen and gradually placed in control. To replace the Self-strengthening policy, various experiments were put to the test by different groups of people. There was to begin with the Hundred Days Reform of 1898, followed by the

---

[1] *Chang Wen-hsiang-kung ch'uan-chi*, ch. 202-203, and J. K. Fairbank and Teng, *China's Response to the West*, pp. 166-174.

[2] Chou Chen-fu, *Yen Fu ssu-hsiang shu-p'ing*, 1940, p. 82.

[3] Quoted from Fan Wen-lan, *Chung-kuo chin-tai shih*, I, p. 311.

Boxer Movement[1] of 1900, the constitutional reform of 1905, the Revolution of 1911, and the attempt to restore the monarchy in 1915. After Yuan's death, the experiments were continued, first by the rule of the Northern warlords and later by Chiang Kai-shek, until the Communist Party took over in 1949.

Such was the trend of events after the 1895 war and peace, and through these experiments, China was seeking an adequate pattern on which to shape her 'state' and to establish a stable central government. At first the Manchu Court looked for ways and means to prolong and to stablize its rule by creating a new army and by enlisting foreign support, particularly financial. The Reform of 1898, led by the more enlightened elements of the upper classes, was not designed to overthrow the Manchu rule. On the contrary, it aimed at strengthening it, but the more conservative wing of the Imperial clan rejected it. The Boxer Uprising of 1900, too, was an attempt to strengthen the country, but it was led by unsophisticated peasants, who relied upon black magic to fight against foreign guns and which (not surprisingly) failed. The Russo-Japanese War of 1905 thoroughly convinced China of the merits of a constitution, with ensuing constitutional reform. This was, however, too late and not quite genuine. With the death of the Dowager Empress in 1908, there came a fatal split in the small ruling circle which ended in the alienation of Yuan Shih-k'ai in the face of the surging tide of revolution.

The Revolution under the leadership of educated and property-owning people and soldiers put an end to the Manchu's role in Chinese politics, yet itself ended in a victory for Yuan Shih-k'ai, thereby introducing the era of warlords. Since it was an armed revolt, it was natural that, immediately after it, soldiers should take control of the country; the tragedy was that the politicians never succeeded in wrenching the power away from them. This was because the soldiers had the backing, especially financial, of the foreign powers and the support of such well-to-do groups as the Communication Clique, the Monarchists, and landed gentry and the conservatives in general.

These people were the *élite* of the Chinese society and were described by Liang Ch'i-ch'ao as follows:

---

[1] The Movement of course had other meanings. See my article, *The Nature and Characteristics of the Boxer Movement*—a *morphological study*, the Bulletin of the School of Oriental and African Studies, June 1960.

'Indeed they are important people, but their abjectness and contemptibility can never be surpassed. In China today only cunning, crooked, vile and ruthless people can flourish; those who have the slightest measure of self-respect have gone down in the race. To become distinguished, one must be skilled in pleasing the evil forces and in serving them well. These people are the upper classes in name, but, in fact, are the lowest and the basest. With them as the *élite* of the society, and with us all under their leadership, do we have to inquire what will become of China?'[1]

Another eminent scholar, Ch'en Tu-hsiu, depicted the Chinese society in these terms:

'What strikes our eyes is the misrule of the soldiers, the emptiness of the Treasury, the evanescence of productive enterprises, the sinking of the moral standards, the corruption of the officials, the infestation of bandits and thieves, the tribulations of droughts and floods and epidemics, etc. . . . . The disdainful remarks about us by foreign observers, humiliating as they are, cannot however be denied. We are said to be "profit-seeking and shameless", "the big and old sick man", "dirty as pigs", "a country of vagrants and trampor' "bribers and bribees", "a nation of mandarins", "pig-tailed people", "gold-worshippers", "skilled liars", "afraid of might not right", "befuddled and sordid", . . .'[2]

H. G. W. Woodhead, like Liang and Ch'en, was also an eyewitness of the deterioration of the Chinese society; he commented:

'Years of domestic chaos have resulted in widespread demoralization. The old saying that "a Chinaman's word is as good as his bond", no longer holds true. Corruption and dishonesty are now as prevalent in commercial as in official circles.'[3]

This was the China at which foreigners exclaimed: 'The pity of it!'; and which the foremost essayist of modern China described as 'cannibalistic'.[4] It was against this background that Yuan Shih-k'ai grew

[1] *Jung-yen*, I, No. 5, p. 9.
[2] *Tu-hsiu wen-tsun*, I, p. 86.
[3] *The Truth about the Chinese Republic*, pp. 268-269.
[4] J. O. P. Bland, *China, The Pity of It*, 1932; Lu Hsün, *A Madman's Diary*, written in 1918, *Lu Hsün ch'uan-chi*, I, p. 281.

in stature and eventually became the supreme leader of the nation.

His first serious political lesson was the Sino-Japanese War of 1894-95 when he saw the ruination of the ageing Li Hung-chang in opposition to a strong foreign power. The lesson was so well driven home to him that, throughout the rest of his life, Yuan never fought against a single foreign soldier—not even during the Boxer Uprising nor when (in 1915) the Japanese presented him with the Twenty-one Demands. An additional reason for his remaining on friendly terms with foreign powers was China's fiscal dependence on loans from the consortium and other foreign bankers. Without the money, Yuan's Government would have been in dire difficulty in paying the officers and officials and would have disintegrated with or without the 1913 Revolution. It was on account of this attitude that Yuan was accused by communist historians of being 'the favourite of foreign imperialism'.[1]

The accusation is ill-justified, not because imperialism did not exist, but because the same historians also admit that the Chinese revolution before 1919 was a part of the *bourgeois* revolution.[2] One can hardly expect a *bourgeois* revolution to be anti-imperialistic or to fight against other *bourgeois* countries, just as one does not expect to see a socialist revolution of a country directing itself against another socialist power. The very aim of a *bourgeois* revolution is to create a strong *bourgeois* state which, in the communist logic, is by definition an imperialist power. It seems here that the communist historians want to 'have their cake and eat it'. In fact, the concept, *imperialism* (*ti-kuo-chu-i*), was not a part of the Chinese language before 1919,[3] and under Yuan Shih-k'ai, or anyone else for that matter, there were simply no effective armed forces to fight against it, nor was there the required money.

Money, or the lack of it, has been frequently referred to in our narratives; the root of the matter lay in China's poverty and the local warlords' refusal to remit tax collections to the Central Government from the time that the Republic began. The financial flexibility achieved in the 1860's due to the establishment of an efficient

---

[1] Hua Kang, *Wu-ssu yun-tung shih*, p. 45; Ch'en Po-ta, *Ch'e kuo ta-tao Yuan Shih-k'ai*, pp. 57 and 62.

[2] This periodization was first put forward by Mao Tse-tung in his now celebrated article *On the New Democracy* (*Mao Tse-tung hsüan-chi*, II, pp. 637-638). The Chinese Revolution after 1919, according to Mao, entered into a new era—the era of New Democracy, and became a part of the world proletarian revolution. Hitherto no historian in China has come forward to challenge this periodization.

[3] cf. Li Ta-chao's view quoted above, p. 345.

maritime customs service and the introduction of the excise tax—
likin—was by now lost, partly because of their being pledged
against foreign indemnities and loans and partly because of corruption
which made the *likin* less yielding. What then about the men? Among
those who were active in politics, there were the Kuomintang and
the Republican Party which later became the Progressive Party.
Both avowed to maintain friendly relations with other powers. The
soldiers were also an important political force, but they knew perfectly
well that a clash of arms with a foreign power would mean their end.
We have seen enough of all their depravity, and yet it was upon the
support of these vile people that Yuan's regime rested.

To say that Yuan Shih-k'ai could have done better by relying on
the support of the common people is simply to be wishful-thinking.
The word 'people' (*jen-min*) has crept into the Chinese history just as
the notion 'Heavenly Mandate' (*T'ien-ming*) did. How exactly it did
so is a mystery. No one denies the existence of the morally healthy,
industrious and tolerant Chinese people, then as well as now, yet the
point remains as to how far they were politically conscious and played
a part in shaping the destiny of their coutnry. Let us quote again:

Ch'en Tu-hsiu, writing immediately after Yuan's death, said this:

'The people have nothing to do with the Government, except in
paying taxes and settling law suits. They have no idea what is politics
or a government.'[1]

Few years later, Lu Hsün, in the preface to his anthology of short
stories, *Nan-han*, argued in reply to a friend who urged him to write
novels and stories:

'Let us assume an air-tight iron room, no ventilation of any kind,
and indestructible. There are many people fast asleep in it, unaware
of being suffocated to death, for they do not feel pain while in a
coma. If you begin to scream and wake up an unfortunate few who
are comparatively clear-headed, they will begin to suffer the pains
of death. Won't you feel sorry for what you have done?'[2]

But Lu Hsün did eventually write; the reason for his giving up a
medical career for writing went back to his undergraduate days in

---

[1] *Tu-hsiu wen-ts'un*, I, p. 55.
[2] *Lu Hsün ch'uan-chi*, I, p. 274.

Tokyo when he saw a newsreel about a number of Chinese being executed by Japanese soldiers in the presence of an inscrutable Chinese crowd, because they spied for the Russians during the 1905 War. Lu Hsün reflected on this event:

'Ignorant people, however strong and healthy, are only good enough to be either the victims or the witnesses of a public execution. Never mind how many of them die of disease, the most urgent task is to change their spirit.'[1]

Even as late as in 1926, four years after T. S. Eliot had written these lines:

> What are the roots that clutch, what branches grow
> Out of this stony rubbish?

a young Chinese scholar and poet lamented his country's plight in a similar tone:

> This stretch of stagnant water, sump of despair,
> Shows not a ripple under the fresh breeze.
> Throw in some more scraps of iron and copper,
> Also any amount of stale slops and left-overs.
>
> The copper will turn emerald,
> The iron will bloom rust,
> Grease will weave a veil,
> And germs ferment patterns of clouds.
>
> The water may brew into green wine
> With white bubbles like pearls.
> The small ones titter and grow,
> But are pricked and burst
>   by mosquitoes that come to steal a drink.
>
> So this stagnant water
> Can at least boast its colour;
> May even decide to sing,
> If the nearby frogs break the silence.
>
> This is a stretch of stagnant water;
> Beauty has no part in it.
> Better let ugliness take it over,
> And see what a world it contrives.[2]

---

[1] ibid, p. 271.

[2] Wen I-tuo, *Ssu-shui*, in *Wen I-tuo ch'uan-chi*, III, pp. 16-17. Professor Wen was assassinated in 1945 for his anti-Chiang Kai-shek speeches.

During Yuan's life-time, the only event in which the people played an active part was the Boxer fiasco and the best description of the Chinese of that period is Lu Hsün's *True Story of Ah Q*. The communist historians praise the *Ah Q*, on the one hand, as a realistic picture, and, on the other, assert that the failure of Yuan lay in his inability to mobilize the strength of the Chinese people and his downfall was due to their robust power. This is certainly *petitio principii*.

So that was the historical background, the kind of people Yuan Shih-k'ai led, and the type of politicians he represented. China was a pariah, bullied left and right by everyone, and yet the only feasible way for her to become strong was to ape one of those who had bullied her. There was no conceivable alternative. Inside the country, people were ignorant of their political rights, soldiers were useless, the Treasury was empty, and ethics and thoughts were confused. Under such circumstances, it would be unfair to blame Yuan alone for the humiliating foreign policies, for borrowing from abroad on usurious terms, for the corruption, and for the violation of the Constitution. The unprincipled politicians and the apathetic people should both take their share of the blame.

In that 'damnable period', as Lu Hsün put it,[1] to escape the stern judgment of history one must stay away from politics. Yuan, being ambitious, took part in the game, and therefore, should be judged also as an individual politician. He proved his worth as the Commissioner for Trade in Korea from 1884 to 1894. His courage, firmness and resourcefulness earned him the trust of his superiors, and these qualities also accounted for his being appointed to take charge of the training of the Newly Created Army. In the 1898 Reform, he showed two other ingredients of his personality—duplicity and realism. He wanted personal success more than anything else, and thus at a critical moment he chose to serve the stronger of two contending forces. He betrayed the Reformers including the Emperor himself and helped the Conservatives led by the Dowager Empress. With this display of loyalty to the Imperial lady and with his outstanding abilities, his future was sure.

A betrayal though it was, it could not mean as much as many people thought it might. The Conservatives were far too strong for the Reformers and Yuan Shih-k'ai to crush. The analysis of the general situation contained in Yuan's 1898 Journal, reproduced

[1] Lu Hsün, *Hua-kai Chi*; see *Ch'uan-chi*, III, p. 49.

above almost in full,[1] was eminently realistic. It would have made no difference, as far as the fate of the Reform was concerned, even if Yuan had joined forces with the Emperor and his entourage. The betrayal of his sovereign should not be taken however to mean a betrayal of the Manchu regime. His loyalty to the Ch'ing Government remained unflinching after that fateful year, and in 1900 he found himself in Shantung as the provincial governor. Once again, he showed his shrewd judgment by driving the Boxers away from his domain, thereby saving himself a world of troubles and disasters.

The Boxer Movement provided for him the opportunity of becoming the pillar of the Empire and he wisely made use of it. He refused to follow the Dowager Empress blindly in her folly; on the contrary, he initiated and led the viceroys and governors in the south-east, including such illustrous persons as Li Hung-chang, Chang Chih-tung and Liu K'un-i, in advocating what was in fact a policy of independence. The movement ended, among other things, in the destruction of four of the five divisions of China's modern army in the north; and thus, after the death of Li Hung-chang, Yuan, in command of the one intact division, became the only man capable of safe-guarding the Manchu Court. He was made the Viceroy of Chihli.

From 1901 to 1908, he appeared to be a satisfied man. As a vassal, his position could not be improved, and his power continued to grow. It was in this period that he showed his mild progressive tendencies. He advocated the adoption of a constitution and the reform of the traditional examination system as well as some other modern measures, with a view to strengthening the Imperial régime so that it could withstand the challenge of a revolution which was becoming more and more apparent. But the death of the Empress and the beginning of Prince Ch'un's regency brought him his first serious set-back. He was unceremoniously dismissed. The dismissal can be reasonably assumed as the most important turning-point in Yuan's life after which he became more selfish, more unscrupulous and more unprincipled. Loyalty either to a man or to a symbol played no further part in his own counsel, for it had proved 'foolish'. It was during his retirement from 1908 to 1911 that the only collection of his memorials and biography were compiled (or written) to demonstrate how loyal he had been to the Imperial House, in the

[1] *Vide supra*, pp. 56-60.

hope that by them the injustice done to him would be eventually
known to posterity. When he re-emerged in 1911, he was a different
man and his turpitude became truly manifest. His sole purpose
then was to obtain the supreme power in the state. Therefore he
played off the tottering Manchu regime against the·weak Revolutionaries in order to fulfil his own mission. But eventually he had to
accept republicanism which he neither understood nor respected,
but was sure that it had no popular support and so could be shaped
to suit himself.

The army and the support of foreign powers caused his rise to the
highest office of the Republic. It was there that his weaknesses also
became evident. Republicanism was beyond his political experience
and knowledge and he simply did not know how to run such a
government. His decrees lacked consistency and his promises were
not made to be kept. In the end his statements and proclamations
lost their meaning and commanded no respect. Being a man of
ambition and action, he hated, in the same way as many others did,
the squabbles of the members of the Senate or later of the National
Assembly. He liked to see things done instead of listening to endless
nonsensical wrangles in the legislature. The legislative bodies
themselves were indeed sometimes hindrances to the smooth
functioning of the Government. Yuan therefore felt the need to
ignore them and even went as far as to flout the Constitution in
order to change them. In such acts he repeatedly showed his lack
of both understanding and respect for republicanism. His ignorance
was the more regrettable when these actions were taken to further
his own amitions and selfish ends. In diplomacy he also showed an
ignorance which was to have disastrous results. He had abundant
admiration for Britain as he had been pro-British throughout his
whole life, yet he failed to understand that in 1912, when he assumed
the highest office, Britain was no longer the strongest power in the
Far East. She was living on her prestige which amounted to no more
than a bluff. It was stupid to Yuan to use the bluff to scare the
maturing imperialistic power of Japan. Although he had the strength
and support to lead the nation, Yuan's ignorance and ambition
made him an anachronism. He was a misfit in post-Revolution
China.

To be perfectly fair to Yuan, we must admit that at the beginning
of 1912 there was no one else who had the slightest chance of holding
the country together. Hence he was repeatedly asked to come out

from his retirement to accept the mantle of authority. His acceptance implied that he was at once the victim of his ambition and of circumstances.

We have seen before what a chaotic country the Manchus and the Revolutionaries had bequeathed to him, and we have also seen what kind of supporters he had. Upon assuming the Presidency his fore-most duties were to maintain the unity of the nation and to strengthen his control over it. Only by the fulfilment of these duties could the new Government earn recognition from others and its credit be established in the international money market. If this were done, the needed money would once again flow into China to make his Government solvent. He had no alternative. But, in maintaining the unity and strengthening his control, he made grave mistakes in the process in handling the 'opposition' and in refusing to accept a limit to his personal power. He engineered a mutiny in order to keep Peking the Capital of China; he murdered Chang Chen-wu in order to please and to exercise greater control over General Li Yuan-hung; he threatened the Senate with violence in order that Lu Chen-hsiang's cabinet could be approved; he had Sung Chiao-jen assassinated in order to weaken the Kuomintang and then used the Reorganization Loan to finance an internecine war against it. During, or after, each of these infamous deeds, he shifted blame on to some of his faithful supporters and jettisoned them. Among them T'ang Shao-i and Chao Ping-chun were the most outstanding. T'ang's estrangement and Chao's murder, and the unfair sharing out of the spoils by Yuan to his generals after the 1913 Revolution contributed to diminish the loyalty and support that his henchmen had been giving him.

The 1913 Revolution marked the decline of the Kuomintang and revealed also the dissension among the Northern warlords. These two groups together with the Manchus had been the three major political forces two years before, and now only the army leaders still flourished. The new situation must have been clear to Yuan, who in consequence of it tried to carry a step further his plan for centralization. He deemed this both opportune and neces-sary, for the Kuomintang was no longer an effective 'opposition' and the unity among his own followers needed cementing. The more he tried this, the more he alienated his supporters, particularly the warlords. His distrust of them thus deepened and he himself became more and more hemmed in by a small circle of sycophants.

The development of his policies after 1913 was plain and consistent. He succeeded in amending the Constitution, creating a 'rubber-stamp' legislature, and making himself a life-dictator. As he progressed in this direction, he was increasingly taken control of by his megalomania, so that finally he decided to found a dynasty of his own. This last attempt was made during the European War when he thought that the foreign powers, preoccupied by the War, could not intervene. It was here that he seriously misunderstood Japan's intentions and calamitously underestimated her influence. He tried to woo her support without knowing that what Japan wanted was his country, not an obedient Yuan Shih-k'ai.

The monarchical experiment clearly showed his unquenchable thirst for power as well as his obsolete knowledge of high politics. He was trained as a statesman under an imperial regime and the two countries which he admired and feared, Britain and Japan, were both kingdoms. A constitutional monarchy was probably his highest political ideal, and hence he tried to impose it on China after she had had enough bitter experiences of both monarchy and constitutions.

While carrying out this experiment he estranged more of his henchmen, and, worse still, lost the support of the Progressive Party. Japan made full use of the internal dissensions, firstly by exacting twenty-one important concessions from Yuan himself and then by turning against him. This double-dealing of hers gravely impaired his authority. Double-dealing was also Yuan's method in realizing his monarchical aim. He and his followers used bribery and threats to enlist what they called 'public opinion' and 'popular support', and, having categorically denied any wish to become an emperor, he eventually, under the pressure of so-called 'public opinion', accepted the 'Heavenly Mandate'. But now, without the loyalty of the Northern Army and many of his erstwhile henchmen, he was isolated and weak, unable to put down the resistance against him. The Yuan Shih-k'ai of 1916 was merely a shadow of the man he had been on the eve of the 1913 Revolution. His troops would not fight and there was no 'Reorganization Loan' to pay them. His lies and his tactical retreats were of no avail. The monarchy collapsed and the Emperor died in despair.

To sum up the above analysis of his times and his political career, we would say that Yuan Shih-k'ai was a typical product of the post-1895 China—a defenceless, impoverished, and morally and ideologically confused China. Yet the country enjoyed a nominal independence with an independent Central Government of which he was first an important minister and then the head. In either role, his main duty was to carry on the administration by relying on the support of foreign powers, inefficient troops, and orgulous and crooked politicians. As the head of the administration he was merely filling a gap and his policies were the only choice under such circumstances. As an individual statesman his career fell into two distinct parts, with 1908 as the turning-point when he was dismissed from all his offices by the Regent. Before that, he had served the Manchus well, and, after it, when he resumed his political activities, he served the Republic ill. His Machiavellism from 1912 to 1916 was chiefly due to his insatiable ambition and his archaic knowledge of high politics. Because of these, he was ill-equipped for the supreme leadership of a nation which he intrigued so hard to acquire.

Had he died before 1911, or had he refused to come out from his hermitage, he would have been a less important historical figure, but a much better man. But hypothesis has a very little part to play in history.

Now let us say a few words about his influences on the evolution of Chinese history.

Yuan was the founder of the Chinese modern army and his legacy to the Republic was a large number of warlords. When he was alive, they supported him; when he was dead, they fought amongst themselves. Therefore his death marked the beginning of a period of warring warlords until the establishment of the Nationalist Government in Nanking.

Another, a more profound influence was that by making a mockery of the Constitution, the parliament and democracy, he also made his successors extremely wary of adopting a similar system, for they deemed that China was not yet ready for such innovations. Even the Nationalist Government under Chiang Kai-shek had neither a constitution nor a parliament. It was not, and did not pretend to be, a democratic government. The democratic experiment, like the Reform of 1898, was a failure and was never repeated.

Yuan's ascendancy and the Kuomintang's failure in the years between 1911 and 1913 taught all Chinese aspirants that, in the last resort, Chinese major political issues could only be solved by force. The wrestling match between Yuan and the Party in those years ended in a victory for the army over the Party. A party without a

R

strong armed force could play no part in Chinese politics. But, on the other hand, Yuan's ultimate defeat might be attributed to his lack of a well-organized party to carry out his political programmes and to fill in the Government posts. This significant lesson was well learnt by Chiang Kai-shek and later by Mao Tse-tung, both being party leaders with the backing of a strong armed force. But these two eminent students differed in that Chiang's party had never succeeded in controlling the armed forces whereas Mao's had always done so.

Chiang learnt another lesson from Yuan Shih-k'ai that a Chinese national leader should never fight against a foreign power. Mao Tse-tung, in a sense, also learnt it, and therefore from 1936 to 1937 he tried all possibilities to urge, to force and even to kidnap Chiang, so that he could make the latter lead the nation to fight against Japan. The result of the Japanese War from 1937 to 1945 is well-known and Chiang's present position is reminiscent of Li Hung-chang's after the earlier Japanese War.

Through all these political changes and crises and their bitter consequences, the common people of China gradually became politically conscious, from negatively distrusting the politicians to being self-reliant. In themselves they found a fountain of strength, and under the leadership of the Communist Party, this robust strength proved enough to free the nation from foreign domination and from the influence of the corrupt elements in its midst. It was through the strength of the honest and industrious people that the phoenix rose again from her own ashes. It is only by an understanding of this that the history of the Yuan Shih-k'ai period can be properly comprehended.

BIBLIOGRAPHY

Chinese Books

aa Ai Shêng, *Ch'üan-fei chi-lüeh*, IHT, I, 443-464 (see bg).
ab Anon., *Ch'ing-ti t'ui-wei kung-ho i-an ho-k'ê*, Shanghai, 1912.
ac Anon., *Jung jao lu*, KTCS, 247-265 (*see* bc).
ad Anon., *Shansi-shêng kêng-tzŭ-nien chiao-nan ch'ien-hou chi-shih*, IHT, I, 495-523.
ae Anon., *Tientsin i-yüeh chi*, IHT, II, 141-158.
af Anon., *Yü-nan jih-chi*, IHT, II, 161-173.
ag Ch'ai O, *Kêng-hsin chi-shih*, IHT, I, 303-333.
ah Chang Chia-hsiang, *Chung-hua pi-chih shih*, 1952.
ai Chang Ch'ien, *Chang Chi-tzŭ chiu-lu*, Shanghai, 1930.
aj Chang Chih-tung, *Chang Wên-hsiang-kung ch'üan-chi*, ed. by Wang Ching-ch'ing, Shuch'êng, 1928.
ak Chang Chung-fu, *Chung-hua-min-kuo wai-chiao shih*, Taipeh, 1953.
al Chang Hsiao-jo, *Nant'ung Chang Chi-chih hsien-shêng chuan-chi*, Shanghai, 1930.
am Chang Yü-lan, *Chung-kuo yin-hang fa-chan shih*, Shanghai, 1957.
an Chao Erh-hsün *et. al.*, *Ch'ing shih kao*, Peking, 1928.
ao Ch'ên Po-ta, *Ch'ê-kuo ta-tao Yuan Shih-k'ai*, Peking, 1949.
ap Ch'ên Tu-hsiu, *Tu-hsiu wên-ts'un*, Shanghai, 1922.
aq *Cheng-fu Kung-pao* (CFKP), from May 1912.
ar Chia Shih-i, *Kuan-shui yü kuo-ch'üan*, Shanghai, 1929.
as Chia Shih-i, *Min-kuo ts'ai-chêng shih*, Shanghai, 1917.
at Chiang K'ai, *P'ingyüan ch'üan-fei chi-shih*, IHT, I, 353-362.
au Chiang T'ing-fu, *Chin-tai Chung-kuo wai-chiao shih tzŭ-liao chi-yao*, 1821-1874, Shanghai, 1931-32.
av Ch'ien Chi-po, *Hsin-hai nan-pei i-ho pieh-chi*, HHKM, VIII, 103-109 (see bf).
aw Chih Pi-hu, *Hsü I-ho-ch'üan yüan-liu k'ao*, IHT, IV, 443-445.
ax Chin Liang, *Kuang Hsüan hsiao-chi*, 1933
ay *Ch'ing Shih Lieh-chuan*, Shanghai, 1928.
az Chou Chên-fu, *Yên Fu ssŭ-hsiang shu-p'ing*, Shanghai, 1940.

ba Chou I-ping & Lo Chih-yüan, *Chung-kuo hsien-chêng fa-chan shih*, Chungking, 1944.
bb Chu Ssŭ-huang (ed.), *Min-kuo ching-chi shih*, Shanghai, 1948.
bc Chung-kuo-k'ê-hsüeh-yüan (ed.), *Kêng-tzŭ chi-shih* (KTCS), 1959.
bd Chung-fang Shih, *Kêng-tzŭ chi-shih*, KTCS, 9-77.
be Chung-kuo Shih-hsüeh-hui (ed.), *Chung-Jih Chan-chêng*, CJCC, Shanghai, 1956.

bf   Chung-kuo Shih-hsüeh-hui (ed.), *Hsin-hai Kê-ming*, HHKM, Shanghai, 1957.

bg   Chung-kuo Shih-hsüeh-hui (ed.), *I-ho-t'uan*, IHT, Shanghai, 1955.

bh   Chung-kuo Shih-hsüeh-hui (ed.), *Wu-hsü Pien-fa*, WHPF, Shanghai, 1953.

bi   Fei Ching-chung (Woch'iuchungtzǔ), *Chin-tai ming-jên hsiao-chuan*, Shanghai, 1920.

bj   Fêngkang chi-mên ti-tzǔ (ed.), *Sanshui Liang Yên-sun hsien-shêng nien-p'u* (Liang, Nien-p'u), Fêngkang, 1939.

bk   Fêng Tzǔ-yu, *San-tz'ǔ kê-ming chün*, San Francisco, 1915.

bl   Fêng Tzǔ-yu, *Kê-ming i-shih*, 1946-47.

bm   Fêng Yü-hsiang, *Wo-ti shêng-huo*, Chungking, 1944.

bn   Fêng Yu-lan *et. al.*, *Chung-kuo chin-tai ssǔ-hsiang shih lun-wên chi*, Shanghai, 1958.

bo   Ho-Han-wên, *Chung O wai-chiao shih*, Shanghai, 1935.

bp   Ho Kan-chih, *Chung-kuo hsien-tai kê-ming shih*, Peking, 1957.

bq   Hsü Ch'i-hêng & Li Hsi-mi, *Chan T'ien-yu yü Chung-kuo t'ieh-lu*, Shanghai, 1957.

br   Hsü T'ung-hsin, *Chang Wên-hsiang-kung nien-p'u*, Chungking, 1944.

bs   Hu Shêng, *Ti-kuo-chu-i yü Chung-kuo chêng-chih*, Peking, 1953.

bt   Hu Ssǔ-chin, *Lü-pei chi*, IHT, II, 483-533.

bu   Hua Hsüeh-lan, *Kêng-tzǔ jih-chi*, KTCS, 99-141.

bv   Hua Kang, *Wu-ssǔ yün-tung shih*, Shanghai, 1954.

bw   Huang Kung-chüeh & Wu Ching-hsiung, *Chung-kuo chih hsien shih*, Shanghai, 1937.

bx   Huang Yên-p'ei, *Chung-kuo shang-chan shih-pai shih*, Shanghai, 1917.

by   Huang Yüeh-po *et. al.*, *Chung-wai t'iao-yüeh hui-pien*, Shanghai, 1936.

bz   Hung Shou-shan, *Shih-shih chih-lüeh*, IHT, I, 87-103.

ca   *Jung-yên* (fortnightly), Tientsin.

cb   Kan I, *Hsin-hai ho-i chih mi-shih*, HHKM, VIII, 116-119.

cc   Kao Nan, *Kao Nan jih-chi*, KTCS, 143-246.

cd   K'ê-hsüeh-ch'u-pan-shê (ed.), *Ti-kuo-chu-i ch'ing-hua shih*, I, Peking, 1958.

ce   Kim Ok Kiun, *Chia-shên jih-chi* (*Kim's Diary*), Hirobumi Ito, *Hisho ruisan*, I, and in CJCC, II, 458-507.

cf   Ko Kung-chên, *Chung-kuo pao-hsüeh shih*, Shanghai, 1927.

cg   Ku Chung-hsiu, *Chung-hua min-kuo k'ai-kuo shih*, Shanghai, 1914.

ch   Ku-kung-po-wu-yüan (Palace Museum), *Ch'ing Kuang-hsü ch'ao Chung Jih wai-chiao shih-liao*, Peking, 1932.

ci   Ku-tê-no (Dr Goodnow), *Chün-chu yü kung-ho*, Ya-hsi-ya (Asia), 19.8.1915.

cj   Kuan Ho, *Ch'üan-fei wên-chien chi*, IHT, I, 467-492.

ck   Ku-chin-t'u-shu-kuan (ed.), *Kung-ho wei-jên ch'ih-tu*, Shanghai, 1912.

cl   Lao Nai-hsüan, *Ch'üan-an tsa-ts'un*, IHT, IV, 449-474.

cm   Lao Nai-hsüan *I-ho-ch'üan chiao-mên yüan-liu k'ao*, IHT, IV, 433-439.

cn   Lao Nai-hsüan, *Kêng-tzŭ fêng-ching I-ho-t'uan hui-lu*, IHT, IV, 475-490.

co   Li Chien-nung, *Chung-kuo chin-pai-nien chêng-chih shih*, Shanghai, 1948.

cp   Li Chien-nung, *Tsui-chin san-shih-nien (1898-1928) Chung-kuo chêng-chih shih*, Shanghai, 1930.

cq   Li Hung-chang, *Li Wên-chung-kung ch'üan-shu*, ed. by Wu Ju-lun, Nanking, 1908.

cr   Li Wên-chih & Chang Yu-i, *Chung-kuo chin-tai nung-yeh shih tzŭ-liao*, Peking, 1957.

cs   Li Hsi-shêng, *Kêng-tzŭ kuo-pien chi*, IHT, I, 9-44.

ct   Li Shu, *Hsin-hai kê-ming ch'ien-hou ti Chung-kuo chêng-chih*, Peking, 1954.

cu   Liang Ch'i-ch'ao, *Yin-ping-shih ho-chi*, Shanghai, 1926.

cv   Lin-lo-chih (Young J. Allen) & Ts'ai Erh-k'ang, *Chung-tung chan-chi pên-mo*, Shanghai, 1897.

cw   *Lin-shih Chêng-fu Kung-pao*, LSCFKP, Nanking, 29.2-4.4.1912.

cx   *Lin-shih Kung-pao*, LSKP, Peking, 26.12.1911-14.3.1912.

cy   Liu Chin-tsao, *Ch'ing-ch'ao hsü wên-hsien t'ung-k'ao*, Shanghai, 1937.

cz   Liu I-t'ung, *Min-chiao hsiang-ch'ou tu-mên chien-wên lu*, IHT, II, 183-196.

da   Liu Mêng-yang, *Tientsin ch'üan-fei pien-luan chi-shih*, IHT, II, 7-71.

db   Liu T'ang, *Tsai Hui chi-lüeh*, IHT, I, 399-404.

dc   Liu T'ang, *Tungp'ing chiao-an chi*, IHT, I, 367-396.

dd   Lo Chia-lun, *Kuo-fu nien-p'u ch'u-kao* (Sun, Nien-p'u), Taipeh, 1959.

de   Lo Tun-jung, *Ch'üan-pien yü-wên* and *Chung Jih ping-shih pên-mo*, *Jung-yên*, Nos. 1-2 and 5.

df   Lu Hsün, *Lu Hsün ch'üan-chi*, Shanghai, 1946.

dg   Ma Hsiang-po, *I-jih i-t'an*, Shanghai, 1936.

dh   Mao Tsê-tung, *Mao Tsê-tung hsüan-chi*, Peking, 1952.

di   *Min-pao*, Tokyo, 1905-1910, 1957.

dj   Pai Chiao, *Yüan Shih-k'ai yü Chung-hua-min-kuo*, Shanghai, 1936.

dk   Pei Hua, *Chung-kuo kê-ming shih*, Shanghai.

dl   P'ing-chiang chü-shih, *T'i-tsao kung-ho ming-jên shih-lüeh*, 1913.

dm   P'u-wei, *Jang kuo yü-ch'ien hui-i jih-chi*, HHKM, VIII, 110-115.

dn   Sawara *et al.*, *Ch'üan-luan chi-wên*, IHT, I, 107-234.

do   Sawara *et al.*, *Ch'üan-shih tsa-chi*, IHT, I, 235-299.

dp   Shên Chien, *Hsin-hai kê-ming ch'ien-hsi wo-kuo chih lu-chün chi ch'i chün-fei*, Shê-hui-k'ê-hsüeh, II, No. 2, January 1937, 343-408.

dq   *Shên-pao*, Shanghai.

dr   Shên-pao (ed.), *Tsui-chin chih wu-shih-nien*, Shanghai.

ds Shên Tsu-hsien & Wu K'ai-shêng, *Jung-an ti-tzŭ-chi*, (JATTC), 1913.

dt Shêng Hsüan-huai, *Yü-chai ts'un-kao ch'u-pien*, Wuchin, 1939.

du Shih Chün (ed.), *Chung-kuo chin-tai ssŭ-hsiang shih ts'an-k'ao tzu-liao ch'ien-pien*, Peking, 1957.

dv Sun Yat-sen, *Sun Chung-shan ch'üan-chi*, Shanghai, 1928.

dw Sung Chiao-jên, *Sung Yü-fu jih-chi*, T'aoyüan, 1920.

dy *Ta Ch'ing li-ch'ao shih-lu*, Tê-tsung ch'ao, 1939.

dz T'ao Chü-yin, *Liu-chün-tzŭ chuan*, Shanghai, 1947.

ea T'ao Chü-yin, *Pai-yang chün-fa t'ung-chih shih-ch'i shih-hua*, PYCFTCSCSH, 1957.

eb Ta-t'ung Hsüeh-hui, *Chung-hua-min-kuo chien-kuo shih*, Peking, 1929.

ec T'ien-hsiao-shêng, *Chung-hua-min-kuo ta-shih chi*, Shanghai, 1958.

ed Ting Wên-chiang, *Liang Jên-kung hsien-shêng nien-p'u ch'ang-p'ien ch'u-kao* (Liang Ch'i-ch'ao, Nien-p'u), Taipeh, 1959.

ee *Tsa-lu*, IHT, IV, 145-152.

ef Ts'ai Chi-ou, *Ochou hsüeh-shih*, Peking, 1958.

eg Ts'ao Ya-po, *Wuch'ang kê-ming chên-shih*, Shanghai, 1930.

eh Tsêng K'un-hua, *Chung-kuo t'ieh-lu shih*, Peking, 1924.

ei Tsou Lu, *Chung-kuo Kuomintang shih-kao*, Shanghai, 1947.

ej Tsou Lu, *Hui-ku lu*, Shanghai, 1943.

ek *Tung-fang tsa-chih*, Shanghai.

el Wang Ch'i-chü, *Yu-kuan I-ho-t'uan yü-lun*, IHT, IV, 171-237.

em Wang Chü-ch'ang, *Yên Chi-tao nien-p'u*, Shanghai, 1936

en Wang Shih-chieh & Ch'ien Tuan-shêng. *Pi-chiao hsien-fa*, Shanghai, 1946.

eo Wang T'ao-fu, *Hsi-hsün ta-shih chi*, Palace Museum, Peking, 1932.

ep Wang Tun-kên, *Pai-pi ts'ung-shu*, Shanghai, 1919.

eq Wang Yün-shêng, *Liu-shih-nien lai Chung-kuo yü Jih-pên*, Shanghai, 1932.

er Wei Chien-yu, *Chung-kuo chin-tai huo-pi shih*, Shanghai, 1955.

es Wei T'ing-shêng, *Ch'ing-chi Chung-kuo liu-hsing chih huo-pi chi ch'i yên-kê*, Ch'ing-hua-hsüeh-pao, Peking, 1924.

et Wei Tzŭ-ch'u, *Ti-kuo-chu-i yü K'ai-luan mei-k'uang*, Shanghai, 1954.

eu Wên Kung-chih, *Tsui-chin san-shih-nien Chung-kuo chün-shih shih*, Shanghai, 1930.

ev Wu Kuan-yin, *Chung-kuo yü-suan chih-tu ch'u-i*, Peking, 1918.

ew Wu Yü-kan, *Chung-kuo kuo-chi mao-i shih*, Shanghai, 1928.

ex Wu Yung, *Kêng-tzŭ hsi-shou ts'ung-t'an* IHT, III, 369-465.

ey Yang Chao-jung, *Hsin-hai hou chih Szechuan chan-chi*, Chin-tai-shih-tzŭ-liao, No. 6, 1958.

ez Yang Sung & Têng Li-ch'ün, *Chung-kuo chin-tai shih ts'an-k'ao ts'ai-liao*, Mukden, 1949.

fa Yang Sung & Têng Li-ch'ün, *Chung-kuo chin-tai shih tzŭ-liao hsüan-chi*, Peking, 1954.

fb Yang Tien-hao, *Kêng-tzŭ ta-shih-chi*, KTCS, 79-98.

fc Yang Tuan-liu, *Liu-shih-nien lai kuo-chi mao-i t'ung-chi*, 1864-1928, Shanghai

fd Yeh Ch'ang-chih, *Yüan-tu-lu jih-chi ch'ao*, IHT, II, 441-480.

fe Yên Chung-p'ing *et. al.*, *Chung-kuo chin-tai ching-chi shih t'ung-chi tzŭ-liao hsüan-chi*, Peking, 1955.

ff Yên Fu, *Hou-kuan Yên-shih ts'ung-k'ê*, Nanch'ang, 1901.

fg Yi Ching Won (Li Ch'ing-yüan), *Ch'ao-hsien chin-tai shih*, Chinese translation by Ting Tsê-liang *et. al.*, Peking, 1955.

fh *Yu-kuan I-ho-t'uan Shang-yü*, IHT, IV, i-122.

fi Yü Yung-ch'un, *Kuan-yü 'Hu-kuo-shih-kao' ti chi-kê wên-t'i*, *Chin-tai-shih-tzŭ-liao*, 1958, No. 5.

fj Yü Yung-ling, *Ch'ing-kung so-chi*, Peking, 1957.

fk Yuan Ch'ang, *Luan-chung jih-chi ts'an-kao*, IHT, I, 337-349.

fl Yuan Shih-k'ai, *Hsin-chien lu-chün ping-lüeh ts'un-lu*, 1898.

fm Yuan Shih-k'ai, *Wu-shü jih-chi*, WHPF, 549-556.

fn Yuan Shih-k'ai, *Yang-shou-yüan tsou-i chi-yao*, ed. by Shên Tsu-hsien, 1937.

fo Yün-lung, *Hu-kuo shih-kao*, *Chin-tai-shih-tzŭ-liao*, 1957, No. 4.

fp Yün Yü-ting, *Ch'ung-ling ch'uan-hsin lu*, IHT, I, 47-55, or *Jung-yên*, 1914, II, No. 5.

Others

fq Abbot, J. F., *Japanese Expansion and American Policies*, New York, 1916.

fr Akagi, Roy Hidemichi, *Japan's Foreign Relations*, 1542-1936, Tokyo, 1936.

fs Allen, G. C. & Doninthorne, A. G., *Western Enterprise in Far Eastern Economic Development, China, and Japan*, London, Allen & Unwin, 1954.

ft Allen, H. N., *Korea, Facts and Fancy*, 1904.

fu Asakawa, K., *The Russo-Japanese Conflict*, Westminster, 1904.

fv Barnes, A. A. S., *On Active Service with the Chinese Regiment*, London, 1902.

fw Beresford, Lord Charles, *The Break-up of China*, New York, 1899.

fx Bishop, Mrs I. L. B., *Korea and her Neighbours*, London, 1898.

fy Bland, J. O. P., *China, Japan and Korea*, London, 1921.

fz Bland, J. O. P., *Recent Events and Present Policies in China* (Recent and present), London, 1912.

ga   *The Boundary Question between China and Tibet*, a valuable record of the tripartite conference between China, Britain and Tibet held in India 1913-1914, Peking, 1940.

gb   Bredon, Sir Robert, *China—The Loan Situation at Date*, April 1912.

gc   *British Parliamentary Debates*, Nos. 185 and 186, 1908.

gd   *British Parliamentary Papers, 1895*: despatch from Her Majesty's Minister at Tokyo forwarding copy of the Treaty of Peace concluded between China and Japan on April 17, 1895.

ge   *British Parliamentary Paper on the Chinese Revolution 1911*.

gf   Cameron, M. E., *The Reform Movement in China*, 1898-1912, Stanford University Press, 1931.

gg   Carles, W. R., *Life in Korea*, London, 1888.

gh   Chang Chia-ngau, *The Inflation Spiral, the Experience in China, 1939-1950*, Massachusetts, 1958.

gi   *China Year Book*, 1912.

gj   *China Year Book*, 1913.

gk   *China Year Book*, 1914.

gl   Chinese Customs, *Decennial Reports*, Shanghai, 1882-1911.

gm   Clyde, G., *International Rivalries in Manchuria*, 1889-1922, Ohio, 1926.

gn   Collies, M., *Foreign Mud*, London, 1949.

go   Colquhoun, A., *China in Transformation*, New York, 1912.

gp   Curtis, L., *The Capital Question of China*, London, 1932.

gq   Curzon, G. N., *Problems of the Far East, Japan, Korea, China*, London, 1896.

gr   Dennett, T., *Americans in Eastern Asia*, New York, 1922.

gs   Dennis, *The Anglo-Japanese Alliance*, California, 1923.

gt   Denny, O. N., *China and Korea*, Shanghai, 1888.

gu   Douglas, R. K., *Europe and the Far East*, Cambridge, 1913.

gv   Dyer, H., *Dai Nippon*, London, 1904.

gw   *Foreign Office Documents (British)*, Foreign Office, 17.

gx   Foster, J. W., *American Diplomacy in the Orient*, Boston, 1903.

gy   Hart, Robert, *These from the land of Sinim*, London, 1901.

gz   Hillier, W. C., *1895 Reports from Korea*, Foreign Office 17, 1247.

ha   Hobden, H., Lawton, L. F. &, 'The Fall of Yuan Shih-k'ai', *Fortnightly Review*, old series, LXXXXIII, March 1910, 420-434.

hb   Hornbeck, S. K., *Contemporary Politics in the Far East*, New York, 1918.

hc   Hoshino, T., *Economic History of Manchuria*, Seoul, 1920.

hd   Hosie, T., *Manchuria, its People, Resources and Recent History*, London, 1904.

he   Hou Fu-wu (Franklin W. Houn), *Central Government of China, 1912-1928*—An Institutional study, Wisconsin, 1959.

hf Hsü, M. C., *Railway Problems in China*, Columbia University, New York, 1915.

hg Hulbert, H. B., *The Passing of Korea*, London, 1906.

hh Hummel, A. W., *Eminent Chinese of the Ch'ing Period*, Washington, 1943.

hi Hummel, A. W. junr., 'Yuan Shih-k'ai as an Official under the Manchus', unpublished M.A. thesis, Chicago, 1949.

hj Ireland, A., *China and the Powers*, Boston, 1902.

hk Ito, Hirobumi, *Official Papers* (Hisho ruisan) Tokyo, 1935-36.

hl Johnston, R. F. *Twilight in the Forbidden City* (Twilight), London, 1934.

hm Jordan, Sir John, 'Private Papers', uncatalogued, 1912-1916, British Foreign Office library.

hn Kawakami, K., *American-Japanese Relations*, New York, 1912.

ho Kennan, G. E. H., *Harriman, A Biography*, Boston, 1922.

hp Kent, P. H., *The Passing of the Manchus*, London, 1912.

hq Kent, P. H., *Railway Enterprise in China*, London, 1907.

hr Lattimore, O., *Manchuria, Cradle of Conflict*, 1932.

hs Lattimore, O., *Pivot of Asia*, Boston, 1950.

ht Lawton, L. F., *Empires of the Far East*, London, 1912.

hu Leonard, H., *The Chinese Army*, ca. 1908, cited as Captain Henry Leonard, USMC.

hv Loan disputes correspndence CMD, 6446, 1912.

hw Longford, J. H., *The Story of Korea*, London, 1911.

hx Lowell, P., *Chöson: the Land of the Morning Calm*, London, 1885.

by MacMurray, J. V. A., *Treaties and Agreements with and Concerning China, 1894-1919*, New York, 1921.

hz MacNair, H. F., *China in Revolution*, Chicago, 1931.

hz MacNair, H. F., *Modern Chinese History:* selected readings, Shanghai, 1927.

ib Matsu, Count, *Memoirs* (in Japanese), Tokyo, 1929.

ic McCordock, R. S., *British Far Eastern Policy, 1894-1900*, New York, 1931.

id McCormack, F., *American and the Chinese Loan*, New York, Scribners, L, 349.

ie McCune, G. M. & Harrison, J. A., *Korean-American Relations*, I, 1883-1886, California, 1915.

if Michie, A., *The Englishman in China*, London, 1900.

ig Millard, T. F., *America and the Far Eastern Question*, New York, 1909.

ih Overlach, T. W., *Foreign Financial Control in China*, New York, 1919.

ii Parker, E. H., *China, her History, Diplomacy and Commerce*, London, 1901.

ij   Pooley, A. M. (ed.), *Secret Memoirs of Count Tadasa Hayashi*, New York, 1915.

ik   Powell, R. L., *The Rise of Chinese Military Power, 1895-1912*, Princeton, 1955

il   Remer, C. F., *The Foreign Trade in China*, Shanghai, 1926.

im   Remer, C. F., *The Foreign Investment in China*, New York, 1933

in   Reid, J. G., *The Manchu Abdication and the Powers, 1908-1912*, 1935.

io   Richard, T., *Forty-five Years in China*, London, 1916.

ip   Reinsch, P. S., *An American Diplomat in China* (An American diplomat), London, 1922.

iq   Reinsch, P. S., *Intellectual and Political Currents in the Far East*, Boston, 1911.

ir   Rockhill, W. W., *The Land of Lamas*, New York, 1891.

is   Sargent, A. J., *Anglo-Chinese Commerce and Diplomacy*, London, 1907.

it   Seymour, Admiral Sir E. H., *My Naval Career and Travels*, London, 1911.

iu   Soothill, W. E., *Timothy Richard of China*, London, 1926.

iv   Steiger, G. N., *China and the Occident:* the origin and the development of the Boxer Movement, Yale, 1927.

iw   Straight, W., *China's Loan Negotiation*, New York, 1913.

ix   T'an, Chester C., *The Boxer Catastrophe*, Columbia University, New York, 1955.

iy   Tenney, C. D., *A Condensed Biography of Yuan Shih-k'ai*, WDGS, Political Conditions in China, No. 7829-17, October 27, 1915.

iz   *The Times*, London.

ja   Tyler, W. F., *Pulling Strings in China*, London, 1924.

jb   Varé, D., *Laughing Diplomat*, London, 1938.

jc   Verbrugge, R., *Yuan Che-k'ai*, Sa Vie-Son Temps, Paris, 1934.

jd   Weale, B. L. P., *Indiscreet letters from Peking*, New York, 1922.

je   Weale, B. L. P., *The Fight for the Republic of China* (Fight), London, 1918.

jf   Weale, B. L. P., The Re-shaping of the Far East, New York, 1905.

jg   Weale, B. L. P., *The Truce in the East and its Aftermath*, New York, 1907.

jh   Wên Ch'ing, *The Chinese Crisis from Within*, London, 1901.

ji   *Who's Who in China*, Shanghai, 1925.

jj   Williamson, H. R., *British Baptists in China, 1845-1952*, London, 1957.

jk   Willoughby, W. W., *Foreign Rights and Interests in China*, Baltimore, 1927.

jl   Winston, A. P., *Chinese Finance under the Republic*, QJE, XXX, August, 1916.

jm Witte, Count, *The Memoirs of Count Witte*, ed. by A. Yarmolinsky, New York, 1921.

jn Woodhead, H. G. W., *The The Truth about the Chinese Republic*, London, 1925.

jo Wright, M. C., *The Last Stand of Chinese Conservatism*, Stanford, 1957.

jp Wright, S. F., *Hart and the Chinese Customs*, Belfast, 1950.

jq *Yuan Shih-k'ai: His Enemies, The Outlook*, LXXXXI, January 16, 1909.

NOTES

The title of a book or an article is given in its alphabetical
order as shown in the bibliography; volume or chapter
in Roman numerals; and pagination in Arabic figures.

Youth:
  dg 45
  ds 1a-4b
  ea 6 and 26
  fn 8b
  hh II 949-950
  je 17-18

Korea before 1882:
  be I 289-95
  ca I, No. 5, 2-3.
  fr 114-18.

Korea Mutiny 1882:
  ai I 3a-4a
  be II 196-97, 207
  ca I, No. 5, 5
  ch III 11a, 17b-18b, 20a, 27a, 32a, 36a-b, 39a, 44a-b
  co 168
  cq Telegram, I 8a
  ds 6b, 8a-9a, 12b
  ea I 6
  eq I 168, 178, 207
  fr 124-25
  hh II 950
  hp 308-09
  ie 103

Korean *coup d'état*, 1884:
  ai I 4a-5a, 6b, 10a
  be II 251-54, 310-11, 315, 459-495, III 57
  ca 7b-8a
  ch V 30a-b, 35a, VI 14a-29a, VII 17b-25a
  cq Telegram X 12a, Translation Bureau XVI 10b-11a, 18b-36b,
       XVII 4b, 8b, XIX 36b
  cv I 27a-28a
  dy CLXLVI 9b-10a, 15b-16b, CLXLVII 16b-17a

eq   I 184, 204, 213, 216-17, 219-221, 223, 230-34, 255-56
fr   119, 127-28, 131-33
gg   290-94
gq   194
gw   17, 962, 979
hg   121, 124-25
hh   II 951
hk   I 297, 299-300, 311, 384-85, 419-20, 424, 503-671
hw   330-31
ie   96-135
je   18-9
jp   502

Commissioner for Trade:
be   II 45, 48-9, 52, 58-9, 65-71, 86, 91-4, 103-04
ch   IX 1a-2a, 9a-10am 13a
cq   Memorial, LXXIV 46b, LXXV 16a-b, 24b-25a, Telegram VII
      24a, 25a, VIII 28a-29a, 30a-b, 31a, 33a-b, 34b, 35a-37a, 38a-b,
      IX 1a-b, 2a-b, 6b-7a, 21b-22a, 23a, 30a-b, 31b, 33a, X 10b, 43b,
      XI 4b-5a, 8b, 9b, 24b, 35b, 40a-b, 43a, 55a, 56a, 57a-b, XII 4b,
      5a, 8b, 16b, XIII 21a, 26a, XIV 1a-2a, 2b, 9a, Translation
      Bureau, XVI 12b-13b, XVII 2cb, 24a-25a, 31a-33a, 50b-51a,
      55a-b, Navy II 3b-4a, 5a-b, 6a, 7a, 7b-8b, :9b, 12a, 13b-14a
ds   15b, 18b, 19a, 20a, 20b, 21a, 26a, 26b, 27a.
dy   CLXXXVI 8a-b
ea   I 6
eq   I 237
fg   28, 62, 73-5, 133-34
hh   II 951
hk   II 5
hw   327
ie   119, 121, 124, 135, 138, 144, 148, 150, 152, 211, 231, 237, 265, 297
je   19
jp   640-41, 506

War, 1894-95:
The Tong Hak—
be   VII 217
cd   I 277, 279
cq   Telegram, XIV 28b-29a, 31b-32a, 37b, XV 31a, 31b, 32a
fg   84-5, 88
fr   136-37
hk   II 332, 643
hw   331-32

Kim Ok Kiun—
be   VII, 7-9
cq   Telegram, XV 25b-26a, 26b, 27a, 29a, 30a

Before the Conflict—
be   VII 150, 219-20
cd   282
ch   XIV 29a-b
cq   Telegram XV 32b-33a, 33b-34a, 34b, 35a, 35b, 36a-b, 37a-b, 38a,
       39a-40a, 40b, 42b, 43a, 43b, 44a-b, 45a, 45b, 46a, 48a, 49b,
       50b-51a, 54a, XVI 3b-4a, 15b-16a, 18a
fg   99, 100-01
fr   138, 141, 145
gg   303
gw   1190
gz   1247
hg   130-31

The War—
be   V 215, 496
bn   30-1
ca   I, No. 5
co   168
cq Telegram, XV 38b-39a, XVI 4b-5a, 22b, XVII 38a, XVIII 12a,
       XIX 26a
eq   I 207
fg   90-1, 102
fr   137, 146
gw   1190
jp   643-45

The Aftermath—
be   VII 495-508
bi   11-12
bj   19
cq   Telegram, XX 52a
cy   CCIII 9512b
fa   365-70
fr   178
gp   95
gz   1247
hk   II 549-50
ib   343

Yuan's Activities—
be   IV 482, 489-90
ds   I 31b, II 1a, 3b
ch   XIV, 37a
cq   Telegram, XIV 42a, XVI la-b, 5b, 8b, 11b-12a, 20-21a, 22b, 25a,
       39a, XVII 14a
ea   I 6
fr   145
gw   1190
hh   II 951
ik   74
iz   7.6.1916
je   20
Peking Gazette: 9.2.Kuanghsü 20, 1.7.20, 10.8.20, 3.10.20, 19.11.20,
       21.11.20, 28.12.20, 12.6.21

Hsiaochan:
an   Basic Annals, XXIV 10b, *Ping*, III 1b-2a, 6b, 7a, X 7b, 8a.
be   IV 505, 511, 517, V 219, 221
bh   I 483
cv   I 28b-30a, IX 24b-25b
cy   *Ping* II 9512b, XVIII 9655b, 9657a
ds   II 5b-8a, 25b
dy   CCCLXXVIII 9a-10a
ea   I 6, 27
eu   I sect. i, 16-38
ez   I 232-33
fl   I 19a-b
fn   I 8b-9a
fw   269, 272
hh   I, 406
ii   253-54
ik   62-3, 79-80, 81-2, 100
iz   4.7.1900, 19.7.1900

The Reform, 1898:
an   Basic Annals XXIV 9a, XXV 22b
bh   I 260-63, 273, 333, 341, 345-46, 349, 351, 377-78, 433-34, 465-66,
       484
bj   31
bm   110-13
cu   I 8, 10
dq   23.8.Kuanghsü 24
ds   II 10b

du 244, 254-55, 258, 275, 365-80
dy CCCCXXVI 1a, 9b
ea I 8-9
fj 10-13
fm *passim*
hl 36
hp 16-22
io 265

Yuan's Role at Hsiaochan and in the Reform:
an XXIV 11a, XXV 22b, *Ping*, III b 6
ao 2
be IV 445, 513, V 221, 231, 303
bh I 348, 513, 518, IV 222, 309
bm 72
ds 5b-10b
eu I sect. i 15
fl I 30a-b
fw 268-69, 270-80, 282-83
gf 28
hh II 951
io 255
iz 21.9.1899, 9.12.1908
je 21
Kuo-wên-pao 11.6.KH 24, 6.8.KH 24, 11.8.KH 24

The Boxer Uprising:
an Basic Annals XXIV 13a, Biography CCXXVII, CCCCLXI,
      CCCCLXXIII
ay LXI
bc:
    ac 257, 265
    bd 13, 16, 18, 22-4, 27, 31
    bu 102
    cc 154, 157, 171
    fb 85, 89, 93, 102, 129-137
bg:
    aa 444
    ae 142-43, 145, 148
    af 161
    ag 303-05, 307-08
    at 354, 360
    cw 443-44

bz 90-1
cj 468, 470, 487, 491-92
cl 452-53, 460
cs 12-4, 15-7, 18, 20, 23, 25-6, 31, 41
cz 183, 188
da 7, 11-2, 24-6, 36
db 399-404
dn 108, 111, 139, 156, 176, 194, 219
do 237-38, 244, 249, 254
el 181, 226
ex 373-74, 376, 386
fd 463
fh 9, 23, 31-2, 48
fk 341, 345-46
fp 47, 52-3
ca I, No. 1, 6, No. 4, 2
co 207
cq Telegram, XXII 6a-b, 33a, XXIII 19a, 20b, 26a, 53a, XXIV 38a, XXXVIII 5b
cy *Pȋng* XXXVIII 9848a
ds II 10b, 11a, 12a-b, 15b, 16a, 17a, 19b-20a, 20b, 21a
dt XXI 19b-20a, 21a-22b, XXXV 22b, 25b, XXXVI 20b-21a, 30a-b, XXXVII 1a, 4b, 17a-b, 18a, 29a, 32a, XXXVIII 21b, 22b-23a, XXXX 1a-1b, 2b, 20b
dy CCCCIV 4b, CCCCLV 11b, 14a
ea I 11-12
eo I 2a, 13b, 48a, 55a, II 26a-b, 27b, 40b, III 5b, 6a, 15b-16a, 23a-b, 24b-25a, 29a-b, 33b, IV 14a-b, 15b, 39b, VIII 53a-b, IX 14a
eu I sect. i, 39
fn I 9a-11b, II 1a-5a, IV 23b, V 1a-b, 4b-5a, 6b-8a, 9a-10b, 11b, VI 2a-b, 3a-b, 7a-b, 8a-b, 12a-b, XIV 8a-12b
fv 31ff, 132
gc China No. 1 (1901), No. 5, and also Nos. 18, 195, 200 and 257
gy 4
hh II 951
hy I 248-252
il 105
it 342-354
ix 49, 50, 51-2, 183
jd 8-9, 29, 33, 49, 85

The Governor:
an Basic Annals, XXIV 12b
s

bi   Chiang Fang-chên's article on military development, 4
br 150
ds II 14-5, 22b-5, 22b-23a, 26a-27b, III 1b
ea I 13, 213
eo II 10a
fn I 2b-5a, 12a-13a, III 3a-5b, 10a-13b, IV 1a-3b, IX 16b-17b,
    18a-b, X 4a-7b, 8a-b, XI 1a-2b, 8b, XVII 1a-b
jj 75-76

The Viceroy:

an Basic Annals, XXIV 17a-b, 18b, 19b
co 216, 230
cq Telegram, XXXVIII 6b, 8b
ds II 25a, III 1a, 2a, 2b, 4b, 5a, 7a, 10a, 14b
dt LVI 27b, 28a-b, 29a-b
ea I 12, 14
fn IX 19a, XIV 13a-15a, XXXXII 1a-2b
ik 126
iz 19.9.1908, 4.1.1909

Defence—
an Basic Annals, XXIV 20a-b, 24a-b, 27b, *Ping* III 7a
bm 82, 90, 94, 95
co 259
cy *Ping* III 9518a, V 9548b, XVIII 9658-60a, XIX 9671b-9672a,
    XXIX 9755a
ds III 4b, 5b-6a, 6b, 8a, 10b, 11b, 14a, 15b, 16b, 18a-b, 19a-b, 20a,
    21a, IV 3a, 5b, 6b, 7b, 8a, 12b-13a, 13b-14a, 14b
dy CCCCCVII 6b-7a, 10b-11b, CCCCCXL 7b, 10a-b
ea 12-13, 15, 16, 17, 19
ek I, No. 2 (1904) 51, No. 1 (1905) 19, No. 4 (1905) 147-48, 181-82,
    197-201, No. 6 (1905) 99, 251, No. 7 (1905) 42, No. 12 (1905) 250
eu I sect. i, 40, sect. ii 2
fn XIII 2a-5a, XIV 15a-16a, XV 1a-4b, XVI 1a-2b, 3a-b, XVIII
    2a-b, 3a, 4b-6b, XXI 4b-5a, XXII 2b, XXIII 1a-b, XXVI
    7a-9b, XXXI 14a-16b, XXXII 4b, XXXIV, 1a-b, XXXIX
    1a-2b, XXXX 1a-b, XXXXI 1a-8b, XXXXII 3a-b, 6a-7b,
    XXXXIII 2b-4a
gl 1902-11, 3rd issue, I 37
hu 170-251, 228, 247-50, 303-322, 373
ik 144, 207-09
iz 7.3.1902, 2.12.1903, 31.10.1906, 3.10.1907, 21.10.1911

Finance and Economy—

an Basic Annals, XXIV 17b, 18a, 19b
bj 53, 54, 58, 67, 68
bq 42
co 296
cu XXI 94-6
cy *Ping* XXXVIII *passim*, *Yu-ch'uan* X 11141-42, XIV 11183a
di No 2 (1905) 10
ds III 2b, 3a-b, 4a, 9a, 10b, 11a, 12b-13a, 16a, 18a, 20b, IV 2b
dt XXXI 32b, LVIII 30a, LIX 5a, 8a, 10a-b, 11a, 15b-16a, 19a-b
eh 53, 66-7, 69-70, 73-4, 76-7, 78, 102-07, 412-13, 499
ek No. 7 (1905) 125-27, No. 10 (1905) 83-7, 241-43
et 2, 3, 7-12, 12-15, 16-18, 27-29, 30, 31, 32, 33-34 35, 38, 101-02, 103-04, 105-06, 109-12
fn XIX 2a-4a, 4a-b, 5b, XX 2b-3b, XXII 4a-7a, XXV 3a-5b, 7a-8b, XXVII 1a-3b, 4a-6a, XXVIII 20a-b, 21a, XXXI 19a-20a, XXXIII 1a-4b
fw 292-303
gc China No. 1 (1899) Nos. 175, 324, 349, 383
gl 1892-1901, 2nd issue, I 306, II 519
hu 165-66, 235-36
ik 302
iz 19, 20, 25, 26, and 28.1.1905, 1, 2, 4, 8, 9, 11 and 13.2.1905, 2.3.1905
ip 812-816

Politics—

an Basic Annals, XXIV 23b-26a, XXV 2a
ax 61
bf IV 4-6, 13, 16-18, 33 *seq.*
bk 50
ca I, No. 6, 3, 5
co 118-119
cr I 215
cy *Ping* III 9527a
di No. 7 (1905), 1, No. 10 (1906) 19, No. 22 (1908) 13, No. 25 (1908), 17-18
ds III 15a-b, IV 11b-12a, 18b-19a, 28a
ea I 17-20, 33-36, 52
ek No. 1 (1905), 2, No. 6 (1905) 116, No. 7 (1905) 58, No. 9 (1905) 65, No. 10 (1905) 170, No. 12 (1905) 203, 216, 379
fj 75, 79, 84-5
fn XXVI 1a-3b, 3b-7a, XXXXIII 2b-4a

S*

dt XIX 54a-b, LXXVII 10a, LXXXVII 13b.
eh 52-3, 75-6, 108-09, 110, 112-13, 117, 415
fe 190
fr 298
hp 117
hq 190-94
ip 96
iw 133
iz 8.1.1909; 7.1, 19.5, 6.9, 27.10.1911

Revolts—
bf I 4, 29, 66-7, 85-7, 133-34, 144-45, 226-30, 231, 235-36, 239, 249,
    315-18, 322-23, 333-35, 349, 367-86, 405, 444-45, 481, 490,
    505ff, 515ff, 530, 540, 547, 572, 573-74, II 3ff, 44, 48-9, 94, 271ff,
    281ff, 283-394, 444-45, 463, III 38, VI 268-70
bi 29-30
bk 51
bm 149-50
ca I, No. 6
co 299, 305-07, 313
cp 97-9, 106
dd 53, 56, 96, 99, 134, 156-58, 195
di No. 1 (1905) 1-3, No. 16 (1907) 3
ea I 8-9, 20, 30-2, 81-4
ef 129
ge Jordan to Grey 5.11.1911
iz 11.11.1911

The Recall—
al 145
an Basic Annals XXV 20a-b, 21a-b, 22b, 31a-b
bf VIII 547
bi 64
bj 100, 103-04, 110-11
co 309
ds 30b-31a
dt CXXXVII 9b-10a
dz 46
ea I 74-6, 78-80, 85-6
hl 84
hp 147
iz 9.10.1909, 17.12.1910, 1.9, 6.9, 8.9, 29.9, 30.9, 23.10.1911,
    20.2.1912

The Revolution, 1911:

War and Peace—
an Basic Annals, XXV 22b, 23a-b, 24a
bf VI 272, 276-79, 285-86, 298, 305, 309, VIII 77, 82, 102-03, 104-07,
      116-19, 129-31, 135-36, 143-44, 308-09, 328-29, 351, 356-58,
      379-80, 544-550
bi III 32
ca I, No. 61
cu XXXIII 107
cw No. 17 20.2.1912, No. 29 5.3.1912
cx No. 1 29.1.1912
cy *Ping* XXXIX 9850b-9851a
dd 279
dr Chiang Fang-chên's article, 4
ea I 16, 82, 87, 89, 90-1, 95-6, 98, 102-03, 106-07, 108, 109, 121-22
ef 157-58
eu I, sect. ii, 4
fz 33, 153, 162, 165, 167, 168, 365
ge Jordan to Grey 1.2, 3.2, 26.11, 28.11.1911
gh 253-55
hl 89
in 150
iz 8.7, 28.10, 1.12.1911
jn 30-31
see also Chang Kuo-kan, *Hsin-hai kê-ming shih-liao*, Shanghai, 1958,
      I 87, 102-04, 105-10, 115, III 269, 278, 281-83, 288, 289, 294, 296,
      298, 299-300, 302-03, 309-10; and Yang Yü-yu (ed.), *Hsin-hai
      kê-ming hsien-chu chi*, Shanghai, 1958, 190-278

The Abdication—
ai III 9b-10a, 40a-41b
al 154-55
an Basic Annals XXV 20b, 22b, 23a-b, 24a-25a
bf VI 288, 308-09, 312, 340, VIII 110, 111-115, 120, 123, 127-28,
      145-46, 173, 183, 187-88, 374-75, 541- 2, 549-50
bg 105-06, 107, 111, 128
bk 52
bl II 328-29
co 361
cw No. 8 5.2.1912, No. 10. 2.1912
cx 3.2.1912, 12.2.1912.
dj 369
ea I 77, 81, 110-112, 120-22

fr 333
fz 155, 161, 166, 168-69
hp 296-97, 311-14
iz 11.12, 23.12, 25.12, 29.12.1911, 11.1, 15.1.1912
je 27

The Capital—
al IV 2a-3b, 8a
bf VI 324, VIII 122, 124-26, 136-38, 514-15, 553
bj 114
bk 60
bm 165
ca I, No. 4, 3
XXV 196
cw No. 20 23.2.1912
cx 9.2, 12.2, 13.2, 15.2, 17.2, 18.2, 22.2, 24.2, 27.2, 28.2, 2.3, 3.3, 4.3,
5.3, 7.3, 10.3.1912
ea I 123-27
ef 177, 188
ei II 956
hp 333-41
ip 3
iz 28.11.1911, 29.2, 1.3, 2.3.1912

The Presidency:

Party Politics—
aq 31.5, 9.7, 12.7, 31.7, 11.8, 19.8, 20.8, 21.8, 22.8, 23.8, 28.8, 30.8,
2.9, 29.9.1912
bf VIII 578 *seq.*, 586-88, 588-92, 598
bj 123
bl I 35
co 209-11, 362-64, 367
cx 30.3, 31.3, 4.4, 13.4.1912
ea I 139-150
ei I 142, 160-61
ej 50, 53-5, 68
fa 574 *seq.*, 687
ip 32
iz 20.8, 27.8.1912, 26.4.1913
je 202

Constitution and Parliament—

aq 26.4, 14.5, 15.5, 17.5, 21.5, 23.5, 27.5, 28.5, 30.5, 31.5, 5.6, 7.6,
10.6, 11.6, 12.6, 17.6, 19.6, 20.6, 26.6, 27.6, 28.6, 1.7, 2.7, 3.7,
4.7, 6.7, 8.7, 11.7, 12.7, 15.7, 17.7, 18.7, 19.7, 20.7, 23.7, 24.7,
26.7, 29.7, 30.7, 31.7, 1.8, 2.8, 3.8, 7.8, 8.8, 9.8, 12.8, 13.8, 14.8,
15.8, 16.8, 19.8, 23.8, 26.8, 27.8, 28.8, 30.8, 2.9.1912; 19.3, 8.4,
10.5, 5.10, 13.11, 26.11, 12.12, 14.12, 15.12, 29.12.1913

bf VIII 595 *seq.*

bk 13

bw I 36, 37-8, 43-6, 48, 57-61

ca I, No. 15, 4-5, II, Nos. 1-2, 2

co 401-03

cu XXX 13, 59

cw No. 35, 11.3.1912, No. 55, 2.4.1912

cx 15.3, 16.3, 17.3, 19.3, 22.3, 26.3, 29.3, 8.4, 6.5, 8.5, 10.5, 13.5.1912

dj 69-79

dr Chiang Jung's article, 1-2

dz 157-160

ea I 123-24, 128, 130, 145, II 5-7, 11-5, 18-20

ei I 145-46, II 958-64

ej 55, 63-66

ep I, II, 1, 4

ip 2

iz 20.2, 9.4, 3.11.1913

je 43

jn 266

Government—

al 153, 161

aq 2.6, 8.6, 17.6, 20.6, 21.6, 24.6, 26.6, 27.6, 28.6, 29.6, 3.7, 11.7, 14.7,
19.7, 21.7, 26.7, 29.7, 2.8, 5.8, 9.8, 10.8, 20.8, 27.8, 16.9, 22.9,
25.9, 10.10, 14.11, 15.11.1912; 1.5, 2.5, 11.5, 16.5, 16.7,
18.7.1913

bf VIII 376-78, 602-07

bj 115, 120-22, 126

bk 46

cg 128

co 376-77

cx 10.3, 13.3, 15.3, 30.3, 30.4.1912

ea I 128, 133, 134, 135-37, 145, II 27

ei II 972

ep I, 1, 40

fz 81, 209, 210, 382

hp 127

Finance and Economy—

aq 25.5, 3.6, 4.6, 6.6, 7.6, 16.6, 17.6, 22.6, 28.6, 29.6, 12.7, 18.7, 20.7,
        9.9, 23.12, 25.12.1912; 5.7, 23.7, 30.7, 21.8, 25.9, 26.9, 2.11,
        7.11, 12.11.1913; 19.2, 7.4, 2.8, 27.12.1914
as 45-66, 154, 158-59, 183-85, 192-93, 219
bb 87, 120-21, 179, 194, 228, 231, 283, 297, 298, 302, 316, 334, 517,
        535
bf VIII 85, 87, 91, 93, 140-41, 562-64
bj 120, 147, 162, 168-176, 178-82, 197, 268-72, 338
bk 22
ca I, No. 5, 1, I, No. 13, 10-11, I, No. 15, 1
cr I, 188, 358-59, II 70 *seq.*, 132-33, 139, 148-49, 47c, 589-99, 617-18,
        620
cu XXIX 111-24
cx 10.3, 16.3, 22.3.1912
dz 20
ei 70-1, 124-25, 402, 416-20, 422-24, 450, 495-500, 567, 570-71, 574,
        567-68, 764
ep I 1, 33, II 16, 17-8, IV 11, 13-4
er 180-206
fe 41, 49, 54, 57-217
fz 200, 279, 378
hm 23.2.1916
ih 238
il 110, 132, 180, 184, 185, 188-94, 199, 250
ip 81-2, 84-5, 86, 90, 150, 162, 166
iz 25.10.1911, 23.11.1912, 16.1.1913, 1.1.1914
je 46-7

Loans—

am 62
aq 19.5, 23.5, 24.5, 29.5, 1.6, 7.6.1912, 24.4, 26.4, 1.5, 10.5, 15.5.1913
as 46, 152, 180-83, 198-201
bf VIII 463, 565-66, 567-68, 569-70, 570-72
bj 187, 194-96, 197-99, 202-04, 216, 245-48, 248-50, 251-52
bk 8-9
ca I, No. 1, 2-3, No. 2, 1-2, No. 4, 3, 7, No. 13, 3, 6-7, 7-12, 13-4, 15,
        20, 23, 25, 25-34, Nos. 13-14, 1-14, II, Nos. 1-2, 3
ea I 133-34, 164, 165, 172
ej 55-7, 60-3
ep I, 1, 18
eq VI, 9, 11-2
fa 705-06

fz 101, 154-55, 162, 216, 251-52, 275-78, 395-98
hm 22.1, 13.2, 6.5.1913; 12.1, 6.4, 10.6.1914; 16.4.1916.
hp 351
hy II 1025
ih 170-72, 223-24, 243, 247-51, 264
ip 91, 187, 191
iw 157
iz 16.3, 25.4, 30.4, 16.5, 7.9, 10.9, 16.9, 19.9, 20.9, 23.9, 26.9, 27.9,
    28.9, 1.10, 4.10, 16.10, 19.10, 25.10, 29.10, 31.10, 2.11, 5.11,
    20.11, 8.12, 12.12, 14.12.1912; 1.1, 30.1, 4.2, 7.2, 8.2, 19.3, 20.3,
    31.3, 25.4, 26.4, 28.4, 22.5, 26.9.1913; 13.5, 15.5.1914
je 15, 34-5, 39
jn 124-25

Sung Chiao-jên and Other Victims—

aq 20.6.1912; 22.3, 30.4, 1.5, 3.5, 4.5, 10.5, 14.5, 15.5, 16.5, 20.5,
    28.5, 6.8.1913
bf VIII 584
bj 131, 340
bl II 215
ca I, Nos. 2, 4, Nos. 13, 1-5, Nos. 14, 1
co 384-89, 394-95
dz 268
ea I 144, 154-183
ef 182
ei II 929-32, 973-74
ej 56
fa 703-04
iz 12.1.1914, 28.2.1914
je 36-7

The Second Revolution, 1913:

The Army—
ao 16
aq 31.5, 16.7, 17.7, 27.7, 8.8, 1.9, 3.9, 5.9, 7.9, 11.9, 6.10, 19.10.1912;
    17.7, 9.8, 10.10, 16.12, 23.12. 1913
bm 167-68
cx 13.3, 16.4, 17.4, 25.4, 26.4.1912
dz 90
ea I 129-131
fa 707
il 172-73
jn 112-13, 114

The Civil War—
ao 22-4
aq 29.1, 3.5, 7.5, 30.6, 7.7, 12.7, 15.7, 21.7, 22.7, 26.7, 28.7, 31.7, 4.8,
    6.8, 14.8, 18.8, 21.8, 3.9, 12.9, 4.11.1913
bf VIII 475-76, 478-80
dz 131, 157-58
ea I 175, 180-96, 205
ei 298-304
ej 67
eq VI 18
fa 702, 707-09
ip 1, 11-2
iz 18.3.1913

The Strong Man:
Diplomacy
ak I 41, 43-46, 50, 54, 77, 80, 81-2, 84, 92, 97-103, 108
aq 12.7.1912; 12.9.1913; 6.8.1914
bf VIII 465-66, 467
bj 45-53, 161-62
bo 274-75, 278-83, 285-92
ca I, Nos. 1, 3-4, Nos. 13, 9
cx 22.2.1912
ea II 7
eh 567
eq VI 8, 19-21, 40-41, VII 20 *seq.*
fz 153, 156, 163-64, 219-20, 293, 326, 337-38, 344-45, 366-67
gc China, No. 2, 1899, CIX No. 25, also No. 1, 1899, CIX, No. 174
gy 167-68
hm 6.5.1913; 6.4, 22.4, 2.10.1914
ih 27, 38, 42, 45, 73, 112-15
ip 77-9
iz 15.7, 3.8.1910; 9.1, 16.2, 11.5, 2.8, 27.8, 30.8, 5.9, 18.9, 5.11, 21.11,
    3.12, 26.12.1912; 21.1, 22.1, 31.5, 1.9, 2.9, 6.9, 26.9, 28.9, 1.10,
    13.10, 14.10, 21.10, 22.10, 24.10.1913; 1.1, 22.5, 7.7.1914.
jb 104
je 14, 51-2, 199
ff 263

Japan—
aq 9.12.1913, 10.5.1914
bj 86-7, 256-58
cu XXXIII 7
dr Chang I-lin's article, 4

eq I 289-300, VI 4-5, 38-9, 87, 91-5, 102-05, 215-18, 262-70, 276, 283-87, 296-305, 309-10
fr 238, 337, 343
fy 45, 137-38, 141
hm 23.2.1914; 26.1, 6.5.1915
ip 87, 123-26, 131-37, 141-45, 169
iz 13.2, 22.2, 5.5, 7.5, 8.5.1915
je 68-70, 77 *seq.*, 92, 98 *seq.*, 105 *seq.*
See also *Chia-yintsa-chih*, I, No. 7, 1-35

Internal Politics—
aq 19.3, 18.5, 1.7, 12.7, 24.7, 26.7, 7.8, 8.9, 28.9, 28.10, 3.11, 22.12, 25.12.1912; 8.1, 1.5, 17.7, 18.7, 19.7, 23.7, 26.7, 27.7, 31.7, 1.8, 3.8, 10.8, 18.8, 3.9, 4.9, 11.9, 17.9, 28.9, 29.9, 11.10, 23.10, 4.11, 5.12, 13.12, 16.12, 18.12, 19.12, 24.12.1913; 11.1, 26.1, 1.2, 4.2, 6.2, 9.2, 14.2, 20.2, 28.2, 9.3, 15.3, 17.3, 18.3, 31.3, 2.4, 3.4, 16.4, 18.4, 24.4, 30.4, 1.5, 8.5, 9.5, 26.5, 14.6, 20.6, 29.6, 30.6, 28.7, 30.7, 3.8, 19.9, 2.10, 8.10, 15.10, 27.10, 22.12, 29.12.1914
bf VIII 592-95, 597, 599
bj 122
bw 44-5, 52-62
ca II, Nos. 1-2, 1-2
cx 15.2, 15.3, 27.3, 28.3, 6.4, 13.4, 26.4, 27.4, 9.5.1912
dr Chiang Jung's article, 2; Chang I-lin's article, 4
ea I 19, 20, 145, 146, 173, 197-98, II 2-3, 5, 8-11, 17, 21-4, 27
ei I 145, 161-63
ep II, X 1-2, 16
fz 254-55
ip 6-7, 43
iz 9.9, 5.11.1913
jb 94, 107, 109
ji 725

The Monarchy:
ai IV 15a
am 41, 51
aq 19.3, 21.7, 26.11.1913; 7.2, 20.2, 4.3, 1.5, 2.5, 3.5, 4.5, 25.9, 30.10, 3.11.1914; 5.10, 8.10, 20.10, 22.10, 27.10, 1.11, 12.11, 20.11, 11.12, 12.12, 13.12, 15.12, 16.12, 17.12, 18.12, 19.12, 20.12, 21.12, 22.12, 23.12, 25.12, 28.12.1915; 6.1.1916.
as 67, 76, 193
az 251, 258-59, 263
bj 183, 187-88, 268, 277, 279, 280-81, 283-88, 299, 331
bl II 239

bm 226
ca II, Nos. 1-2, 9-10
ci *passim*
co 418, 420-21, 439-40
cu XXXIII 22, 56, 100-04, 143-44, XXXIV 4-6
dg 14
dj 255-56, 270-73, 346-48
dr Chang I-lin's article, 4
dz 211-12, 217-18, 233, 264, 271-72, 338
ea I 130-31, II 21, 24-6, 28
eq VII 23, 27-8
er 182, 194-95
ey 41
fy 48
hl 120-21, 128-29
hm 8.2, 8.3, 4.5, 1.6.1914; 7.9, 23.9, 4.11.1915
ip 6, 24-5, 68, 171, 173-4, 177, 179-82, 186
iz 20.11.1911; 25.6.1914; 9.2, 11.8, 9.9, 15.11, 17.11, 7.12, 11.12, 14.12, 17.12.1915; 11.6.1916
je 41, 50, 64-5, 111, 128-29, 142, 161, 163, 165 *seq.*, 168-70
ji 109

The Downfall:

aq 10.11, 11.11, 21.11, 24.11, 30.11, 26.12, 29.12.1915; 5.1, 7.1, 6.2, 7.3, 21.3, 22.3, 23.3, 25.3, 21.4, 22.4, 23.4, 23.5, 29.5, 6.6.1916
bj 320-30, 333, 341, 345
bm II 7, 11-2, 20
bn 45
co 432-33, 442, 447-49, 452, 460, 462-65
cu XXXIII 2, 6-12, 15, 24-6, 29, 32, 34-36, 44, 48, 50, 53, 121-22, 124, 144, 145-46
dj 301, 327-29, 333, 339, 341, 349-50, 361, 370, 372-75
dr Chang I-lin's article, 4
dz 270, 277-78, 290-96, 300, 303, 313, 320-23, 331-37, 349
ea I 206-09
ed 419-20, 461-62, 465, 467-69, 471, 473, 475, 477, 484, 487, 491, 493
eq VI 82, VII 6-9, 12-5, 17-8, 20, 23-5, 27, 33, 35, 36-8
er 196-98
fi *passim.*
hm 20.10, 21.12.1915; 14.1, 10.2, 23.2, 28.2, 5.4, 11.4.1916
ip 178, 188-94
iz 1.11, 4.11.1915; 18.4, 21.4, 6.6, 7.6.1916
je 181-82, 196-97, 203
ji 27, 641

DATE DUE

RESERVE			
MAY 7			
MAY 9 '67			
NOV 8 '72			
NOV 24 '75			
AP 15'81			
DE 7 '81			
NO 21 '83			
GAYLORD			PRINTED IN U.S.A